THE INVENTIVE WRITER: A Discovery-Based Rhetoric

THE INVENTIVE WRITER

A Discovery-Based Rhetoric

G. Scott Cawelti, *University of Northern Iowa*

Jeffrey L. Duncan, *Eastern Michigan University*

Mayfield Publishing Company
Mountain View, California
London · Toronto

Library of Congress Cataloging-in-Publication Data
Cawelti, Scott
 The inventive writer : a discovery-based rhetoric / Scott Cawelti and Jeffrey Duncan.
  p.   cm.
 Includes bibliographical references.
 ISBN 1-55934-060-6 (paper)
  1. English language—Rhetoric.   2. Duncan, Jeffrey L.   I. Title.
PE1408.C2927   1992
808'.042—dc20   92-26824
                                                   CIP

Manufactured in the United States of America
10 9 8 7 6 5 4 3 2 1

Mayfield Publishing Company
1240 Villa Street
Mountain View, California 94041

Sponsoring editor, James Bull; production editor, Carol Zafiropoulos; manuscript editor, Mark Gallaher; text and cover design, David Bullen. This text was set in 10½/12 Bembo by G&S Typesetters and printed on 50# Finch Opaque by R. R. Donnelley and Sons.

Acknowledgments and copyrights
Pages 3, 4 Reprinted by permission of Running Press, 125 S. 22nd Street, Philadelphia, PA from *Writers on Writing,* edited by Jon Winokur, copyright 1988 by Running Press.
Page 92 From "When Nice People Burn Books" by Nat Hentoff by permission of Progressive, Inc.
Page 168 From *The Poetry of Robert Frost* edited by Edward Connery Lathem. Copyright 1942 by Robert Frost. Copyright © 1970 by Lesley Frost Ballantine. Reprinted by permission of Henry Holt and Company, Inc.
Page 181 "Metaphors" by Sylvia Plath. Copyright © 1960 by Ted Hughes. Reprinted by permission of HarperCollins Publishers.
Page 207 Excerpts from "In Bed" from *The White Album* by Joan Didion. Copyright © 1979 by Joan Didion. Reprinted by permission of Farrar, Straus & Giroux, Inc.
Page 215 Excerpts from "Los Angeles Notebook" from *Slouching Towards Bethlehem* by Joan Didion. Copyright © 1967, 1968 by Joan Didion. Reprinted by permission of Farrar, Straus & Giroux, Inc.
Page 218 Dylan Thomas: *Poems of Dylan Thomas.* Copyright 1952 by Dylan Thomas. Reprinted by permission of New Directions Publishing Corp.
Pages 246, 247 From *Thinking With a Pencil* by Henning Nelms. Reprinted by permission of Ten Speed Press, Berkeley, California.
Cover: ©Joe Tilson. *OH!* Oil on wood, 48″ × 36″, 1963.

TO THE INSTRUCTOR

When we try to help students learn to write, we don't merely want them to write correctly but to write well, with clarity, honesty, and grace. To write like that, students must care, both about writing and the subject of their writing. As a rule, the latter comes first: first they care about the subject, then they learn to care about writing because they want to do the subject justice.

Many students, however, get stuck before they get started. They seem unable to come up with a subject, an idea to develop in writing, much less one they care about. And if they do happen to find a subject they care about, they don't know quite what to do with it. Instead of an occasion, a subject becomes an obstacle.

We have found that students often have trouble writing because they haven't been empowered to generate and develop ideas. Once they learn to do so, they get excited about ideas and what they are able to do with them. Then they begin to care about writing, about doing their ideas justice.

Thus, we must ask writing students to start at the very beginning, at the source, the place where ideas are begotten, born, and raised. We must begin with invention itself, the process of discovering and developing ideas. This is hardly news—the importance of invention is now a truism among writing instructors, and the word itself has become a technical term of the profession, a buzz word—yet most textbooks mention invention as a kind of add-on process. None take sufficiently into account, for instance, that different minds work in different ways. Some students are highly intuitive, others verbal, others visual—and often these traits tend to be mutually exclusive. Highly intuitive people find formats and outlines confining, preferring free association as a way of generating ideas. Visual people flounder if they have to work exclusively with words, while verbal people don't usually get much out of extensive visual aids. Each mental style needs strategies appropriate to its patterns and predispositions. Writing teachers and students need a text devoted primarily to invention, a text which recognizes that no two writers approach (or should approach) writing the same way.

Hence, this book. It is a comprehensive and detailed account of invention strategies ranging from freewriting to intuiting to revising (as a means of invention) to collaborating to breaking writing blocks. Some are familiar: the reporters' questions and the rhetorical modes, for example. Some are not so familiar: creative actualization, ranking tables, and prompted connections may seem strange and challenging.

We have tried to write an eminently useful book, one that will serve a variety of instructor and student needs. Every chapter includes numerous "Applications," writing exercises and suggestions that range from individual practices to more extended group activities, and every chapter ends with "Invitations for Extended Writing," where students apply what they've discovered to realistic writing contexts. We include only those strategies that writers (whether student or professional) actually use successfully and, wherever possible, strategies that we ourselves or our own students have found useful.

Chapters 1 through 5, "Foundation Strategies," offer all the major strategies that students need to begin their work as writers. Chapter 1, "Writing as Discovery," takes as its premise that there is no single approach that works for all writers. Still, writing that focuses on exploration involves preparation, incubation, illumination (an "Ah-Ha" experience), and verification. This chapter also contains an extended discussion and applications of freewriting, the most basic of invention strategies.

Chapter 2, "Concentrating and Intuiting," first offers seven strategies to help students develop their powers of concentration. Then we discuss three further strategies that encourage students to use and trust their intuitive powers: daydreaming and dreaming, creative actualization, and incubating.

Chapter 3, "Gathering," covers three essential research strategies—inquiring, searching, and formulating—and includes detailed advice about using primary and secondary sources, along with a brief overview of source citation and documentation formats.

Chapter 4, "Revising," covers four essential revision activities—cutting, adding, rearranging, and rewording—with special emphasis on how writers use revising to discover, develop, and refine ideas. In this chapter we also cover the concept of *audience* and how writers go about anticipating reader response.

Chapter 5, "Collaborating," contains extensive suggestions for getting feedback from writing partners or writing groups while working with drafts. Here we have also included strategies for writers working together in a formal group to produce a single document.

Chapters 6 through 9 contain further discovery strategies for extending the range and complexity of invention. Chapter 6, "Questioning," offers three questioning patterns: reporters' questions and Burke's pentad, cubing questions, and questions derived from an abbreviated version of the tagmemic grid. Chapter 7, "Mapping," contains four strategies that rely on visualizing information: clustering, outlining, flow charts, and ranking tables. Chapter 8, "Connecting," introduces students to metaphors, analogies, and prompted connections—techniques that apply equally to writing and thinking. Chapter 9, "Forming," describes a variety of forms and formats that writers use to help them discover ideas: traditional ABA form, the rhetorical strategies, line and circle exploratory forms, and a number of common professional formats.

At any time in their use of this book, students may wish to refer to the three appendixes. Appendix A presents eight quick steps that writers might use when faced with a rush writing job. Appendix B focuses on how writers can enhance their creativity. Appendix C offers eighteen techniques for breaking writing blocks.

Our treatment of each invention strategy is essentially self-contained, so that instructors can choose to cover any strategy individually, apart from the rest of the chapter. Our discussion of each strategy ends with a set of exercises called "Applications" that suggest various ways students can practice using the strategy on their own. Many of these applications are sequenced within a chapter and lead to a particular "Invitation for Extended Writing."

A word about the "Invitations for Extended Writing": these are designed to help students write finished pieces for various readers and purposes—essays, letters to a group or person, newspaper and magazine articles, reports, reviews, memos, classroom research papers, and the like. They invite students to begin a crucial process that leads beyond the classroom into the world of business and professional writing.

Although the chapters may be taken up in various orders, you may find it useful to follow the order of the book. Not every strategy need be assigned every student; you may wish to assign particular sections according to individual students' needs. For further suggestions about ways of ordering and using the material, see the Instructor's Manual.

If education means anything, it means connecting with one's deepest thoughts and feelings about a variety of subjects. The range of strategies in this text offers multiple alternatives for discovering, developing, and communicating ideas. When students discover how much they think and feel about a subject, they inevitably feel liberated from the damaging perception that they haven't anything to say and are anxious to explore their ideas further. The ultimate goal of this book, then, is to help students enhance their education by showing them the power and joy of discovery.

Acknowledgments

G. Scott Cawelti would like to thank the University of Northern Iowa for an eight-week summer research grant to get started, and to the many faculty and friends who commented on the text as it evolved: Mac Eblen, Mike Dargan, Mike Janopoulos, Robert Waller, Linda Kettner, Jim Hiduke, Sally Hudson, Kent Meyers, and Anne Johnstone. And my hearty applause to the 120 or so UNI students who used the "Gathering" chapter as a text for several sections of a short research writing course; you made wonderful guinea pigs. Also thanks to the students in my Exploratory Writing and Invention seminars. You made me a believer in discovery as the truest joy of writing.

Finally, thanks are due the Cawelti kids, Christa and Jason, who heard enough talk about invention to last them several years, and to Martha Waterman, whose enthusiasm for the project at times nearly outshone my own.

Jeffrey L. Duncan would like to thank the Graduate School of Eastern Michigan University for a Faculty Research Fellowship to help him get this book going, and Eastern's Board of Regents for a Sabbatical Leave to help him get it done. He would also like to thank Barbara and Tyler for hanging in there.

Both of us extend our warmest thanks to Paul Nockleby, whose abiding belief in the power of writing as a means of discovery made this text possible. His perseverance kept us going through several inevitable discouragements, and we're grateful for his continuing support. Also thanks to Jim Bull at Mayfield, whose questions strengthened the text in several areas; to production editor Carol Zafiropoulos and copyeditor Mark Gallaher, whose suggestions (always tactful) added immeasurably to the quality of the text.

In addition, we are grateful to reviewers Kathleen Evans, San Jose State University; Cheryl Fontaine, California State University, Fullerton; Arlene Kuhner, University of Alaska, Anchorage; Sonia Maasik, University of California, Los Angeles; and Patricia Murray, California State University, Northridge, whose thoughtful criticisms and suggestions improved several sections of the text.

TO THE STUDENT

Let us say first what this textbook is not. It is not a reader—a collection of essays. Nor is it a handbook containing rules of grammar and usage for you to follow. Nor is it a traditional "rhetoric," a book that focuses on how to write effective sentences and paragraphs.

Instead, this book is a guide designed to help you generate and develop ideas. You may think that only creatively gifted people can generate and develop ideas, and only natural-born writers come up with fresh and exciting material, but that's not the case. One or another of the techniques in this book can enable anyone to generate and develop the kind of ideas that good writing requires.

You'll find that certain techniques work particularly well for people with certain dispositions. You may be highly intuitive; if so, there are techniques here that will help you to capitalize on your intuition. You may be highly visual; if so, there are techniques here that will help you develop your thoughts visually. You may not be certain how your mind works, but with all the strategies available here, you should be able to find out. In fact, you may find that sometimes your mind works one way, sometimes another, sometimes several ways at once; this book includes all the strategies you need to take full advantage of your mental multidexterity.

Often you need to find ideas within yourself, the whats and hows and whys of your own mind. What interests you deeply? How do you think and feel? Why do you hold certain attitudes and beliefs? To develop material out of your own experiences and observations, you will find *freewriting, intuiting, mapping, questioning,* and *metaphors* to be useful strategies.

Equally often you need to gather information on a particular subject. It may be well and good that you think the stock market is exciting, but if you don't know how it works you can't write about it. More than most people realize, professional writers (including novelists and poets) do considerable research to generate and develop the material they wish to write about. Chapter 3, "Gathering," contains a number of strategies for finding sources quickly in order to formulate your ideas.

Common though the analogy is, ideas aren't like seeds. A seed, once planted, grows into something quite predictable. A tomato seed (providing it germinates) produces a tomato, come hell or high water. An idea, though, is anything but predictable: it can turn into something else at the stroke of a pen, something completely unforeseen.

Hence, the need to explore and commit oneself to an idea. Hence, also, the need to revise, to find out what your idea really means, where it fits best and for whom. Writing means revising to understand the idea yourself and to make it clear and persuasive for a particular audience. Thus Chapter 4, "Revising," presents various strategies of revision with which you can generate still further ideas (for the piece of writing you are working on or for others) and develop the ideas you have generated into a finished form.

Putting writing into a finished form means observing various criteria. For many kinds of writing, in fact, you must follow a particular form. In Chapter 9, "Forming," we show you how to use various conventional forms not only as a way to give structure to your ideas but also as a means of further discovery, of generating even more ideas and developing them as effectively as possible.

In sum, this book offers a comprehensive array of strategies for generating and developing ideas and material for various readers and occasions. For each strategy there are a variety of "Applications," exercises that allow you to practice and learn to use that strategy. In addition, every chapter ends with several "Invitations for Extended Writing," where we offer ways you can go beyond these brief Applications to write polished pieces for particular readers and purposes.

In addition, we offer three appendices. Appendix A, "Eight Steps for Quick Writing" will help when you must meet a sudden deadline (notes, memos, short papers) and know most of what you need to say before starting. Appendix B, "Conditions for Creating" offers suggestions to enhance both the physical and mental conditions for your own creativity. And Appendix C, "Blockbusting" describes eighteen techniques for breaking writing blocks that can help whenever you find yourself stuck (and who doesn't at some time or another?).

We feel sure that if you explore these strategies regularly and intensely, you'll soon find that instead of wondering how you can come up with 500 words on a subject, you'll be wondering how to write about all you've discovered in *just* 500 words, or even 5,000. The strategies in this book—which can also help solve the problem of having too much to say—will allow you to see your subjects as rich, varied, and worthy of sustained attention. In other words, with these strategies as your guide, you can find yourself immersed in the joy and excitement of discovery as you never have been before.

CONTENTS

PART ONE

FOUNDATION STRATEGIES

CHAPTER ONE

Writing for Discovery

Writing, like life itself, is a voyage of discovery.

—HENRY MILLER

I write books to find out things.

—REBECCA WEST

All writers work in their own way. How they write depends on whether they're morning people, afternoon people, or night people; whether they prefer a keyboard or a pad and pencil, white paper or blue, a splendid view before them or a blank wall, background music or silence. Often the way they work also depends on whomever they're writing for: themselves, instructors, friends, relatives, colleagues, employers, potential employers, or general readers. Their method may also depend on what they're writing: a note to the cleaners, a letter of recommendation, an essay on the state of the liberal arts, a poem.

If you believe that great writers must eventually find one perfect way to write or that they agree on anything relating to how to write, read these quotes from several professionals:

WRITERS' ATTITUDES TOWARD WRITING

William Styron: "Writing is a form of self-flagellation."

Jane Smiley: "I *like* writing. I'd rather write than do anything else. I'd rather write than clean house. I'd rather write than grade papers or go to the store."

Pete Hamill: "Writing is the hardest work in the world not involving heavy lifting."

Flannery O'Connor: "No writer is a pessimist; the very act of writing is an optimistic act."

WHY WRITERS WRITE

Joan Didion: "In many ways writing is the act of saying *I*, of imposing one-self upon other people, of saying *listen to me, see it my way, change your mind.* It's an aggressive, even a hostile act."

John D. MacDonald: "My purpose is to entertain myself first and other people secondly."

Blaise Pascal: "Anything that is written to please the author is worthless."

Beverly Cleary: "I write because reading meant so much to me when I was growing up, as it still does. I love reading, so naturally I like to write."

WRITERS' ATTITUDES TOWARD CRITICISM

Jean Cocteau: "Listen carefully to first criticisms of your work; note just what it is about your work the critics don't like—then cultivate it. That's the part of your work that's individual and worth keeping."

John Berryman: "I would recommend the cultivation of extreme indifference to both praise and blame because praise will lead you to vanity and blame will lead you to self-pity, and both are bad for writers."

WRITERS ON KNOWING ENDINGS

Toni Morrison: "I always know the ending; that's where I start."

Isak Dinesen: "I start with a tingle, a kind of feeling for the story I will write. Then come the characters, and they take over, they make the story."

Scott Spencer: "I try to know as much as I can about a book before the beginning, but I never know exactly where it's going to end."

Katherine Anne Porter: "If I didn't know the ending of a story, I wouldn't begin. I always write my last line, my last paragraphs, my last page first."

As you can see, writers don't agree on much of anything. Some write during the early morning, but not all. Most, it would seem, write sitting at a desk or table, but some (like Truman Capote and Winston Churchill) write lying down, and others (like Ernest Hemingway and Virginia Woolf) write standing up. Some know exactly where they are going when they begin, others write to find out. Some write their first drafts nonstop and then revise, others revise as they go. Some write a few hours at a time, while others (like Aleksandr Solzhenitsyn and Isaac Asimov) write twelve, fifteen, even eighteen hours a day. Some write primarily for their readers, others for themselves. Many use computers nowadays, but some still type or write in longhand. As Bernard Malamud says, the most important thing is to find out how *you* write best, then do it.

Exploration, Illumination, and Commitment

As much as their work habits may vary, however, all writers do a certain few things in common. They define a subject and *explore* its possibilities by some combination of researching, talking, and thinking, depending on the subject and their acquaintance with it. The less they know about it, the more they need to learn through research and talk. Much thinking goes on through writing: as E. M. Forster asked, "How do I know what I think until I see what I say?"

In exploring, writers hope for *illumination,* the discovery of something (a connection, an angle, the figure in the carpet, the missing link) that usually prompts an exclamation and so is sometimes referred to as the "Ah-Ha experience." In psychology such illumination is called a *gestalt,* an insight or revelation wherein things fall into place making a pattern visible, as when you look at a silhouette of two chalices and suddenly see that they also define two faces in profile.

Illuminations can range from major visions that change the shape of the world (the theory of relativity, for instance) to more personal insights (suddenly understanding an axiom in geometry or realizing why a friend has been acting oddly). Illuminations can happen at any time and place. They often occur when you're not thinking about the subject, when you have put it aside and are doing something else. They may be so sudden as to take your breath away or so gradual and subtle you hardly realize they're happening. Wherever and whenever they strike, whatever their size and form, they are always the result of exploration. No exploration, no illumination; no illumination, no discovery—it really is that simple.

At some time or other, ranging from the moment they define the subject until after they have done considerable research on it, writers decide to do it— that is, they make a *commitment.* Implied in such a decision is another possibility: deciding *not* to do it. Few people appreciate how often writers explore a subject only to reject it, because it incites no riots of illumination. They find it has been done and re-done and over-done, and they can't come up with a new angle or slant on it; or they realize it requires research in areas that don't interest them as much as other subjects they have in mind; or they discover it requires more work than they have time for; or they come to see it just doesn't keep their juices flowing the way a subject should. Writing is hard work, so it requires real commitment, a hard-core decision to do the job.

Having made the commitment, writers explore the subject some more, the means of exploration depending on what they need to find out. Some subjects require considerable research in the library or the laboratory. Others require considerable interviewing and field studies. All require thinking, which means, as we have seen, writing.

It would be a mistake, however, to assume that from this point writers simply push on until the job is done. Often they run into difficulties they had not foreseen—dead ends, traffic jams, gridlocks, writing blocks—and the illuminations necessary to solve the difficulties are not forthcoming. Sometimes they shelve the project for a while and go on to something else. "When I feel difficulty coming on," explains Isaac Asimov, "I switch to another book I'm writing. When I get back to the problem, my unconscious has solved it." Sometimes they reconsider it, a process that involves re-exploring the project, then deciding (possibly with the benefit of more illumination) whether it is worthwhile and doable. If so, they make a recommitment to it and push on to the end. If not, they might shelve it again, perhaps permanently. (Non-writers would be amazed at the number of projects writers chuck even after putting in a great deal of time and effort.)

As varied as the process of writing may be, then, it usually requires exploration, commitment, re-exploration, and recommitment—in short, a great deal of back-and-forth movement, charging and retreating. And when it seems done, it's often still not done. At some point, writers show their work to others—colleagues, editors, people whose judgment and honesty they trust—for their critiques. Then they revise some more, a lot or a little depending on what it takes to make the piece effective for an audience and purpose.

There are other ways to analyze the writing process. Many who study creativity break it down into four parts: *preparation, incubation, illumination,* and *verification.* Or we could talk about writing as a three-fold process: *exploring, composing,* and *revising.* We want to stress that however one spells it out, the actual process of writing is not nearly so neat. We make the process look like a simple sequence because the result of the process—a piece of writing—is necessarily linear: one word, one sentence, one paragraph after another. But the *act* of writing is "recursive"—that is, the various activities of the process overlap and repeat until the writer finally declares the piece done and hands it over.

Yes and No Voices

We all have two voices within ourselves, a "yes" voice and a "no" voice. The yes voice tells us we're okay; the no voice tells us we're not quite all we might be. The yes voice is what gets us started on an endeavor and keeps us going. The no voice keeps telling us that what we're doing is not very good and that we ought to make it better or just drop it. As novelist Dorothea Brande and many others have pointed out, a writer needs an internal creator and a critic, a supportive yes voice and a firm no voice. To write well, you must stay in close touch with both.

To get in touch with your two voices, try this. Find a quiet space, sit down with a pencil and paper, and write at the top "My yes voice usually tells me _____." Now time yourself for three minutes and write *nonstop* out of your yes voice. When things are going well—when it feels as though you are doing something worthwhile and you are doing it right—what do you hear inside? Many students write comments such as "I'm fine, I'm doing well, I'm enjoying my life, everything will turn out well, I'm capable and confident, people like me. . . ." Write all the internal comments that give you confidence to keep going.

Next, take another sheet and write at the top "My no voice usually tells me _____." Time yourself again, and write nonstop everything that comes to mind when you worry that a project is not worthwhile, that you can't finish, or that even if you do, it won't be any good.

Compare the two pieces. Did one come more easily than the other? Does one seem more "true" than the other? Did one voice want to interrupt the other? ("I'm doing well, I'm a great person, but I usually don't finish what I start," wrote one student while supposedly focusing on his yes voice.)

If your no voice consistently overshadowed your yes voice, tell it to go away until you need it and do the exercise again. (Your voices *will* eventually cooperate with your needs, by the way, if you keep after them.) You don't have to suppress either voice completely at any time, but you want to be able to use them when they're most helpful: the yes voice when you're initially composing, the no voice when you're revising.

If your no voice is still giving you trouble—stifling you with doubts so that you find it difficult to let your yes voice go—keep in mind novelist Kurt Vonnegut's comment. Speaking of all writers, he points out that writing enables those "who are patient and industrious to revise their stupidity, to edit themselves into something like intelligence." By turning your yes voice loose, if only a little, you begin turning up material. If it seems stupid, don't worry. As Vonnegut says, you can, with patience and effort and the help of your no voice, edit it into something like intelligence. That's what writers do.

Freewriting

The kind of nonstop writing you've used to help you contact your yes and no voices is called "freewriting." It requires no sources other than your own mind, so you can do it anytime, anywhere. It offers an extraordinarily powerful means of exploring a subject, although you can freewrite without a particular subject in mind. It's like taking a walk in a field and finding fossils and arrowheads: when you freewrite, you turn up ideas, one after another.

The directions for freewriting are absurdly simple, and the benefits almost immediate. Basically, you turn your no voice down, turn your yes voice up, and then follow where it seems to lead. If your no voice insists on being heard, put down what it has to say, too. Do not get hung up on spelling, punctuation, grammar. Just write the thoughts going through your mind as fast as you can. (Some suggest ten-minute freewrites as a minimum. We think three minutes is enough for starters, since it's brief enough to prevent fatigue, but long enough to produce results.)

If you find you have trouble laying down words freely—without stopping to correct spelling, punctuation, and grammar, to revise words and phrases—and if you have access to a computer, we suggest the following exercise: compose at the keyboard, typing as fast as you can, *with the monitor screen darkened or turned completely off.* The effect is to force you to write quickly, with *no* editing whatsoever.

The benefits of freewriting are several. First, it gets you writing. If your knee-jerk reaction is to say that the writing isn't any good, just remind yourself that at this point quality isn't an issue. That will come later, when you have something definite to say and to shape.

Freewriting also raises your awareness of subjects that concern you but that you may have suppressed or repressed: the woman or man next door, the chemistry paper due at the end of the semester, your behavior at the party last weekend. Such discoveries don't always happen, but they often do, and if you learn to freewrite with an open mind, with genuine abandon, they almost always do. In other words, freewriting helps you discover what's really on your mind.

Freewriting has another benefit: it captures your consciousness in motion. Impulses, observations, frustrations, contradictions, secrets, irritations, joys, hopes, disappointments, fears, hankerings, anticipations—they are all part of the flow we call consciousness. Freewriting lets them flow onto the open page, so that you can get a good idea not only of what's on your mind at that particular moment in your history, but also of how your mind works, the kinds of associations and leaps it characteristically makes. This knowledge can help you find and refine an effective writing style, and to develop your own voice.

Still another benefit of freewriting: problem-solving. Say that something is bothering you, a problem of some sort (personal, intellectual, social) that you can't figure out. Freewriting may help you figure it out. It can get you from the outer skin to the inner heart of the problem, from confusion to comprehension, often quickly.

There are two basic kinds of freewriting, *open* and *responsive.* An elaborate variety of responsive freewriting, *circling,* can help you generate and develop ideas whenever you have a little free time.

Open Freewriting

Open freewriting means what the name implies: you let your yes voice go, and write down anything and everything it says. Here is an example of a three-minute student freewrite (as with all examples of freewriting, mechanical errors remain uncorrected):

> Okay, here I am at my desk writing away for three minutes. Hmm, what is there to say? Boy, three minutes is going to go by fast, and I won't have much of any value unless I write fast. Or should I write slow, since I don't have much to say, there shouldn't be any hurry. What a gloomy day outside. It looks like rain or maybe even snow. That means I can't go for the jog I wanted this afternoon. Ah well, maybe I'll get something else done. What a waste of time this is. I'm really not getting anywhere—just a lot of words on the page. Is that all this is about? I sure can't see any value here. Well, I'm supposed to keep writing anyway and I guess I will. That's me, always one to follow directions no matter how stupid. I'd probably just follow all the little lemmings over the cliff if I could. What a total, utter, complete waste of time. But at least I guess I'm writing. Is that enough, just to write for three minutes? (TIME)

In three minutes this writer wrote eighteen sentences, nearly 180 words. Had he kept on for nine more minutes, he could have written almost three pages. Your no voice might be protesting that nobody would want to read it, but free-writing is where a good deal of writing begins:

> *Frank O'Connor:* "I write any sort of rubbish which will cover the main outlines of the story, then I can begin to see it."
> *Vladimir Nabokov:* "I have rewritten—often several times—every word I have ever published. My pencils outlast their erasers."
> *James Merrill:* "The words that come first are anybody's, a froth of phrases, like the first words from a medium's mouth. You have to make them your own."

These three writers (and hundreds more) insist that one's first words should tumble out, fresh and fast and virtually nonstop whether they make any sense or not. It's all part of discovering what one is up to. After all, *some* words on a page are better than none, because they can lead to more and other words, even words that strangers might want to read. And in the freewrite above, the writer uncovered an idea rich with possibilities: "That's me, always one to follow directions no matter how stupid."

Be careful not to let your freewriting reinforce the destructive side of your no voice. Suppose you're convinced that you can't write at all, that you hate writing from the word go. Then you try a couple of open freewrites that don't lead anywhere: no insights, no discoveries—just a lot of semi-coherent prose loaded with spelling and grammatical errors. Now your internal critic can say with reason (you think), "*See!* I *told* you that you couldn't write. Now you've gone and proven it!" Should you find yourself giving in to such sentiments, remember that you can choose to listen to a less negative side of your no voice (everyone struggles at times, even to the point of incoherence) or—if you possibly can—tune in to your yes voice for a while.

Keep in mind that open freewriting often can seem like mere psychic noise:

> What a lot of stuff I have to do tomorrow. Oh, how I hate that feeling of having too much to do and not enough time. What was that? Oh, the wind pushed the door open again. I really ought to fix that door latch one of these days. O yeah, I'm supposed to fix supper tonight. I had better get that fish out of the freezer. Oops, that's right, I took it out last night. I wonder what I should fix with it? I wonder if Charlie's busy tonight. . . .

And so on, and on. You can write for hours and never get beyond the daily aches and pains that bother everyone. This is fine; it's all potentially rich mental compost. Often such freewrites serve as a prelude to breakthrough thoughts, so don't worry if your open freewrites seem trivial.

In our experience, open freewriting is most effective for journal writing, especially if or when you are having trouble coming up with ideas to write about. Sitting down periodically, two or three times a day, and turning your mind loose on paper for a few minutes can jostle the brain, making it release the ideas that are there for your consideration. Moreover, sometimes open freewriting is good therapy. Expressing all those private complaints, those psychic aches and pains, seems to be good for people, whether anyone ever reads them or not.

Responsive Freewriting

You've already tried responsive freewriting when you wrote about your yes and no voices. In responsive freewriting, you begin by spelling out a subject of concern in an incomplete sentence, such as "My yes voice usually tells me _____." Then for a set length of time, you respond specifically to that concern nonstop, putting down all the thoughts, examples, images, metaphors, and anecdotes that come to mind. Your mind may wander off the topic. Psychic noise may intrude. If so, don't stop writing: include the noise, the wandering. Who knows? The noise may turn into music, the wandering lead to a more promising subject. The point is, given your initial focus, there will be *less* noise and wandering than in an open freewrite, therefore a *greater* chance of discovery.

Here's an example of a three-minute responsive freewrite in which the writer, a high-school student, made a couple of discoveries. She began with, "To me, the prospect of writing in college is _____."

> To me writing in college is pretty much the same as writing anywhere else. Maybe more intimidating if its going to be graded—other people critiquing your ideas and searching for missing commas, run-on sentences, spelling errors. If college writing means writing long papers—up late at night researching topics I don't care about and endless hours of notecards and references and footnotes—if that's what it is—then I guess that I'm not very interested in it. It's not so much writing that I enjoy as thinking up ideas. I could spend hours thinking up ideas but the actual process of writing them down is a real pain. In fact, I can think of very few things that I anticipate less. . . .

She discovered that what bothered her the most about writing in college was the prospect of having to research topics that didn't interest her. She also discovered that she enjoyed "thinking up ideas."

The ways to express a concern you can respond to are endless:

I am looking forward to _____ because _____.
I am dreading _____ because _____.
I am puzzled about _____ because _____.
My spouse/roommate/parent/significant other/sibling is angry because

_____.

I am interested in _____ but have the following reservations:

_____.

Some instructors use responsive writing at the end of a class to help the students solidify what they've covered that hour: "I've learned today that General Grant _____."

The great advantage of responsive freewriting is that it gives your mind a focus, a subject at the outset to develop. (In contrast, the great advantage of open freewriting is that it helps you *find* something to develop.) Having a focus, you can gauge how fully you're actually developing the subject. Another advantage of responsive freewriting is the way it allows you to take a quick inventory of your thoughts on the subject at hand. Such an inventory can be particularly helpful when you feel bogged down. You can begin the freewrite with something like, "I'm stuck at this point because _____" or "Right now it seems as if the subject is _____," and then write away. Often something will turn up that will get you out of the bog. If nothing turns up, set the piece aside for your unconscious to chew on for a while: with the freewrite you have given it food for thought.

Circling

Circling is a demanding form of freewriting, requiring you to write virtually nonstop for 24 minutes, shifting perspectives every three minutes. You may think of it as eight consecutive three-minute responsive freewrites on one subject. It's a strategy designed to get you to look at the subject in different ways for different audiences. We call it circling because you keep returning to three activities—expressing, explaining, and persuading—from different perspectives.

Circling works best with issue-oriented subjects—college athletics, political correctness, the effects of divorce on children, the effects of television violence. To circle effectively, you should have some ideas about opposing viewpoints. Circling is especially useful in preparing to write a persuasive or argumentative essay, because argument requires making a case *for* one position and *against* others *to* a particular audience.

Here are the eight circling activities:

1. *Express Neutrality.* Without worrying about an audience, you say what's on your mind in a matter-of-fact way, as though you aren't emotionally committed to any particular position for *or* against.
2. *Explain to Novices.* In this activity, you *do* need to worry about audience. The goal is to write for readers who know little about your subject so that they can understand the subject in one reading.
3. *Persuade a Reader to View a Certain Position Favorably.* Here you imagine an audience who takes a neutral or negative position on some aspect of the subject. Your goal is to convince them to see that position more positively.
4. *Express Negative Feelings.* At this point you stop worrying about readers and come up with as many negative statements about your subject as you can. If you don't really feel negative about it, pretend you do.
5. *Explain to General Readers.* In this freewrite you explain the subject for readers who know something about it but aren't themselves experts.

The goal is to increase their knowledge, improve their understanding, or both.

6. *Persuade a Reader to View a Certain Position Unfavorably.* Now you imagine readers who advocate a certain position regarding the subject or are neutral about that position. The goal is to persuade this audience that the position is questionable.

7. *Express Positive Feelings.* Once again, you forget about any reader, and enumerate all the good things you can say about the subject. As before, if you don't really have anything good to say, you pretend you do.

8. *Explain to Experts.* This last activity can pose a challenge. Here you write to readers who know the subject as well as (or better than) you do, trying to tell them something new or enlightening.

Figure 1.1 shows what circling looks like when diagrammed. To see what an actual circling freewrite looks like (and to see how much work circling can help you do in 24 minutes) look at this one by a second grade teacher as she explored how her students learned from her example:

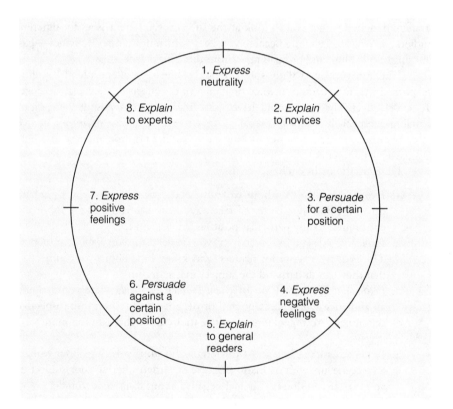

Figure 1.1   Circling Diagrammed

1. EXPRESS NEUTRALITY

Modeling is a strong form of instruction. It is an act of setting an example of what is expected of the learner. For example, if a teacher wants his/her students to do a freewrite, he/she should first demonstrate this and share it so the students know exactly what to do. Then the teacher needs to consistently do the act with his/her students to show the importance of the activity.

2. EXPLAIN TO NOVICES

Whatever we do, someone is watching. From their watching they are learning and making or allowing that learning to be a part of their entity. This is called modeling or model/learning. Whether it is at home fussing over a glass of spilled milk or at a grocery story listening to an older child beg for candy, the three year old is forming a concept of how to act by how others treat the same situation.

3. PERSUADE A READER TO VIEW
   A CERTAIN POSITION FAVORABLY

Modeling is a very strong and positive way to teach students or children within the social/home environment. It is natural. Show the children what is expected and desirable and then let them practice it. It is easy. If we believe in what we are modeling then it does not take any more time or energy because it is a part of us. We model cleanliness by dental hygiene. Our child follows our modeling example by doing this.

4. EXPRESS NEGATIVE FEELINGS

What is so scary about the naturalness of learning through seeing a model is that there are so many negative models in this society that children are also picking up on. We can not turn on and off the modeling avenue of learning. We can not shelter our children or students from learning negative actions or thoughts. We have to be totally aware of our actions due to the eyes on us. Many people are not aware.

5. EXPLAIN TO GENERAL READERS

We are all teachers. We are all being watched—be careful. When you do an act, or share an emotion or opinion a young person is picking up on your example. You are modeling a behavior to an audience. You are teaching a concept. If you always show partiality toward a subject, your enthusiasm will be picked up on.

6. PERSUADE A READER TO VIEW A
   CERTAIN POSITION UNFAVORABLY

How on earth can we constantly monitor our actions so those around us see an exemplary model? Why, we would have to pre-think every move like an actor. This idea of eyes are watching you and learning is placing the burden on adults for all the negative or unproductive incidental learning that takes place. We are now expected to be perfect, to be God-like. The demands of this response is too (TIME)

7. EXPRESS POSITIVE FEELINGS

Modeling is so easy and natural. All you have to do is show the most positive side possible. If you want your children or students to act in certain
ways, you then need to be a part of that. If you do it by modeling along
with the children in a consistent way, then whammo—learning is happening through your giving it credibility and importance by doing it yourself.
Also all actions, not just specific learning/teaching objectives are teaching
young eyes.

8. EXPLAIN TO EXPERTS

We are advocates of modeling. We want our youth to see the best examples
possible. Do you wonder how long it would take to demolish a negative
learned behavior by wiping out all of the negative models? For example, if
we got rid of all smoking yet had cigarettes still around, do you suppose it
would gradually rebuild to a smoking society?

When you have finished 24 minutes of circling (three minutes for each of
the eight perspectives), the next step is to read through them all, noticing which
flowed naturally so that you might have continued for several more minutes. This
writer discovered that she was most concerned about the effect she had on her
students and about the pressure to "model" ideal adult behavior. She found that
despite her reservations about modeling (perspective 4), she still saw it as offering
a crucial reinforcement to learning and wanted adults to be more aware of its
importance.

After examining which sections flow most easily, it's important to notice
which seem least natural, the least in line with your sense of the subject. The elementary teacher realized that she was "putting on" a voice when she tried to persuade others of the dangers of modeling (perspective 6). She didn't really believe
that "we would have to pre-think every move like an actor. . . ." However, in
considering that aspect of modeling, she prepared herself to understand at least
one negative position regarding the subject. Doing so could help her prepare to
answer objections from those arguing against the value of consciously modeling
behavior.

Circling, then, is particularly valuable when you have some acquaintance
with a subject but no clear sense of how to write about it. By noticing which circling perspectives seem natural and which seem forced, you can discover your
best approach to your subject and define a specific audience.

APPLICATIONS

1. Keep a journal for a week in which you write five-minute open freewrites daily. Then look back over the entries. Write a paragraph about your
major concerns as suggested by this week of journal entries.

2. Do a five-minute responsive freewrite with the following openers:

I usually wish I were _____ instead of _____.
In five years I hope I'm _____.
Whenever I _____ I feel _____.

When you finish, look over all three, and make a list of the items you find most interesting and surprising. Write a paragraph on what those items, taken together, say about you that you hadn't realized before.

3. Take any problem that's been bothering you and freewrite about it. Begin with "I'm really bothered by _____," and write nonstop for three or more minutes. Read what you've written. If you discover anything about the problem, write a paragraph summarizing what you discovered.

4. Take any subject in which you have a strong interest and circle it, writing for three minutes from each of the eight perspectives described earlier. Keep in mind which perspectives flowed naturally and which didn't. Then, write a brief essay for your classmates and teacher about how the method worked. Include what you discovered about your subject and your attitudes toward it.

5. With a group of friends or classmates, do individual circle freewrites on a single agreed-upon topic that everyone knows something about. Read your circlings to one another, and compare the results. Help each member of the group define his or her best approach and audience for an essay on the subject.

Concentrating and Intuiting

Nothing interferes with my concentration. You could put on an orgy in my office and I wouldn't look—well, maybe once.

—ISAAC ASIMOV

Concentrating

Concentration contributes mightily to success at anything. Sports, math, science, business, law, medicine, religion, fund-raising, child-raising, even word-raising (otherwise known as writing) all require sustained, profound attention. Writing requires concentrating anywhere from a few minutes for journal entries to several hours a day over a number of days for extended essays and reports.

If you are like most people, you probably wish you could concentrate better. Take heart: here we offer seven steps to better concentration. Practice them, and you will see a significant improvement in your concentration that can make a considerable difference in your writing.

Set Your Own Deadlines

Most writers agree that if they don't have a definite time to finish, their concentration flags. Donald Murray, a Pulitzer-prize winning writer and writing teacher, insists that "whenever I stop giving myself a deadline—a minimum number of pages by a certain hour on a certain day—then I stop writing. Without deadlines I do not write." Deadlines are important not only for finished drafts but for everything, from journal entries to first drafts to polished essays and reports. And they must be your own deadlines. Instructors give deadlines for papers, but they're not your deadlines until *you* decide when you will finish.

What do deadlines have to do with concentrating? It's quite simple: because we're all busy people, we don't work seriously on most assigned tasks until a deadline looms. Then we begin paying attention.

If it's 9:00 A.M. and you have yet to start a paper due today at noon, you will probably become a world-class concentrator for a couple of hours. However (as you may already know from bitter experience), this is not the best way to operate. It's better to set your own deadlines that will allow you to finish writing before the "official" deadline, and thus to take care of any unforeseen problems that may arise.

We suggest that you set both short- and long-term deadlines. If you work better in bits and pieces, then write your essays in bits and pieces: start the paper far enough in advance of the official deadline so you can spend an hour or so each day writing a paragraph or two. If you work better in extended stretches, then set aside several hours for writing and impose short-term deadlines for yourself within each extended stretch: a paragraph every half-hour, a page every hour, whatever your pace happens to be.

Follow Your Interests

If a subject interests you, you probably have little trouble concentrating on it. Obviously, therefore, when you can choose your own subject, you should write about something that interests you. The things that interest us most are generally those that have given us great pleasure or those that have given us great pain. The former probably speak for themselves: when you enjoy something—a rock star's singing, movies, cats, whatever—you learn about it and like to think and talk about it. Therefore you have no trouble mustering the concentration necessary to write about it effectively. Although they may not be so obvious, those things that have given us great suffering preoccupy us as well, and we can turn them into remarkably positive accounts. Losing a loved one to drugs or AIDS or anorexia, for example, can lead not only to grief but also to a deep and valuable understanding of drugs or AIDS or anorexia, that one can share with others through writing. Although you may find it difficult to write about things that have made you suffer, the problem won't be concentration, and the result may well be worth the difficulty.

On the other hand, when you have to write on a particular assigned topic, perhaps even in a particular way, you may have more trouble concentrating, especially if the topic or approach doesn't interest you at all. On the job, people often are assigned writing tasks that don't fit their interests. So what do they do? What can you do?

Here are five strategies. Next time you have trouble concentrating on a writing assignment, try any that appeal to you. If one doesn't work, try another: one of them should do the trick.

1. *Shift your point of view entirely.* Instead of the indifference or boredom you feel about the subject, pretend that you absolutely love the subject and can't get enough of it, or that you hate it and wish it could be eliminated

forever. Take any extreme point of view and start writing. The voice that emerges won't be your own, but it will be interesting, most likely, and you'll be concentrating.

2. *Free associate, using lists of words and phrases.* List everything that comes to mind about the subject in any order. Put down anything, however remote and indirect its relation may be. Finding personal connections can help you see a relevance for the subject, and a sense of relevance can help you concentrate.

3. *Freewrite without thinking about the subject at all.* Write nonstop for five or seven minutes on anything that comes to mind, and look over the freewrite for any connection to your subject. The connections may be oblique, but they are generally there.

4. *Talk about the subject with someone.* Ask a friend to listen for five minutes, and explain the subject as best you can. Just gathering your thoughts enough to discuss a subject will help you concentrate on it, and you may well find yourself more interested than you thought.

5. *Write your instructor a letter explaining why you don't want to write about the subject.* You may not send such a letter, but it is an unsurpassed means of concentrating. You have a definite audience and purpose, and something to say about the subject, after all. If the letter makes sense and actually falls within the guidelines of the assignment, you'll be done. If not, you will have at least begun to think about the subject in a way that interests you, and you can then try some of the other strategies here.

Know Your Goals

If you are having trouble concentrating on a writing assignment, ask yourself *why* you are writing it. "Because it was assigned" is not much of an answer: that it's an assignment doesn't mean you have to do it. You have at the very least the options of dropping the class or failing. So ask yourself: what difference will it make to you or anyone else that you finish?

Then answer the question, in writing. Be honest. If your goal is simply to get a good grade, say so, but then ask another question: what difference will a grade make? For example, is graduate study of some sort on the line? Keeping in mind the difference the grade will make may help you concentrate better on the paper.

It may be that you want to do a good job for the sake of your self-esteem, to do better than everyone else or someone in particular. Such motives may not be noble, but good things can come from less than noble motives. Whatever the personal motive, get it out in the open, so that you know exactly why you are writing—exactly what it means to you.

It may also be that, even though you are having trouble concentrating, you still want to understand the subject better. If so, explain to yourself what it is about the subject that you want to understand, and why. Maybe you'd like to show certain people something they hadn't seen before, or change some minds about a problem you think is serious. You might even regard the paper as an opportunity to improve your writing because it involves a subject you've never written about before or a format you've never followed.

Whatever your reasons for writing the paper, you are more likely to become aware of your goals by writing about them. And the clearer your goals, the better you will concentrate.

Know Your Best Places and Times for Concentrating

You're going to be sitting at a desk or table for fairly long periods of time, so you need to get rid of all your usual preoccupations and external distractions—your roommate, your spouse or significant other, your pets, even your refrigerator if you're a hard-core snacker. Find a special spot for concentrating—a corner of the library, a secluded study lounge, a nook in the cafeteria, a cubby in the cellar—wherever you can put your normal world out of sight, out of sound, and therefore out of mind.

But don't neglect your quirks and magic charms. We all know people who can't concentrate unless they're surrounded by people—in a cafe, a hotel lobby, a subway, wherever there is hubbub. Sigmund Freud couldn't write without his cigars at arm's reach. Marcel Proust couldn't write unless he was in his room, which he had soundproofed with cork and perfumed with rotting apples. So if you need caffeine, have coffee or cola nearby. If incense helps, burn a stick or two. If you can't work without Bach in the background, put on the Brandenburg Concertos. In short, do what helps you concentrate.

Next, consider your best time to concentrate and schedule yourself accordingly. Everyone has a best time to work—when the mind is sharp, the memory strong, the energy high—and it may not fit ordinary schedules. Morning people ("larks") may be ready at sunrise. Night folks ("owls") don't hit their stride until after dark. Whenever your peak times occur, use them for writing. That's when you'll concentrate best.

Plunge In

You've set your own deadline, found what interests you, clarified your goal for writing, and now you're sitting at your desk, which happens to be your favorite place to concentrate. It's your best time, so you're alert and ready. Now: plunge in.

This may seem easy, if not self-evident. But don't be so sure. At this point you will almost certainly be tempted to doodle and dawdle, to jump up and fix more coffee, to call a friend, to adjust the thermostat, to open a window. Writers are famous for finding dozens of reasons to avoid actually starting. So don't hesitate. Start writing.

Stay with It

You may want to stop after only a few minutes of concentrating. Distractions abound, both from without (phones, visitors, mail) and from within (hunger, intrusive daydreams, frustration). But stretch yourself; go just a little beyond the urge to quit. The most common internal distraction is your no voice, which tells you that it's no use to keep writing. When that voice intrudes—as it sometimes will when you're doing your best to concentrate—tune it out. With practice, you can learn to bring it back when you're getting a draft ready for final submission. But for now turn it off, and listen instead to your quieter and vastly more productive yes voice.

Stop Where You Can Start Again Easily

When you absolutely must stop, be sure you're at a place where it will be easy to start again. Usually the worst place to stop is at the very end of a major section or where you've just completed a major point. Faced with starting at the very beginning of a whole new set of ideas, you may well find the temptation to put off starting again overwhelming. Ernest Hemingway often stopped in the middle of a sentence. Most writers find it's better to quit after they've begun a new section or paragraph. The important thing is to stop where starting again will be easy.

APPLICATIONS

The following are designed to help you notice things you may not have noticed before and respond to them, all by way of helping you learn to concentrate. You don't have to write polished prose here; just engage your attention for a while, turn down your no voice, and let your thoughts flow.

1. Look carefully at the photograph in Figure 2.1 for one minute. Then turn the page and list every object visible in the photograph. Hint: count articles of clothing as separate objects.

If you can list ten objects or fewer, look again. If you can list twelve to fifteen, good work. If you can list twenty or more, congratulations. There are actually twenty-two separate items in this relatively simple photograph: three women, three bathing suits, three violins, three bows, six flippers, water, bubbles, light patterns in the water, shadows in the water.

When you've finished your list, write a paragraph decribing the photograph for someone who hasn't seen it. Try to make your description precise enough so they can "see" it from having read your paragraph. Show your paragraph first to members of your writing group for discussion, then to someone who hasn't seen it.

Figure 2.1

Now write two or three paragraphs that explain what you think might be going on in the photograph. Write for members of your writing group and discuss your speculations in detail.

2. Figure 2.2 reproduces an upside-down signature. Take three minutes to copy it in the space below, left to right, exactly as it appears.

Figure 2.2

You may be surprised by how accurately you could copy the signature. Most people can do so quite well, no matter how untalented they may be at drawing. The act takes intense concentration, in part because the signature is so unfamiliar when it's upside-down. Ironically, it's precisely because you don't perceive a whole signature, but a sequence of loops and squiggles, that you are able to draw it.

Based on your experience drawing the signature, write a paragraph explaining why you think it's possible to reproduce an image so accurately. (If you don't have any ideas, speculate.) You might consider writing out a set of instructions for copying other drawings, after trying out the technique with your favorite cartoon, for example.

3. In two minutes, write five or more sentences that will give your classmates a clear picture of the top of your desk.

4. Take five minutes to recall your most recent full meal, and make a list of everything you ate, explaining whether you really liked it, hardly noticed it, or actively disliked it. Then, write a paragraph describing your ideal meal—both how it would look and how it would taste.

5. Consider where you go or have gone regularly to relax and enjoy yourself. Choose one of these favorite places, then close your eyes for a few minutes. Try to recall the place so fully that you go there mentally. In your mind, see it, smell it, feel it. Stay for a few minutes, then come back and open your eyes.

Once you open your eyes, write a paragraph describing the place so that your classmates can see it as well as you did, including, if you wish, some explanation of why it gives you pleasure to go there. As an alternative, write a page or so speculating about how your favorite place may change over the years, if you think it will; if you think it probably won't change much, speculate about why this is the case.

6. If you're taking another class where some writing is required, practice using the seven concentrating steps described earlier in this chapter as you work on your next writing assignment. Then, for your classmates and instructor, write a page reporting whether the seven steps made any difference, positive or negative, in your writing for that class.

7. With your writing group, discuss when you concentrate best—what are the conditions that foster concentration? When do you find it difficult to concentrate? Gather everyone's responses and report your findings to your instructor and/or the class.

Intuiting

For some people, the very notion of intuition is suspect. It smacks of oracles and muses, of crystal balls and tarot cards. The knowledge intuition delivers is therefore also suspect. Because it's just a feeling, a hunch, difficult to explain precisely in words or formulas, it isn't really knowledge.

The truth is, however, that everyone relies on intuitive knowledge much of the time: such knowledge is not only a matter of feeling, but often a matter of fact. It's extremely difficult, for example, to imagine the concept of "face" without imagining an individual human face, of which we recognize hundreds. And this recognition is factual, genuine knowledge upon which we rely daily.

In the last decade or so, researchers have begun to study intuition. After taking a poll of some 2,000 managers in corporate and agency settings, political scientist Weston Agor concluded that managers who trusted their intuition were the most successful decision-makers. The fact is that many decisions *require* the assistance of intuition because rationality easily gets overloaded by all the elements that need to be considered. (Imagine, for example, trying to hit a fastball by using your reason.)

When scientists conduct a formal study, they first have to decide what to study, what area or angle will best help them solve the problem with which they are concerned. That decision is a function of intuition, a gut feeling. When business people conduct a feasibility study, the purpose is to check out (as best they can) the validity of an intuition, a hunch or belief that they should develop their business along certain lines. When a football coach calls a certain play, he is relying, even when he follows a game plan, on intuition, a felt sense of what will probably work.

Intuition can even amount to premonition. Mary Kay Ash, founder of the Mary Kay cosmetics company, recounts this case:

> We were starting out with nine people—eight women and one man. The women were inexperienced. But the man sounded like a marketing whiz, spouting enthusiastic plans for getting Mary Kay Cosmetics off the ground. I had already promised to hire him. But as I stood talking to the man outside the office, I suddenly changed my mind. I had no reason. Just intuition. Six months later I read in the newspaper that he had been indicted for a felony.

While intuition is subjective and often spontaneous, it is also a mental skill that can be developed. The more you study something, the keener your intuition about it: your ability to sense opportunities, to come up with valuable hunches and flashes of insight, to make fruitful connections that deliberate rationality alone cannot reveal. But keep in mind that intuition (like rationality) is far from infallible. Scientists often choose unfruitful lines of research, business people wind up with losing propositions, football coaches goof. Mary Kay *could* have been wrong—such impressions are sometimes misleading.

The idea, then, is not to develop a foolproof intuition but rather to develop a *keen* intuition, one capable of providing exciting leads, hot tips, fruitful lines of inquiry, mind-opening connections—the sorts of leaps and turns that help make your writing not only competent, but genuinely good.

Developing intuition requires learning to pay attention to what's already going on within, the little tugs and pulls and pushes at your mind, the warms and colds around the heart, the inclinations and misgivings in the solar plexus, the heat lightning on the horizon of your consciousness. To help develop your intuition, we will explore three strategies: (1) *inventive daydreaming and dreaming;* (2) *creative actualization;* and (3) *incubating.* The key to developing intuition is the same key that unlocks other skills: practice. Our discussion of each intuitive strategy concludes with applications to help you practice; to increase your powers of intuition, try these activities. Not all of them will work all of the time, but some will, especially when combined with your yes voice. When this happens, you will undoubtedly expand your intuitive powers, and this in turn will improve your writing.

Inventive Daydreaming and Dreaming

Both daydreaming and dreaming are rich sources of intuitive knowledge. Every culture appreciates the value of dreams, interpreting them as a key to understanding personality, the times, and the future. Indeed, many cultures designate certain people as dream-interpreters: witch doctors, psychoanalysts, and the like. Artists, writers, composers, and scientists habitually pay close attention to their dreams for ideas and insights, and they allow themselves to daydream for the same reason: musing in reverie on its own, the mind can turn up all sorts of things that otherwise would escape its owner's notice.

Writers are often adept at harnessing their dreams and daydreams. William Faulkner, for example, explained that for him "a story begins with a single idea or memory or mental picture. The writing of the story is simply a matter of working up to that moment to explain why it happened or what caused it to follow." In describing how he wrote *The Sound and the Fury*, Faulkner explains the process in detail:

> I wrote it five separate times, trying to tell the story, to rid myself of the dream which would continue to anguish me until I did. . . . It began with a mental picture. I didn't realize at the time that it was symbolical. The picture was of the muddy seat of a little girl's drawers in a pear tree, where she could see through a window where her grandmother's funeral was taking place and report what was happening to her brothers on the ground below. By the time I explained who they were and what they were doing and how her pants got muddy, I realized it would be impossible to get all of it into a short story and that it would have to be a book.

People like Faulkner, who are creative by profession, do not have a monopoly on dreams and daydreams. We can all use our dreams and daydreams as a means of generating and developing ideas. In this section we offer a beginning.

Daydreaming Daydreaming means slipping away from your immediate surroundings and going into your head. We all take such mental vacations, sometimes deliberately, sometimes inadvertently. A good daydream usually requires nothing more than unfocusing the eyes and gazing out and away, drifting off into wide open spaces of the mind where you just let what happens happen. Disconnected images, colors, patterns, memories, words, stories, ideas—all occur in a jumble, a stream of consciousness loaded with flotsam and jetsam.

To see the difference between a normal daydream and an applied daydream, try a brief exercise. Finish this paragraph, then stop reading and look at the ceiling or out the window or up at the sky, or just close your eyes. Let your mind wander to the most pleasant place you can imagine. Put yourself there: sense how it would look, smell, feel. If there's a beach or mountains or rolling fields, let yourself enjoy them. Stay there for a few minutes; don't return to your normal surroundings immediately. And don't try to control the dream—remember that you're along for the ride.

This is ordinary daydreaming, the sort we all do and enjoy often. Such daydreams are necessary to our mental health; the mind needs regular short breaks.

Now try this. Imagine yourself at your probable career five years from now. Where are you? In an office? A classroom? Alone? With people? Listening? Talking? If you're inside, look out a window. Are there mountains? Is it warm and sunny? Are you happy or worried? Relaxed or tense? Content or wishing you could go or do something else? Stay with this fantasy for several minutes, letting your mind wander about your surroundings. Avoid making quick judgments about your situation. Just go there as though it's real and look around.

If you don't get upset or impatient, chances are that in ten minutes or less you'll find yourself with a fairly clear set of images that seem likely, given your current goals. If not, *you haven't wasted your time*. Your mind is still working, and you may go on to daydream about your future occasionally and effortlessly. This seems to be the way applied daydreaming works: when you define a specific goal, the mind keeps working on it whether you're consciously aware of the process or not. Daydreaming in this manner, though you may look merely distracted, can be one of the most productive activities of your day.

When you have larger, more difficult problems to solve, you can integrate deliberate thought and daydreaming. That is, you work on a problem consciously, concentrating, thinking, using whatever formulas are at hand, writing down the results of your labors. But you also let your unconscious mind work on the problem, taking breaks for as long as several hours or several days, and letting yourself daydream regularly. When ideas pop up, write them down, then turn away from the problem again until more pop into view for you to write down. Keep this up until you have enough material to return to deliberate thought again.

To put daydreaming to work, then, give your mind a specific orientation by defining a problem. Then let go, cut the mind loose from its everyday moorings. And be ready to write down the ideas that will come. The more familiar this process, the easier and more productive it will be. It involves trusting yourself at first, but after a few successes, the process becomes almost automatic.

Dreaming You may find that sleep dreams are beyond your powers of recall, much less your conscious control. But a great deal of evidence proves that with practice you can not only learn to recall your dreams more effectively, you can also program them to help solve problems, gain insights, provide new perspectives, suggest entirely new approaches.

First, you need to take your dreams seriously. As Patricia Garfield points out in *Creative Dreaming*:

> Dreams are what you make of them. If you believe them to be meaningful, you will have and remember meaningful dreams; if you believe them to be

creative, you will have and remember creative dreams. Dream states respond to waking attitudes.

If you have never taken dreams seriously and find yourself skeptical now, try to assume a belief in them for the moment, a deliberate faith, just to see what happens. After all, what have you got to lose?

Next, to put dreams to work, you have to remember them. The most profound dream is of no value if it never sees the light of conscious recall. Two measures help most people who have trouble recalling their dreams. First, tell yourself during the day that you *will* recall your sleeping dreams. Literally say this: "Tonight I am going to have dreams I'll remember. I will wake up in the morning able to recall my dreams." Repeat this several times a day for several days. And be sure to say it just as you're falling sleep.

Then, instead of leaping out of bed when you wake up, lie still for a few minutes with your eyes closed. See if you can begin to recall some of the dream you've just experienced. (Usually you wake up toward the end of your longest dream of the night, a dream that may have been running as long as 45 minutes.) Don't start thinking about the day ahead; rather, just muse on what was in your mind as you woke up, dwell on it. One memory usually leads to another. In time, if you practice faithfully, you will find yourself recalling more and more of your mind's nocturnal pursuits.

You will find that a dream log helps. Keep a notebook by your bed to record as much and as many of your dreams as you can. Writing down what you remember helps you remember more. Also, writing dreams down can help you realize their meaning, help you see the important insights they may offer. (You may prefer to use a cassette recorder.)

Finally, it's not enough just to wish for pleasant and useful dreams. To get dreams to help solve problems, you must immerse yourself in the subject and actively prepare your mind by telling it what you'd like to dream about. If you stay with it, your mind will oblige.

If you don't get results in a day or two, keep trying. In time—a week or two, perhaps even longer—you will get results you never dreamed of.

Suppose, for example, that you're faced with writing an extended paper in a Western Civilization II class. Your assignment is to choose any subject covered in the class that you would like to research further. Western Civilization II happens to cover everything from the Renaissance up to World War I, so chances are, you will be faced with a bewildering variety of subjects. If none comes immediately to mind, you have a dilemma. What should you choose? You can't avoid the question long without risking some serious procrastination.

We suggest that you try dreaming about it. Just before you go to sleep for several nights, tell yourself that you will dream specifically about this dilemma, that you will learn which subject would work best for you from your dreams. Astoundingly enough, most people find that they really can use their dreams for just such everyday problems and options.

APPLICATIONS

1. Keep a dream log for at least two weeks. Tell yourself during the day and right before falling asleep that you will remember your dreams. Avoid alcohol, especially before going to bed (it fogs the memory), and keep a notepad nearby. Try to wake up naturally, without an alarm, and lie quietly for a few minutes, going back over the dream you woke up to and any others that come to mind. "Grow" them into the fullest form you can. If you wake up without any recall, shift your position: doing so often seems to jiggle dreams into consciousness.

Record in the notebook (or into a recorder) everything you recall. Leave nothing out. If you wish, venture an interpretation.

2. If you have a problem that's been on your mind for some time, try both dreaming and daydreaming about it. To daydream, turn your mind loose several times a day, imagining yourself solving the problem. Toward the end of each daydream, tell yourself that you will dream about the problem in your sleep. Keep a notebook and pencil by your bed, and record as much as you can recall when you wake up. If you wish, after two to four weeks write a brief explanation of what you learned for your instructor and classmates.

3. Ask members of your writing group about their dreams. Have their dreams helped them solve problems? Given them insights? Do they ever deliberately daydream? Are they ever disturbed by dreams? Share your own thoughts about your dreams as well, and then write a summary of what you learned for your instructor and/or the class.

4. The work of Carl Jung, one of the most prominent psychologists in the twentieth century, centered in the interpretation of dreams and still influences students of psychology, as well as literary critics, anthropologists, therapists, and sociologists. Chapter 4 of his autobiography *Memories, Dreams, and Reflections* deals specifically with dreams. Read it (it's only 29 pages) and write a two- or three-page reaction—in any form you choose—for your classmates.

5. If you have any recurring dreams or daydreams, explore them in a brief essay for your classmates. Tell them about the dream or daydream, how often you have it, when it began, and what you think it might mean.

6. For college students who are not in your class, write a two-page set of instructions, based on your own experiences, for dreaming and daydreaming creatively. Be sure that the instructions are in your own words, so you will know that you understand what you're talking about.

Creative Actualization

Although you may find the term strange, creative actualization is extremely common. It's a way you make decisions every day. Say you are going out to dinner and want to decide on a restaurant: you imagine yourself (often very briefly) in different places eating different things. The image you find most appealing and suitable usually determines where you go. You do the same thing when you decide what to wear, what route to take on a drive, what to buy as a gift for a friend.

Using the imagination in such ways is creative actualization. We use creative actualization for long-term life goals as well: we imagine where and how we would like to be in ten or twenty years—the work we would like to be doing, the place we would like to live, the lifestyle we would like to lead—and we bend our efforts accordingly. Creative actualization, in fact, is *how we hope,* by creating images of the future. We choose majors and careers and marriage partners accordingly.

Creative actualization, then, is a technique that puts your imagination to work, visualizing a specific situation that does not exist in order to help make it exist, to become actual. It involves seeing, hearing, and feeling some outcome *as though it is in the process of occurring or has already occurred.* Studies have shown that the more intensely you can create such a "present" image, the more likely you are to make it a matter of fact.

Athletes use creative actualization to very good effect: they improve their skills by imagining how they want to perform a certain feat—a tennis stroke, a jump shot, a skiing maneuver—and then by practicing to fulfill the form they imagine. (Golf legend Jack Nicklaus has said that he visualizes every shot he takes, and he doesn't take a shot until he has visualized it in its entirety, from beginning his backswing until the ball stops.) Dramatists imagine the different ways a scene can play onstage or in a movie or television show and then write the one that they think will work the best. Actors, directors, choreographers, and dancers also use creative actualization—without it they wouldn't have a clue where to begin.

Perhaps less obviously, poets, novelists, and writers—both student and professional—use the technique, too. When they're writing well, they imagine people, places, activities, incidents, and ideas as they search for words that will evoke their mental patterns for readers. In his essay "Politics and the English Language," George Orwell writes directly about this process:

> Probably it is better to put off using words as long as possible and get one's meaning as clear as one can through pictures or sensations. Afterward one can choose—not simply *accept*—the phrases that will best cover the meaning, and then switch round and decide what impression one's words are likely to make on another person. This last effort of the mind cuts out all stale or mixed images, all prefabricated phrases, needless repetitions, and humbug and vagueness generally.

Those who do not use creative actualization when they write have no idea what they are writing toward—a distinct disadvantage. It's worse than trying to draw a picture in the dark; it's like trying to draw a picture with none in mind. If, then, you have not used creative actualization when you write—or if you have used it only occasionally or tentatively—you owe it to yourself to practice the strategy. Once you begin using it, you may well wonder how you ever wrote without it.

APPLICATIONS

1. Think of someone you know, and visualize that person as completely as you can. Imagine you're a video camera, taking first a full-body shot, then a waist-down shot, then a waist-up shot, then a facial close-up. Note everything you can—all features, expressions, gestures, clothes. Look at this person in different contexts—with family, with friends, at a party, at a picnic—noting the differences. Then write a two-page description of this person for someone who does not know him or her, a description so detailed and accurate that the reader would recognize this person immediately.

2. Using creative actualization, *listen* to someone you know well, to how she or he talks in different situations and to different people. Listen to the expressions the person characteristically uses, to the way he or she puts sentences together and deals with a subject (directly or indirectly, with an anecdote or philosophical lecture). Then write two pages on a topic of particular interest to this person, using the *person's own voice.* Have someone who is a good reader read the piece aloud to you, to see if it sounds the way you intended. If not, revise it and have it read aloud again. Do this until you have captured on paper the voice of the person you are imitating. Then show what you've written to that person.

3. Visualize the last fight you had with anyone. Then actualize it on paper, using description and dialogue, as accurately as you can for your classmates and instructor.

4. Visualize the last really funny episode you were involved in. Then actualize it on paper for general readers.

5. Create in your mind the perfect writing place, a place that will support all your thinking needs: the right color, lighting, music, chair, and desk, free from interruptions, not too hot or too cold, well-ventilated. Imagine that everything you write in this place reflects your true thoughts and feelings and gives you a sense of accomplishment. To help your imagination, read the following slowly to yourself:

> *The place in which I sit now supports my ideas and feelings perfectly. The walls are _____ (your favorite color), the decor matches my mood, my favorite chair holds me, and I can relax completely here. Whatever I think about feels right here, and my ideas and feelings seem enhanced by being here. In this place I lose myself in the flow of work, so I work more effectively without fatigue. The work that results is the best I've done. Whenever I work on any writing project, I will return to this place.*

You can mentally re-create this place and return to it, no matter where you're really sitting.

6. With members of your writing group, discuss how you each "see" your future. If the "future" seems too vague, consider your next weekend. Describe your plans, how they make you feel, and whether your vision usually works out as you see it. Write a brief summary for your instructor and/or the class.

Incubating

Americans tend to equate work with activity, with hustle and bustle, jamming in the fast lane from one deal to the next. The word *business,* after all, comes from *busy-ness.* If you're sitting around with a book or staring off into space, you're not *busy.* It's hard to break the demand for busyness, which is why we saved this technique for last: it goes against the grain, yet it can be crucial for concentrating creatively. It amounts to backing off from the problem or subject of concern—laying it aside, putting it to rest for a while, not concentrating on it—not thinking about anything much, in fact, but instead just *incubating,* or *waiting and seeing.*

Waiting for what? To see what turns up. There is more to the mind than enters your consciousness. To give a problem or subject the benefit of complete attention, you must let the unconscious have a go at it. And you do that by turning your conscious attention off. According to one study, most creative people—artists, composers, poets, and such—sleep a lot, a good eight or nine hours a night plus a nap during the day. It's not because they're lazy. It's because they're working.

Don't get the wrong idea. The unconscious does not work unassisted, and it never starts from square one. You must first concentrate on the subject consciously, investigating it through thought and intuition, and then often through research—reading, experiments, surveys, interviews. *Then* you set it aside for the unconscious mind.

For the unconscious to work effectively, you need to undertake relatively mindless activities that you do alone: gaze out a window awhile, noticing whatever seems interesting, take a long hot bath, take a nap, take a walk, jog, ride a bike, drive a car, put on a CD, play solitaire—do whatever it is you enjoy doing alone while your mind meanders through its own countryside like a lazy river. Then wait and see what happens.

The great German physicist Hermann Helmholtz wrote that ideas never came when he was at his working table: "They came particularly readily during the slow ascent of wooded hills on a sunny day." Likewise, playwright and novelist Thornton Wilder said, "My springboard has always been long walks." In fact, walking seems the perfect incubation exercise for writers. You can drift from thought to thought, daydream, note sights along the way, but you can't do much else. Walking seems to require just enough mind power to keep the consciousness occupied but not so much that it distracts the walker from other matters.

Don't be afraid to drop a piece of writing right in the middle and take a walk (or pursue some other incubating activity, such as biking or just sitting by a creek watching the water). Ernest Hemingway often stopped writing for the day in the middle of something, putting his writing out of his mind so it could sink into the well of his unconscious. Then, when he began the next day, ideas for new developments emerged immediately, as a rule, into his awareness.

Note, however, the phrase *as a rule.* The mind is its own boss and delivers its goods as it sees fit, not on command. You may be sure that neither Helmholtz nor Wilder received great ideas every time they took walks, any more than Hemingway got one every morning when he began writing. Sometimes you have to wait a good long while before the unconscious does its natural work. But it will turn up something eventually if you meet three conditions:

1. *Prepare.* You must work hard on the subject first, concentrating, investigating, and pondering.
2. *Have patience.* Insights worth knowing and communicating must be stalked, in much the way photographers seek whitetail deer or great blue herons.
3. *Have faith.* Unless you believe you actually have an unconscious that can and will turn up ideas, it won't.

You may find the last condition the hardest to meet. We all feel at times that for a brain we have nothing but a big wad of cotton or a pit of quicksand into which insights sink forever. These nasty pictures of your brain are not to be trusted. Rather, trust that you have a perfectly fine mind with all its conscious and unconscious faculties intact, quite capable of giving you good service. For proof, remember that you are able to speak and listen, to read and write, to add and subtract—all activities that require remarkable intelligence. Remember, too, that you have had ideas before—exhilarating insights and revelations that popped into your consciousness as you were shaving or kneading dough or changing your oil. You will have them again, especially now that you know how to prepare for them.

Sometimes the unconscious delivers an idea in comic-book form: a flash of light that illumines the whole subject at once. At other times it delivers an idea piecemeal, as a train of associated thoughts that slowly but surely keeps making more and more sense of the subject. However the idea comes, the next step is *verification*—subjecting what your unconscious delivers to the searching criticism of your no voice. The unconscious is hardly infallible. It can deliver the right goods to the wrong address or the wrong goods to the right address. But even though you may find errors, you'll also find that you won't have wasted your time puttering around the apartment while your unconscious was puttering around with your problem. It will come up with workable ideas more often than not.

This brings us to what may be your first objection concerning incubation: time. How can anyone expect to have the *time* to set problems aside for unconscious incubation? After all, you have assignments, deadlines, people to see. You live in the pressure-cooker of the real world, not in some mythical ivory tower.

First of all, you have no choice. To come up with *good* ideas—the kind that solve problems brilliantly, please professors, impress bosses—you must follow at least approximately the procedure we have outlined: preparation, then incubation, followed sooner or later by illumination, and finally verification.

Second, you *make* the time. Pulitzer-prize winning political cartoonist Bill Mauldin produces a nationally syndicated cartoon daily, but he makes time for incubation. Every night, after reading the newspaper and watching the news, he jots down ten ideas for the next day's cartoon. Then he puts the list out of mind and goes to sleep. In the morning he starts work by going over the list. He says he almost never uses any of the ideas on it for his cartoon, but as he studies them, other ideas come tumbling to mind out of the unconscious where they have been incubating all night long. Mauldin doodles now with one and now with another, still waiting for the right idea, and when it happens, he transforms that into his cartoon for the day. If Mauldin has time for incubation—to put his preoccupation aside and to wait and see what his unconscious will do with it—so do you. And you will find that the time you take to do it is worth every minute, for you will get results: illumination, and excitement to boot.

APPLICATIONS

1. Everyone has an illumination now and then—a sudden insight into something or other while not even thinking about it. If this has happened to you, write one or two pages reflecting on the experience. Explain the preparation you did—even though you weren't aware of it as such at the time—and describe what you were doing when you got the illumination, what it was, how it worked, and how you felt. Discuss any verification you may have done.

2. Take a long walk—an hour at least—alone, during the day, either in the country or the town. Notice the sights and sounds, the smells, the people and other creatures, the various structures—everything you can. Don't force your attention: let your mind wander freely. But shift it occasionally and gently to some subject you've been interested in and puzzled by: Chinese cooking, drag races, grades, loopholes, coffee, sex, the gross national product, marriage, money, the stock market, fraternities and sororities—whatever. Then, let your mind wander off again. Wait and see if anything happens—an illumination. Write a brief reflection on the experience, describing what did or didn't happen.

3. Before going to sleep, jot down ten ideas concerning a paper you have to write for another class. Next morning, before you begin writing the paper itself, freewrite about the ten ideas for five to seven minutes, seeing which seem better and which worse and taking down new ideas as they occur. Then, examine the freewrite, jot down the ideas you want to use in the paper, and begin writing the first draft.

4. Talk to members of your writing group about their illuminations. When did they get sudden insights that they later used in their speaking or writing? What activities do they regularly engage in when incubating? (Most people have something they turn to when they need to get away from their work and let it "cook.") Write a brief report on your research for your classmates and instructor.

INVITATIONS FOR EXTENDED WRITING

In any activity that counts, you have to move at some point from rehearsal to performance, from practice to game. In doing the applications for this chapter you have been rehearsing or practicing. Now it's time for the real thing: using concentrating and intuiting strategies to write an essay proper for an audience.

In writing specifically for an audience, consider three things: readers' *knowledge, attitudes,* and *needs.* We discuss these concepts in greater detail in Chapters 3 and 4, but, for now, here is an overview.

> *Knowledge.* How much are your readers likely to know about your subject? How little? Which terms will you have to define? Which concepts will you have to explain?
>
> *Attitudes.* How are your readers likely to feel about your subject and your point of view? Will you need to answer some objections? Which ones? Will you be able to assume some agreement and lead a few cheers?
>
> *Needs.* What will readers need in order to understand your subject and be persuaded to your point of view? What details will they relate to? Should you use graphics—diagrams and illustrations? Should you include quotes by famous people? Should you be formal, friendly, intimate?

As you begin to write drafts, call on your yes voice for support. (You might want to review pp. 6–7.) Remember to set your no voice aside for a while; you will need it as you revise and edit, but as you generate, gather, and develop your ideas, rely on your yes voice.

1. Tackling a Problem Choose any problem which you've approached through concentration, dreaming, actualizing, or incubating. Unleash your yes voice and write about the problem for your classmates, a friend, or your parents—whomever you're comfortable with. Explain what it is, how it affects you, what you've learned about it, how you hope to solve it. If possible, write about the problem so that your readers may learn something about it as well. Try to write about it in your own most natural voice.

2. Your Ideal Career Imagine yourself ten years from now. What do you want to be doing for a living? Where? Realistically, how much money do you want to make? What kinds of satisfactions and frustrations do you anticipate? Using as many of the concentrating and intuiting techniques as you have found compatible, write the following three pieces (remember to listen to your yes voice!):

- a two- to three-page explanation of your ideal career for your classmates.
- for an appropriate professional journal, a three- to five-paragraph advertisement for your ideal position. (Imagine yourself as a personnel director trying to attract the best qualified candidates.)
- a letter of application in response to the ad, detailing your qualifications for the position. (Try to be positive but realistic about the qualification you will have amassed in the next ten years.)

3. A New Experience Try something you've never done before—something legal that you'd be willing to explain to strangers in a feature magazine or newspaper story. Eat some nutritious but unappetizing food, such as baked grasshoppers; sky-dive or go bungee-jumping; fast; panhandle; try out for a play; sing in an amateur night at a local hangout.

Then (as you listen to your yes voice), examine what you've done, using as many of the concentrating and intuiting techniques as you like. Write a three- to five-page story about your experience—what you did, what you liked about it, what you didn't, what surprised you, what met your expectations, what you learned from it, what it meant. Consider submitting it as a feature story to a local newspaper.

4. Another Assignment If you have a writing assignment for another class, use any of the concentrating and intuiting strategies as you work on it. Remember to listen to your yes voice, and try various kinds of freewriting, concentrating, daydreaming and/or dreaming, creative actualizing, and incubating strategies. Also remember your audience: the instructor and his or her particular requirements.

5. Autobiographical Sketch Using freewriting and any of the concentrating and intuiting strategies, write in detail about your life up to now. Try to answer any of these questions: What made you the way you are? What do you value? How have you changed? Who do you spend your time with, and why? What do you hope to do to make money someday? What fascinates you the most?

Remember to listen to your yes voice, and write in your own most natural voice for your classmates and instructor.

For Further Reading and Research

Bosnak, Robert. *A Little Course in Dreams.* Boston: Shambhala, 1988.

Cowley, Malcolm, ed. *Writers at Work: The* Paris Review *Interviews.* First series. New York: Viking, 1958.

Edwards, Betty. *Drawing on the Right Side of the Brain.* Los Angeles: Tarcher, 1979.

———. *Drawing on the Artist Within.* New York: Simon, 1986.

Garfield, Patricia. *Creative Dreaming.* New York: Ballantine, 1973.

Gawain, Shakti. *Creative Visualization.* New York: Bantam, 1978.

Hughes, Elaine Farris. *Writing from the Inner Self.* New York: Harper, 1991.

Jung, Carl. *Memories, Dreams, and Reflections.* New York: Vintage, 1965.

Nachmanovitch, Stephen. *Free Play: Improvisation in Life and Art.* Los Angeles: Tarcher, 1990.

Rowan, Roy. *The Intuitive Manager.* New York: Little, 1986.

Ueland, Brenda. *If You Want to Write.* St. Paul: Greywolf, 1987.

Wallas, Graham. *The Art of Thought.* New York: Harcourt, 1926.

CHAPTER THREE

Gathering

"The greatest part of a writer's time is spent in reading, in order to write; a man will turn over half a library to make one book."
—SAMUEL JOHNSON

Gathering—finding material to write about—is a third foundation skill for writers. The first, *concentrating,* underscores the need to give your whole attention to a subject. The second, *intuiting,* underlies all the operations that writers do, including seeing new patterns and making fresh connections. Gathering gives you material upon which your intuition can go to work.

Even when you're asked to write about your own observations and ideas— a sketch of your favorite person or how your run-in with the law changed your attitude toward police officers—you will use the gathering processes described in this chapter. Writers need facts, observations, ideas, and opinions—either their own or others'. Indeed, writers rely on sources constantly. Autobiographers rely on their own memories and observations, as well as on interviews and reading to corroborate their memories and fill in the blanks; newspaper and television reporters rely on interviews and observations; editorial writers rely on facts drawn from reference sources and newspaper reports; academic writers rely on previously published research and information gathered from a variety of primary reference sources. In a sense, writers are latter-day hunters and gatherers.

You've probably already used a number of gathering strategies to answer questions: Which word processing programs include graphics? How safe is the drinking water in our area? What cities rate high on "quality of life" charts? What are scientists currently thinking about global warming? How have budget reductions affected faculty morale? To find answers, you can't stay in your armchair. Sources are often scattered far and wide, and the answers they provide may lead to more questions and thus to other sources.

Even such a seemingly mundane problem as buying a used car requires research, in addition to the skills of concentration and intuition we've already discussed. First, you concentrate on the problem, asking such questions as "What is the car for?" and "How much can I pay?" As you answer such questions, you will certainly call on intuition, seeking "gut feelings" about particular cars' suitability, letting the problem incubate as you go about your other business, perhaps even receiving flashes of insight as you daydream or dream—using the self in such instances as your primary source. Yet none of what you gather in this way would be enough without material from other sources as well. You would want to visit car lots, talk to salespeople, call previous owners, get a mechanic to look at the prospective car. Secondary sources such as *Consumer Reports* would also be helpful. Without some research, in addition to concentration and intuition, you won't have a car, or at least not a car you're satisfied with.

Gathering, then, means finding useful information from others so we are not stuck with the limitations of our personal knowledge. Everyone does it, except people who choose to put themselves out of touch with the larger community to which they belong (which is the original meaning of the word *idiot*). We know it's possible—and necessary—to learn to research in a systematic manner and to become more successful at it. That's what this chapter is about. For a start, let's examine four traits that professional gatherers have in common.

Four Traits of Professional Gatherers

Gatherers—whether private eyes, lawyers, scientists, engineers, scholars, accountants, poets, or consumers—have four things in common if they're successful: they're *objective, accurate, thorough,* and *systematic.*

Objectivity

Gathering only evidence that supports one's presuppositions and stereotypes is an exercise in bias, not investigation. Of course, complete objectivity is impossible; humans can't help but register their biases in dozens of ways, from what they select to notice to how easily they forget what they don't want to notice. Indeed, the investigator always affects the investigation, just by how he or she selects what to investigate and what to emphasize.

Nevertheless, genuine investigation means following your sources even if they take you places you may not expect. As Anton Chekhov put it: "A writer must be as objective as a chemist; he must abandon the subjective line; he must know that dungheaps play a very respectable part in a landscape, and that evil passions are as inherent in life as good ones."

Accuracy

In his book *On Becoming a Novelist* writer John Gardner insists that "all human beings see with astonishing accuracy, not that they can necessarily write it down. . . .The trick is to bring it out, get it down. Getting it down precisely is all that is meant by 'the accuracy of writer's eye.'" So observe whatever it is you are looking at with all the care you can, and record your observations with the same care, so that others can see it as well as you.

Good investigation, however, involves more than just looking at things and events with care. It involves getting the facts—whether visible or not—and getting them right. Doing so usually means checking every supposed fact against a minimum of three separate sources. If such a check isn't possible—and often it isn't—a writer may still incorporate the information, but must treat it as opinion or rumor, using labels such as "so-called" or "alleged" until the information can be verified.

Thoroughness

Every successful investigator closely examines all leads or sources that might be helpful, however slender the possibility. Police investigators call this aspect of investigation "foot work." It requires discipline to scrutinize closely all sources—the sort of patient attention one gives to a love letter. As Don Murray suggests in *Write to Learn,* "we need far more information than we can use so that we can pick and choose, connect and reconnect, as we make meaning."

A Systematic Approach

Sometimes fictional sleuths—Detective Columbo from the long-running television series comes to mind—seem to be delightfully haphazard; but the appearance is misleading. Such characters are really following a system, which includes the pretense of being haphazard. In fact, they know exactly what they are doing. All good gatherers have a plan of action, a procedure they try to follow. This does not mean they refuse to follow hunches, only that they follow them as part of a procedure. Haphazard investigation relies on luck and turns up unreliable results. Good investigation minimizes luck in order to find the most probable truth.

For an example of a systematic approach, consider the work of nonfiction writer John McPhee, a regular contributor to *The New Yorker* whose dozen books are widely considered among the best nonfiction writing on the scene. In his introduction to *The John McPhee Reader,* William Howarth describes McPhee's approach to writing.

McPhee's inquiry begins when a subject catches his interest. He focuses on a question or issue he'd like to investigate further. Once McPhee settles on a subject, he undertakes extended research. He visits his subject's locale and interviews people (primary sources), and he reads everything about the subject he can get his hands on (secondary sources). After he "starts to hear the same stories a third time," he begins formulating. He transcribes his notes from all the interviews, "occasionally adding other details or current thoughts as he goes." McPhee's writing processes are interesting enough to examine at length. According to Howarth:

He [McPhee] likens this process to a magnet's attraction of iron filings; as the notes take shape, they draw from him new ideas about placement, phrasing, or possible analogies. When finished, he may have a hundred typed sheets of notes, enough to fill a large spring binder. He makes a photocopy of the original set and shelves it for later use. He then reads and rereads the binder set, looking for areas he needs to flesh out with research and reading at Firestone library [at Princeton, near where he lives]. The reading produces more notes, the notes more typed pages for his binder. Finally, he reads the binder and makes notes on possible structures, describing patterns the story might assume.

While its structure is forming, or when he senses how the story may end, McPhee often writes out a first draft of "the lead," a term journalists use to describe openings. . . .

Having read the lead via telephone to an editor at *The New Yorker,* he goes back to the binder and begins to code it with structural notes, using titles like "Voyageurs," "Loons," or acronyms—"GLAT," "LASLE." These are his topics, the formal segments of narrative, which he next writes on a series of index cards. After assembling a stack, he fans them out and begins to play a sort of writer's solitaire, studying the possibilities of order. . . .

McPhee's approach mirrors that of all gatherers: they *inquire,* they *search,* and they *formulate.* That's the whole process: deciding what questions to answer, searching sources for answers, and formulating the best answer from the sources. The process works whether you're writing an essay about yourself or an extended report on the workings of the Federal Reserve System.

The rest of this chapter will be devoted to examining the processes of inquiring, searching, and formulating. You will see that the activities are interdependent, so that as you work with one, you will return to the others: inquiring leads to searching, which in turn leads to further inquiring, which leads to formulating, then further searching and inquiring, and so on.

Inquiring

To become a good inquirer, it helps to follow five rules of thumb.

First, *start with your deepest interests.* Find a question or problem that truly fascinates and excites you, that overwhelms you with the need to find answers or solutions. The more passionate you are in your inquiry, the more eager you will be to continue your research despite occasional setbacks.

Of course, you often have limited choices as a writer. You are assigned to write about the causes of the Civil War or the influences on Hemingway's prose or the buried feminist ideas in George Eliot's novels, and that's all there is to it. Even within an assignment, however, you must search for your own angle, your own interests, in order to write with as much involvement and concentration as possible under the circumstances. If you're having trouble writing on an assigned topic, consider trying a different format: a letter to the author or to the author's publisher, for example, or a dialogue between a husband and wife, one of whom is trying to explain the subject to the other. Sometimes format makes all the difference.

If you're lucky enough to have a wide range of choices concerning an assignment, shop around for your topic. Look at databases, using various key words. Look at various magazines that carry articles you might not agree with, such as the *National Review* if you're a political liberal, or *Progressive* magazine if you're a political conservative. Or read *Ms.* if you're a man, *Esquire* if you're a woman. Consider how you might explore points of view to which you normally pay little attention.

Look for topics that have personal relevance. You might have a friend or relative afflicted with the so-called "yuppie flu," for example. Why does this "new" disease make people so tired they can hardly get out of bed some mornings? What are doctors doing about it? How many people get it? Or suppose you heard that director George Lucas once made a striking science fiction film called *THX 1138* that few people have seen. When did he make it? Is it anything like Lucas's *Star Wars* films? Or maybe you've heard of a computer that can translate the voice into onscreen writing with no typing. Who makes it? Does it really work? When will it be commercially available? How much does it cost? Consider anything that really interests you as a possible subject for research.

Second, *narrow your focus.* Consider your deadline and length limitations. The narrower the inquiry, the more manageable the searching and formulating. What do we mean by a "narrow" inquiry? Compare these two questions:

1. How much progress is being made in the medical fight against cancer?
2. How much progress has been made in the last three months in the medical fight against cancer?

The second question is much "narrower" than the first, simply because it calls for examining only the most recent medical research, rather than all cancer research from its beginnings to the present. (Even that question presents a challenge, however, since so much cancer research occurs in three months.)

Now consider these two questions:

1. How much progress has been made in the medical fight against children's leukemia in the last year?
2. How much progress has been made in the medical fight against children's leukemia at the Sloan-Kettering Institute for Cancer Research in the last three months?

If you have months with little else to do and want to write a lengthy report, you might try to answer the first question. However, if you have a deadline and can only write a few pages, you had better narrow the question. Articles in newsmagazines offer clear models. They usually attempt to answer fairly narrow questions. Such an article might consider just one particular researcher's discoveries over a few months, a topic narrow enough to be researched and written about in a limited time.

It may take some experimenting, some trial and error, to find a question that's narrow enough but not too narrow. You know that "What was World War II like?" is much too broad. But what about "What material were GI socks made of in World War II?" Probably too narrow, right? Once you've learned that all GI socks were woven from wool, there's not much more to say. That all GI socks were woven from wool is a fact, not an issue. As interesting as facts can be, they usually need to be part of a context, an issue, a recommendation, a point of view, an opinion. Except in reference works, very seldom do we read—or write—facts for their own sake, without a larger purpose.

An issue that included this fact about GI socks might arise from research on, say, how U.S. Army combat uniforms have changed since World War II. For certain audiences and purposes, this would be a fascinating topic, and probably not too broad or too narrow to research and write about in a reasonable time.

Third, *inquire awhile.* Don't settle for the first interesting question that pops into your mind. Often students jump into research and start digging away because time seems so limited. But the time it takes to find just the right questions is time well spent.

Take time at the outset to list several problems or questions that interest you. Give yourself at least a couple of hours of discovery. Then, listen to your gut feelings, your hunches. Let your intuition tell you which one to jump into.

That said, it's a good idea to start looking for sources even if you aren't sure about your inquiry. You can always change your problem as you go; it's not carved in stone. In fact, most researchers find that their original inquiry becomes more precise and pointed—even quite different—after they examine some sources.

Fourth, *localize.* If possible, work first with local issues of immediate concern. Instead of charging into questions about abortion or capital punishment or first amendment rights or the conduct of the Vietnam War (all of which are interesting but overworked, and usually not of much local interest), consider questions about your campus food service, relations between your university and the local community, whether a liberal arts education makes students on your campus more employable, places in town where you can get a decent tune-up, what various local restaurants have to offer for various tastes, or potential pollution caused by popular lawn chemicals that people spray on local neighborhood lawns.

Fifth, *seek fact-based questions or issues.* "Why is blue such a pleasant color?" or "What makes pecan pie so delicious?" probably won't work as topics for inquiry because they're based on personal preference rather than on facts—evidence—you can research. Less obviously, while "How did Ford come up with the best-looking cars during the late 1980s?" is seemingly a question for research, it actually needs further definition. You can't really claim that one manufacturer's cars "look better" than others' without examining the whole sticky issue of automotive aesthetics. Better would be "What do we mean by 'style' in car design?," since "style" can be defined and discussed as actually existing "out there" in the world. Here are other questions based essentially on personal preference:

> Why are robins a favorite bird?
> What makes Italian food so special?
> Why is *Gone with the Wind* a memorable film?
> Why is blue the most popular color for evening wear?
> Why is "slim" so much more desirable than "fat" in America?

All of these questions might result in interesting personal or autobiographical essays. That is, you could answer them successfully by researching your own feelings, ideas, and observations—but they would require little research outside yourself.

This is not to say that there aren't genuinely researchable inquiries related to these subjects. Here are questions worthy of research:

- How well protected are robins in America? (Are they a state bird anywhere? Can they be hunted legally anywhere? Have they ever become a nuisance bird that had to be eliminated?)
- What *is* Italian food? (Do Italians agree on what their national cuisine really is? What are the typical ingredients of an Italian meal? Are there any recent experiments with new kinds of Italian food?)
- How well received was *Gone with the Wind* at the time of its release, and what is the current critical opinion of the film? (What did critics say about it in 1939? How did the film do at the box office? What have critics said about it since? On what are their judgments based? How well does it sell as a videotape?)
- What do specific colors symbolize in American culture? (What events and moods are customarily accompanied by certain colors? How do these associations differ across cultures?)
- How have Americans' attitudes toward obesity changed in the last few years? (How have the physical features of women models changed in the last two decades? What is the current image of the ideal man, and how is this image different from the ideal at the turn of the century or in other decades?)

Dealing with questions that grow out of researchable topics will require you to seek out information beyond your own immediate experience.

SUMMARY OF INQUIRING

1. Begin with a question or questions you're genuinely interested in answering.
2. Narrow your questions so that they're manageable.
3. Inquire awhile to discover just the right question.
4. Focus on local issues of immediate concern, if possible.
5. Focus on issues for which you can find evidence other than personal preference; use facts to develop and support your answers.

Searching

Outside of your observations and experiences, you will probably examine three kinds of sources in your research: primary, secondary, and reference sources.

Primary sources are first-hand sources, based on immediate experience and observation. Primary sources do not rely on other sources for information. They are the sources others rely on to develop arguments, support opinions, create histories, and so on. Letters, bills, journals and diaries, trial transcripts, inscriptions on books (or even pottery), photographs, video and audio recordings all may be primary sources. But here we will be concerned primarily with interviews and certain kinds of newspaper sources.

Secondary sources often rely to some extent on primary sources as well as on other secondary sources. Essays, opinions, arguments, reports, histories, editorials—are all secondary sources, whether the writers rely on primary or other secondary sources.

In addition to primary and secondary sources, there are various kinds of dictionaries, almanacs, encyclopedias, and bibliographies to help you locate information quickly. These *reference sources* serve as shortcuts to both primary and secondary sources, and they may be used as sources themselves, either primary or secondary.

Using Primary Sources

You are surrounded by primary sources—your professors, parents, friends, the salesperson at the used car lot, the mail delivery person, the food service worker, the local newspaper. Various publications in the library also constitute primary sources—a journal writer's impressions of Chicago, an eyewitness account of Lincoln's death, William Bradford's *Of Plymouth Colony.* A primary source is an original, *raw* source—a direct report of information based on personal experience and observation—as opposed to a *cooked* or *digested* source, which reports other people's experiences and observations. *Original* research means primary source research.

For most topics there are two main primary sources: direct interviews with knowledgeable individuals and first-hand reports in newspapers and other periodicals.

Interviews Reporters are always looking for eyewitness accounts. Interviews with eyewitnesses are a staple source for newspapers, magazines, television, and radio. Interviews, both in person and over the telephone, have several advantages over print sources:

- They are current.
- They often provide information on items of local interest unavailable anywhere else.
- Because they are personal, they are almost guaranteed to be interesting.

Interviews have certain disadvantages as well:

- They are often superficial; even experts often speak off the top of their heads, making points that they would probably revise if they were writing.
- They require skill on the part of the interviewer.
- They are subject to the biases of personality; the interviewer and the interviewee may be responding to each other as much as they are to the subject at hand.

At their best, interviews offer the possibility of making real discoveries. Good interviewers start out with an open mind, ready to hear what they do not expect. For example, Marlyn Schwartz of the *Dallas Evening News* was assigned a routine profile of the winner of the 1982 Miss America Pageant. But by interviewing the winner with an open mind and ear, she discovered that in order to improve her chances in beauty pageants, Miss America had had extensive plastic surgery. Schwartz wound up with a superb story on the obsession with winning that illustrates one of the major values of the interview: asking questions directly of others is an extraordinary means of generating and developing material worth writing about.

To conduct successful interviews, you need to follow six steps.

First, *consider the people you'd like to interview.* Make a list of several people, arranging them if possible by category. Suppose you've decided to look into the food service in your campus dining hall. Perhaps you are impressed and want to give credit where it's due. Perhaps you're depressed and want to see how it can be improved. Whatever your motive, there are a number of people you could interview who might know about the food service and its operation.

In most such situations there are four kinds of people who would be useful to interview:

> *Executives,* or decision-makers. In the case of food service, these might include the vice president for student services and his or her assistants in charge of budgets and management decisions about policies and procedures.
>
> *Experts,* or those people who know most about actual processes and products. In the case of food services, these would include dietitians and menu planners.
>
> *Technicians,* or those people responsible for actually doing what the executives and experts order. In our example, these would include the kitchen supervisors, the cooks, the student help.
>
> *Laypeople,* or those people who use the product or service and thus know about it from the perspective of an interested outsider.

If possible, find two or three people in each category in order to get as balanced a picture of the whole operation as you can.

Second, *write out a list of questions.* Usually five to seven is enough for starters. You can always add more as they occur to you. Try to anticipate key points and ask questions centering on those points. If you were going to write about the campus food service, for example, and knew you would likely be most concerned about how the food service plans meals, here are some opening questions:

- What principles are followed in meal planning?
- How have these principles changed over the years?
- What student input have you gathered about meals?
- What kind of training do the dietitians have?
- What provisions do you make for persons with special dietary needs and preferences, such as diabetics and vegetarians?
- How are costs kept down?
- Who inspects kitchen facilities? How often?
- How much does food quality vary, and why?
- Would people be willing to pay more for higher quality meals? How much more?

Some of these questions are more appropriate for one category of interviewees than another. Suit your questions to the person you're interviewing whenever possible. Also try to avoid questions that can be answered "yes" or "no" and questions that are answered in easily available brochures or handouts.

Having made a list of questions, determine how much time the interview will take. If the questions are few and require fairly quick answers, so that the entire interview will take no more than ten minutes, arrange a telephone interview. If, however, the interview is likely to take longer, and if it would help you (as it often does) to see the person you're going to interview—the setting, the dress, the facial expressions, the body language—then arrange for an interview face-to-face.

If you are in doubt, conduct the interview in person. By seeing as well as hearing, you always learn more about the person you're interviewing, and you are more likely to come up with new leads and discover the unexpected.

Third, *call for an appointment*. Begin by introducing yourself by name, explaining your project and the reason you're calling. If you're calling for a phone interview, explain that it will take no more than ten minutes and ask if you can conduct it right then or if you should call back at a more convenient time. Emphasize that you will be happy to call back later: no one likes to answer questions over the phone at an awkward time, when dinner's on the table or the kids are screaming, or a meeting or a quarrel is in progress. If you're calling for an in-person interview, explain the length of time you need (but no more than an hour; if it happens to take more, you can arrange for a follow-up). Make every effort to be available at the interviewee's convenience. End with a thank-you and a reminder of the date and time of the interview. After you hang up, write down the time for the interview.

Fourth, *prepare for the interview*. Read any literature that's available concerning the subject of the interview—the person, the company, the campaign, the party, the service. Note the points in the literature that answer any of your questions and the points you might want to ask questions about. Decide whether you want to use a tape recorder or to take notes. With a tape recorder you have the advantage of recording the exact quote; you have the disadvantage of relying on the machine instead of your own ear, so that you might miss certain nuances of tone that could lead to the unexpected and thus end up stringing together quotes you only half understand. (Incidentally, be sure to ask for permission to tape, preferably in writing. It is unethical to tape anyone without their permission.)

Keep in mind the overall purpose of the interview. What are you trying to find out? What do you hope to gain? Having your purpose clearly in mind helps you know when you've met your objective, and when the interview is over.

Make a final list of appropriate questions for the person you're interviewing. These need not necessarily be agreeable or disagreeable but should be questions the person is likely to understand and answer. You are trying to make neither a friend nor an enemy in an interview. Rather, you are trying to get information not available elsewhere.

Fifth, *conduct the interview.* Show up on time, introduce yourself, and begin asking questions. (This visit is business, not a chat.) Maintain eye contact without staring. Take notes, but try to avoid asking the interviewee to repeat an answer— people find it annoying to do so and will begin to question your competence. Try to notice when the interviewee has finished an answer, and have the next question ready, to avoid long awkward pauses.

Above all, listen. Don't focus your attention on the next question you're going to ask—you should have a list in front of you for that. Focus rather on what the interviewee is saying, so that if something unexpected comes up you'll be able to notice and follow it up. Don't try to force the interview along a certain line. If it starts acquiring an interesting dynamic of its own, go with the flow. Help it along with a "segue" or transition: "Let me follow up on that point. . . ." or "Does that mean you think . . . ?"

On the other hand, don't let important questions go unanswered. If the interview begins to wander, bring it back into line by returning to the questions you've prepared. Finally, don't forget to thank your interviewee for his or her time.

Sixth, *"debrief."* Immediately after the interview, find a quiet place and rerun the interview in your mind. Reporters agree that this is a crucial phase of the interview. It enables you to find any missing points, to clarify your notes, to discover other questions you'd like to ask, either of the interviewee in a follow-up session or of someone else. (If you should discover, for example, that the food service staff includes no trained dietitians, you would want to ask the executives involved a question or two.)

In your debriefing session, *write down* the points you've learned and any questions or other observations that come to mind. If you trust your memory, you may learn some hard lessons about how imperfect that faculty can be.

As a summary of interviewing, let us return to John McPhee again. His interview techniques comprise a large part of his research. Here's William Howarth's description of McPhee's interviewing style:

> When McPhee conducts an interview he tries to be as blank as his notebook pages, totally devoid of preconceptions, equipped with only the most

elementary knowledge. He has found that imagining he knows a subject is a disadvantage, for that prejudice will limit his freedom to ask, to learn, to be surprised by unfolding evidence. Since most stories are full of unsuspected complexity, an interviewer hardly needs to *feign* ignorance; the stronger temptation is to bluff with a show of knowledge or to trick the informant into providing simple, easily digestible answers. Neither course is to McPhee's liking; he would rather risk seeming ignorant to get a solid, knotty answer.

As a result, some of his interviewees have mistakenly believed he is thick-witted. At times his speech slows, his brow knits, he asks the same question over and over. When repeating answers, he so garbles them that a new answer must be provided. Some informants find his manner relaxing, others are exasperated; in either case, they talk more freely and fully to him than they normally would to a reporter.

SUMMARY OF INTERVIEW STEPS

1. Make a list of people you want to interview.
2. Write out questions.
3. Call for an appointment.
4. Prepare for the interview.
5. Conduct the interview.
6. Debrief.

Newspapers For all their flaws—and they are numerous—portions of newspapers can be indispensable primary sources. First, newspapers provide a daily record of the world, containing information unavailable from other sources on local, regional, national, and international events and issues. You will be hard pressed to find anything in history books on the Garden Club of Paul's Valley, Oklahoma. You can't interview people about events that took place a hundred years ago; in fact, people have difficulty remembering the specifics of events that happened last year or even last week. For such facts and figures and for responses to events and issues—the way people felt and thought—newspapers provide as accurate a record as we have.

Second, newspapers are widely available. Every library—whether city, county, or college—keeps back issues on file. For example, the public library in Cedar Falls, Iowa (a town of about 35,000) contains microfilm issues of a local daily newspaper dating back to 1860, at the start of the Civil War. Large libraries keep microfilm collections of a number of newspapers, from local weeklies to the *New York Times.*

Finally, through editorials and letters, through classified and commercial advertising, through cartoons and illustrations, newspapers provide a sense of the "style" of a time, what Germans call the *Weltanschauung* or worldview—the thoughts and feelings, the concerns and controversies, the hopes and fears, the popular opinions and biases and prejudices of an era. Look at newspapers from the turn of the century and you will find (from illustrations and advertisements) that white, middle-class women wanted to look soft, rather plump, and untanned;

look at papers today and you will see that white middle-class women want to look lean and tan. The difference reflects a radical shift in values concerning the body, beauty, and leisure (a shift that will almost certainly occur again as the sun gains a reputation for causing various forms of skin cancer). Newspapers provide a surprisingly clear record of cultural and social values.

Newspapers also have disadvantages. Most notably, material presented as factual may be erroneous, even fabricated. Some reporters are notorious for making up facts in lieu of the hard work of chasing them down. Writer Norman Mailer once complained that newspaper "facts" should be called "factoids" until cross-checked and verified with other sources. You'll see Mailer's point if you read two different newspaper accounts of the same story; while purporting to be objective, they will differ in ways ranging from minor details to major issues.

In addition, because of space and cost, small and medium-sized libraries are quite selective about the papers they collect. Most will have the local paper and the *New York Times*, perhaps the *Christian Science Monitor* and the *Wall Street Journal*. But unless you live in Denver or Des Moines, you're not likely to find the *Denver Post* or the *Des Moines Register*. Consequently, you may have difficulty cross-checking stories, especially older ones.

Another practical disadvantage is that reading microfilm or microfiche is tiring, and taking judicious notes is challenging. You will be tempted to take either too few notes, just to get away from the glare, or too many notes, to avoid missing something important. (We recommend that you take notes on everything you find important or interesting: when in doubt, take notes. Make photocopies of whole pages only when you need the entire story to analyze closely.)

To use newspapers as a primary source in your investigation, keep in mind the following six recommendations:

First, *try to begin with a fairly clear question*. Thoreau, who explored the woods and fields around his home every day, noted that when he wasn't looking for anything in particular he found nothing but when he was looking for something in particular he almost always discovered something, whether what he had in mind or something else. To see, we must look; to look, we must have something to look for.

Before combing newspapers for information, then, remember the need for an early focus. Define a question you'd like to answer or a problem you'd like to investigate, no matter how odd or remote it may seem. How much local protesting occurred during the height of the Vietnam War? What were local attitudes toward racial integration during the early sixties? What did people think of the McCarthy hearings in the early 1950s? What vaudeville shows were performed in the old downtown movie theater before it began showing movies? What sorts of recipes were considered fashionable a hundred years ago? What breeds of dogs were popular? How were garbage and trash disposed of?

Newspapers can help you answer just such questions.

Second, *consider which newspapers and dates will be appropriate for your inquiry*. If you are concerned about local matters, for instance, you will not need to look at national papers like the *Christian Science Monitor* or the *Wall Street Journal*. Local papers will do. If you are concerned about a matter of state-wide significance, you will want to look at several large-circulation papers in the state. If your subject is of national or international significance, you will probably want to read the *New York Times,* the *London Times,* the *Washington Post,* the *Christian Science Monitor,* and the *Wall Street Journal,* among others.

In deciding on dates, make sure you define a span large enough to encompass the subject you are investigating: if you are interested, say, in local responses to the Supreme Court's 1954 *Brown v. Board of Education* decision (which declared that laws establishing separate but equal educational facilities for blacks and whites were unconstitutional), you should not limit yourself to the year 1954 but look into at least the first six months of 1955.

Once you have the papers and dates in mind, check with your college or university library, your hometown library, and the local newspaper office. For libraries, call the reference librarian and find out whether newspapers are available for the dates you want. In the case of the local paper, explain the topic and ask permission to visit their archives to look at old copies.

If the papers are available, you're ready to begin. (If they're available in one place, you've got it made.) If some are not, you will either have to settle for less or take a trip to a different library. If none are available—and, alas, this happens— you might have to find a different subject. (If you know the exact dates you need and no library in the area carries the particular paper you want to see, you can look into obtaining copies through interlibrary loan, but this process can be slow and expensive.)

Third, *be prepared to take notes.* Use two sizes of note cards: 3 x 5 inches and 4 x 6 inches. The 3 x 5s are your bibliography cards: include on them the exact title of the newspaper, the date, and the title and page numbers of the story you're reading, one story per card. (Entering only one item per card will make it easy for you to list your sources alphabetically for the bibliography.) Your bibliography cards should look something like Figure 3.1.

The 4 x 6s are your note cards: at the top of these, write a quick reference to the particular source, then make a note about that source, one note per card. Resist the temptation to fill the card up, front and back, to save space and time and trouble. You will save yourself time and trouble in the long run if you enter only one piece of information on each 4 x 6 card: when it comes time to write, you will be able to arrange and rearrange your material freely until you find the right form. Your note cards should look something like Figure 3.2. In general, you will use many more 4 x 6 note cards than 3 x 5 source cards.

Different size cards help keep sources and notes from being confused. And labeling all cards clearly means you won't have to backtrack for necessary bibliographical information, a serious nuisance that you should spare yourself in advance. (Incidentally, more and more researchers are now relying on laptop word processors to take notes; if you have one, or can afford one, you can keep notes and references in different files.)

Cushman, Deborah.   Road Rollin.
Des Moines Register   23 July
1991: Section T, 1-2

Figure 3.1   Sample Bibliography Card

Fourth, *look for facts, inferences, and judgments as you read.* Keep in mind here that not all stories in the newspaper are primary sources. Editorials, feature stories, and reports from multiple witnesses are secondary sources, filtered through the reporter's consciousness. Primary sources include first-person accounts, transcripts of events, legal announcements, journals, diaries, and letters, all regularly printed in newspapers. Even such primary sources, however, may contain hidden inferences and implied judgments.

What are facts, inferences, and judgments?

Facts are data that are presented as true, and that can be corroborated by other sources. While you can't believe everything you read, even from eyewitnesses, statements about what happened during and after a plane crash that come directly from the pilot and the flight attendants are likely to be more reliable than statements from a reporter who writes about it from a distance. A reporter is likely to add inferences and judgments, sometimes inadvertently.

Inferences are conclusions about the unknown based on facts that are known. For example, you see a student staggering along the sidewalk, falling down, and vomiting in the gutter: you conclude that he is drunk. Your conclusion, however, is not a fact; it is based upon certain facts (staggering, falling, vomiting), but it may be wrong: the poor guy may have the flu. To be certain, you need more facts: a whiff of his breath, a breathalyzer test, eyewitness accounts from people he may have been with ("He just downed three six-packs." "He's been complaining of feeling feverish and achy and nauseated."). An inference should be stated as such ("Because he staggered, fell, and vomited, he seemed to be drunk."), but you cannot assume that newspaper writers will always extend

Cushman — 1

Cushman asserts that people who use
in-line skates must wear heavy padding ——
  like ice hockey players wear. (Knee
pads, elbow pads, wrist pads and
helmets.) Also, many in-line skaters
use bike helmets.

Cushman — 2

Cost —— Cushman says $250 for new
in-line skates and all the protective
gear you will need. (Rent for $6 an
hour before you buy —— up to a week
for $25.)

Figure 3.2 Sample Note Cards

this courtesy to their subjects. They often present inferences as facts, and they
may, when they find certain facts disagreeable, present facts as inferences.
(Imagine a lawyer representing our sample student: "He seemed to be staggering,
and it would appear he fell, and he may have vomited.") As a reader, then, you
must be on the alert for the difference, sifting facts from inferences so that you
know which you are using.

Judgments are votes of approval or disapproval expressed either explicitly or implicitly.

Approval: "This legislation is long overdue."
Disapproval: "This legislation is unnecessary."
Explicit: "I'm in favor of it!"
Implicit: "Do we really need another piece of legislation on this issue?"

Such value judgments can be made with considerable subtlety, by using certain words (movie "mogul" or "czar," for instance, instead of "producer") or by omitting certain facts (the mogul's work with the blind, the producer's association with the mob). Note that a judgment can overlap with an inference—indeed, a judgment amounts to a value inference—but an inference doesn't have to involve a judgment. The inference that the student is drunk, for instance, may lead to radically different judgments: "The jerk is drunk." "The poor guy is drunk."

Fifth, *read comparatively whenever possible.* Look up more than one account of the same event to cross-check facts and to note what one writer emphasizes and omits compared to another. Note also any differences in word choice between or among the accounts you're comparing. In other words, try to understand an event from as many perspectives as possible.

Be aware, though, that older and local events usually cannot be corroborated by other sources. A forest fire in Peshtigo, Wisconsin, on October 8, 1871 (the same day as the Great Chicago Fire) did not, you may be sure, get wide coverage from several sources, as the Chicago Fire did. And simply because most libraries have larger collections of more recent newspapers than of older, you would probably be able to find more reports about the 1980 fire at the MGM Grand Hotel in Las Vegas than about the Chicago Fire of 1871. If you can find only one newspaper account of an event, read carefully to distinguish fact from inference from judgment from unfettered imagination. Note the facts you might be able to cross-check with other kinds of sources—newsmagazines, historical journals, history books.

Sixth, *when you finish a session with newspapers, debrief.* See if you have gaps in your notes, or areas of possible confusion. If you find such, and if it's possible, try to fill in the gap or resolve the confusion before you leave the library; if not, make a note right on the card about what the difficulty is and where you were when you left off, jotting down the title, date, and page of the paper, along with the number on the roll of microfilm. If you don't blaze your trail carefully, you can waste precious time backtracking.

SUMMARY OF USING NEWSPAPERS

1. Begin with a clear purpose.
2. Consider which newspapers and dates are appropriate for your purpose and available to you for research.
3. Take notes on two sizes of cards: 3 x 5 for bibliography, 4 x 6 for information.

4. Look for facts, inferences, and judgments.
5. Read comparatively when possible.
6. Debrief.

APPLICATIONS

1. Every campus has famous and infamous features: the accounting department for its high percentage of graduates who pass the CPA exam, the student union for its lousy hamburgers, the area around campus for its dirt and noise, the library for its collection of children's literature. Choose one such feature of your campus, and begin an investigation by listing the various people you might interview about it—laypeople, technicians, decision-makers, experts. Based on your lists, begin investigating: make appointments for interviews and conduct them. Take notes. Look for new leads.

2. Take any well-known personality you admire, and plan an investigation into how he or she has been treated by the press. Select several major newspapers available to you—the *New York Times,* the *Chicago Sun-Times,* the *Christian Science Monitor,* the *Wall Street Journal*—as well as all the local papers you can find. Focus on three or four episodes in the celebrity's personal life and professional career, and look up the stories dealing with these in various newspapers. Compare and contrast the stories to find basic similarities and differences, and to see how the press's treatment of the subject developed over time. Take notes. Remember that the more famous the celebrity, the more material you'll have to deal with.

3. Choose any important event that has taken place in the lifetime of people you know—the bombing of Pearl Harbor, the Rosenberg executions, the Kennedy assassinations, the King assassination, the Nixon resignation, a local disaster. Plan a series of questions for various people: when they heard about the event, how they first responded, what they did, how they feel about it now that it has become history, what difference, if any, the event has made in their lives. Conduct several interviews based on your questions, taking careful notes. (For a classic of this genre, see Studs Terkel's *The Good War.*)

4. If you follow fashions, investigate the fashion ads and layouts in several older issues of various newspapers and magazines (especially, of course, fashion magazines). Choose a five-year period, and make notes about what people were wearing—the popular shapes, colors, materials, textures.

5. Investigate any local issue that has made the news: the mayor's hiring practices, women in local positions of power, alcohol ordinances, towing illegally parked cars, the push for a winning football team. Make a list of people to interview and of questions, then make appointments and conduct the interviews.

Read and take notes about various news stories concerning the issue. See if you can discern basic schools of thought, the agreements and disagreements.

6. With members of your writing group, investigate newspaper ads over a period of ten years or so from newspapers printed before 1940. (You will probably use microfiche or microfilm.) Have each member examine several issues for a designated period and bring back information to the group concerning how the ads were worded, frequency of ads for certain kinds of products, use of illustrations, layout—whatever seems worth noting.

Using Secondary Sources

Many sources you will use for research include information gathered from other research, in addition to the writer's own observations and experience. These secondary sources interpret, take sides, draw conclusions, make recommendations. Because they attempt to understand the subject rather than just compile data about it, we might also call them *cooked* or *digested* sources. For example, the text of the President's State of the Union address is a primary source, but columnist David Broder's commentary on that address is a secondary source. Similarly, if you examine advertisements from old newspapers, you are making use of primary sources; if you read an article or book on advertising practices, you are using a secondary source.

Why use secondary sources? Three reasons: (1) to gather more information, (2) to examine how others understand your subject, and (3) to help you arrive at your own understanding of the subject and formulate your own conclusions.

Using secondary sources offers several advantages:

- You get the benefit of work already done—research, study, and thought.
- You get the chance to read writers who know how to make difficult material understandable, interesting, entertaining, sometimes absolutely compelling (writers like Carl Sagan, Lewis Thomas, Joan Didion, Rachel Carson, James Baldwin, and John McPhee).
- You often get visual aids—photos, drawings, tables, graphs, and the like —that primary and secondary sources rarely include.

There are a couple of disadvantages, too:

- The very charm of a writer's style can make it difficult to spot lapses of logic, insufficient data, flights of fancy pretending to be fact.
- The work of professionals, because it seems so authoritative and complete, often intimidates beginning investigators, making them feel that there is nothing left for them to do, no other information to find, no other position possible to take.

To cope with these potential problems, reserve judgment for a while. Remind yourself that no one has the last word on anything, that other points of view are always possible, and that, after you've done some looking around, you will be able to assess the relative strengths and weaknesses of the sources you are using.

In dealing with secondary sources, consider three factors: (1) source credibility; (2) facts, inferences, and judgments; and (3) readers' needs.

Source Credibility Credibility means believability. How do you determine whether the person you are reading or listening to is believable? In the flesh you take into account a number of things—expression, demeanor, gesture, dress, tone, and pitch. Further, if you know the person speaking, you already have a sense of his or her credibility. In reading, though, you can't see the writer's expression and demeanor, and you may well know nothing about the person. So how do you determine credibility? By taking into account several considerations, some of which you can assess right away, others only after you've done some research. In determining source credibility, keep the following considerations in mind:

First, *consider the context,* that is, the place of publication. As a rule (to which there are always exceptions) an article in *Atlantic* is more reliable than one in, say, a fan magazine. A book published by major commercial publisher is more reliable than one published by a vanity press (where the writer pays the costs of publication). Take into account religious and political affiliations: Catholic and feminist magazines approach abortion with definable biases; liberal and conservative presses deal very differently with third-world revolutions. If you don't know anything about a particular press or publication, ask your instructor or reference librarian.

Second, *consider the writer's use of sources and documentation.* Are the sources recent? Are they well-known or obscure? Where were they published? Are there enough of them for the size of the investigation, or did the writer take shortcuts? Is the documentation clear? Could you easily look up the sources cited?

Third, *consider the writer's use of facts.* Are there enough to warrant the conclusions? Are some facts actually inferences and judgments in disguise? Have any of the "facts" asserted been discredited elsewhere?

Fourth, *consider the writer's knowledge of background information.* Does the writer know what other studies have been done, what is already known?

Fifth, *consider the writer's attention to language and the mechanics of written English.* Many mistakes bespeak carelessness, a cavalier disregard for precision and accuracy.

Sixth, *consider the writer's style and organization.* Walker Gibson has identified three basic styles expressing three basic attitudes toward material and readers: "tough," meaning clipped, factual, dry; "sweet," meaning agreeable, warm, familiar, ingratiating; and "stuffy," meaning formal, academic, official, bureaucratic, often riddled with jargon. Like any classification scheme, Gibson's is too simple for the complex reality it describes, but it can be useful.

When examining sources, observe which of these styles predominates. Pay particular attention to how the style affects you. Sometimes a sweet style can persuade you to accept a position not warranted by the facts (which is why advertisers favor the sweet style above the other two); a stuffy style may put you off valuable material; a tough style may make you receptive to inferences and judgments that you might otherwise dismiss as sentimental.

Organization refers to the writer's arrangement of material. All kinds of arrangements are possible depending on subject, purpose, and audience: least to most important (or vice versa), chronological, spatial, general to specific, specific to general, familiar to difficult, agreeable to controversial. Whatever the organization, it should seem appropriate to the subject and help you understand the material.

Finally, *consider the writer's reputation.* Do you read the writer regularly with certain expectations? Have you found him or her trustworthy in other essays? If you haven't read the writer before, have you heard of him or her? Is the writer a respected authority on the subject, or a newcomer? (If no information is given in your source, you might consider looking the writer up in a reference work such as *Current Biography* or *Contemporary Authors.*)

Facts, Inferences, and Judgments Just as when you read first-person reports in newspapers, when reading secondary sources you must differentiate among facts, inferences, and judgments. Early on in a project you may have trouble distinguishing, but as you progress you will acquire the knowledge necessary to read critically, to see if an author is omitting facts or asserting an inference as if it were fact.

To help yourself read critically, try to label at least some of the assertions in secondary sources as F (for facts that can be corroborated from other sources), as I (for inferences about the unknown based on the known), or as J (for judgments of value). To illustrate, here is the opening paragraph of an article from the June 1984 issue of *Nursing,* a professional journal for nurses:

> If ever the "herd instinct" is powerful, it's during adolescence. [I] Teen-agers hate to be different from their peers. [I] But 13-year-old Katie *was* differ-ent because she had a rare, disfiguring disease, ateriovenous malformation of the leg. [F] Guiding her through a long, complicated treatment meant helping her accept one setback after another. [F] It wasn't easy. [J] She was hospital-ized for 8 months and we had to tailor her expectations almost weekly. [F]

Not every reader will come up with the same labels. Whether an assertion is seen as an inference or a judgment is sometimes a matter of personal perspective. But by labeling each statement, you force yourself to weigh it carefully and assess just what it is you're reading.

Readers' Needs As you read you have to decide what's worth taking down and what's not. The major criterion for choosing has to be your own sense of what's true and what's significant, because the point of doing research is to dis-cover and communicate what you see as the truth.

But to communicate your points effectively you have to take into account your probable readers. More specifically, you must consider their knowledge of the subject and their attitude toward it. For example, how much can you assume they already know about alcoholism and Alcoholics Anonymous? How much (and how little) will you need to explain about the physiological effects of alco-hol? About prohibition and its repeal? How are they likely to feel about the posi-tion you're taking? If you approve of AA, for instance, and your readers think it's radically overrated, you will need not only strong evidence of its value, but also strong arguments in its favor.

You will also need to consider the "style" of information you should use: if your audience is a no-nonsense, to-the-point sort of group, you will need the sort of information they will find persuasive—hard facts. If, however, you will be addressing elementary-school children, you would probably want to present anecdotal information suited to their level of interest.

Whatever your audience, be sure to take careful notes. As with primary sources, use 3 x 5 inch cards for bibliographical information, 4 x 6 inch cards for the notes themselves. When you write something down verbatim, make sure you're accurate. Always take down the page numbers of the material you're recording, whether you're setting it down verbatim or summarizing it in your own words. Careful citation will increase your credibility with eventual readers. If in doubt whether to record something or not, record it: good researchers always wind up with considerably more material than they use, because with ample material they improve their chances of having good, strong, telling support for each and every point. If and when the sources you're examining provoke ideas of your own, write those down, too: if you trust your memory you may be putting yourself in the hands of a fickle friend.

APPLICATIONS

1. You may have conducted interviews on some campus feature you find interesting, following the directions for Application 1 on page 53. Now search for secondary sources on that feature: news articles, maybe a book or a chapter in a book, possibly an essay. Take notes on these secondary sources.

2. Look for secondary material about the celebrity you may have researched following the directions for Application 2 on page 53. Start your search with the year he or she first became noticed (you should know this from your investigation) and see what various writers had to say about your celebrity. Take notes.

3. Read as many historical essays, reports, and arguments as you can that deal with the event you may have examined following the directions for Application 3 on page 53. Pay attention to the various writers' points of view, and watch for facts, inferences, and judgments. Take notes.

4. After completing Application 4 on page 53, investigate what various writers say about fashion. Start with general works on fashion that catch your interest, then try to focus on some aspect of fashion that connects to what you noticed as you examined newspaper ads. For example, you may have noticed how often ads use certain female facial and body types for all clothing ads. You might want to examine Naomi Wolf's *The Beauty Myth* to follow up on this observation.

5. Search for case studies, arguments, research reports, essays, and editorials on the *kind* of local issue you may have examined following the directions for

Application 5 on page 53. Read them as possible sources for your own use, taking notes on any information that seems worth knowing and remembering.

6. If members of your writing group have examined newspaper advertising (see Application 6 on page 54), now find secondary sources that discuss various aspects of advertising. You might begin with marketing texts, then find more specialized works that appeal to various members of your group. Take notes, and discuss whatever ideas seem to emerge.

Using Reference Aids

For many subjects you will need to gather statistical and other factual information, as well as the kinds of information found in magazine and journal articles, government publications, monographs (brief scholarly books on narrow subjects), and books. Yet there is such an abundance of these sources, literally thousands, that groping through library stacks will get you nowhere. You need help in finding the materials you require. And such help exists in a variety of reference sources and in search aids that serve as indexes to many published works. We will show you how to select and use reference sources and search aids in any general investigation. While every specific field—microbiology, corporate law, orthodontia, coin collecting, rhetoric—has specialized reference sources of its own, we will focus on the basic reference sources that every general investigator needs. There are three kinds:

1. Fact references compile information about people, places, events, and ideas—atlases, almanacs, historical surveys, brochures, encyclopedias, yearbooks, dictionaries of biography.
2. Literature/language references include dictionaries, thesauruses, dictionaries of quotations, concordances to various works.
3. Search aids include catalogs, readers' guides, indexes, and bibliographies.

Using these reference sources offers several advantages.

- They are genuine shortcuts, saving you time, trouble, even money.
- They are usually reliable.
- They help you narrow your investigation quickly from the big picture (often about the size of the world) down to the close-up that most investigators find most productive.
- They help you generate more material, different angles, other possibilities.
- They're readily available in libraries, in paperback versions at local bookstores, and on computer databases designed for both home and library.

Reference aids do have some disadvantages, however:

- They tempt beginning researchers to rely on them exclusively, resulting in "cut-and-paste" research papers that lack both depth and insight.

- They are not absolutely reliable; you may need to cross-check even such "factual" material as birth and death dates.
- They vary widely in quality—some are poorly designed, hard to use, and therefore not very useful.

Certain reference books are so important you should have copies of your own: a dictionary, a thesaurus, a handbook of grammar and style, and a manual for documenting research sources. You might also find it worthwhile to buy your own dictionary of biography and desk encyclopedia. (Don't, however, grab any book off the shelf. Like cars, some reference books are lemons. Check with your instructor or reference librarian for specific titles.)

To use reference aids effectively, keep the following six points in mind:

First, *always begin with a question you want answered or an issue you want to investigate.* If you look around for nothing in particular, you won't find much, and what you do find may amount to little more than unrelated odds and ends—a trivial pursuit.

Suppose, for instance, you were at a party recently where a number of people got drunk and acted like idiots. But they didn't act like the *same* idiots. Some got silly. Some got mean. Some got sad. And all acted unusual, as if they had been transformed. The silly ones were usually serious, the mean ones nice, the sad ones jolly. So you wondered: how does alcohol alter people's personalities? And that question leads to another: how does it alter personalities in such radically different ways? These are your questions; this is your inquiry.

Second, *jot down two lists, one on what you already know about the subject and one on what you need to know.* Let's continue with the inquiry on alcohol:

WHAT I ALREADY KNOW ABOUT ALCOHOL

1. Effects vary: some people become hostile, some sentimental, some happy, some silly, and so forth.
2. Effects change from first drink to last: some may start silly and wind up mean; some may start mean and wind up sentimental.
3. People often drink specifically for the changes in their personality, especially the early changes.
4. Heavy drinkers require more and more alcohol for the changes to occur.
5. Serious problems, physical and psychological, can result from prolonged heavy drinking.

WHAT I NEED TO KNOW

1. What is alcohol, exactly?
2. Are there different kinds of alcohol?
3. How does alcohol operate on the brain?
4. Is there any correlation between the effects of alcohol and personality type?
5. How long have people used alcohol as a recreational drug?
6. How can one tell when alcohol is becoming a problem?

Third, *examine your "need to know" list and decide where to go for answers.* Remember that there are three basic types of reference sources: fact sources, language sources, and search aids that list further sources. Fact sources will give you basic information about the subject—historical, sociological, psychological, cultural. Language sources will help you understand the terms used. The lists of further sources will give you titles of works dealing with the subject—books, monographs, and articles.

Usually you can begin with the two most common sources, the dictionary and the encyclopedia. The encyclopedia is especially useful because it serves as both a fact source and a list of further sources.

Students often forget the dictionary, perhaps because it is so common or because they don't realize the value of definitions. Here is a standard dictionary definition of alcohol:

> Alcohol—n. [ML. < Ar. *al kohl,* powder of antimony: the change of meaning occurred in European usage] 1. a colorless, volatile, pungent liquid, C2H5OH, synthesized or obtained by fermentation of sugars and starches, and widely used, either pure or denatured, as a solvent, in drugs, cleaning solutions, explosives, and intoxicating beverages.

Look up any words you don't understand. What, for instance, is "denatured" alcohol? You'll find that it's ethyl alcohol (that is, common alcohol) made unfit for drinking by the addition of a substance such as methanol. One thing leads to another when you are investigating: what is methanol? If you don't know, look it up—you can't afford to overlook any leads. Here is what you would find:

> Methanol—n. [< *methyl* + *-ol*], a colorless, volatile, inflammable, poisonous liquid, CH2OH, obtained by the destructive distillation of wood and used in organic synthesis, as a fuel, and in the manufacture of formaldehyde, smokeless powders, paints, etc.: also called *wood alcohol.*

So *that's* the stuff people get blind drunk on, literally! Note how much information we've obtained from looking up only three words. If you look up more—*ferment, synthesize, distill, volatile*—you will come up with even more information.

So start with the dictionary. Then turn to an encyclopedia (or two or three). They will give you the basic information to launch your investigation effectively.

Fourth, *take notes.* Remember to use two sizes of cards: one 3 x 5 inch card for each source (including any listed in the encyclopedia) and one 4 x 6 inch card for each note (any information you consider worth saving, either in direct quotes or your own words). Don't forget to include the source and the page number on every note card.

Fifth, *based on what you've learned, make another list of what you still need to know.* Chances are, you're discovering more questions, and you're beginning to develop an interest in one particular aspect of the subject. If not, start looking for an aspect to focus on. Alcohol, for example, is simply too large a subject to manage, even in a long research paper or report.

Suppose you've read something in an encyclopedia that has sparked your interest in the history of alcohol in this country: Alcoholics Anonymous was founded in 1934, one year after the repeal of prohibition. You'd like to look into that, so you make a list of questions:

- Who founded AA, and why?
- What are its tenets, its principles?
- Are its principles applicable to other kinds of addiction?
- How successful has it been?
- Are there any offshoots of this organization?

Sixth, *go to the lists of other sources.* You may already have noted some further sources from the encyclopedia, but now that you've developed a more specific focus, you need to consult more extensive reference aids to lead you to the publications that contain the answers to your questions. Here are the main reference aids for finding sources (all of which may be available in your library on-line or on CD-ROM, which can be a real time-saver):

- the library card catalog
- *Reader's Guide to Periodical Literature*
- *Humanities Index*
- *Social Sciences Index*
- *Monthly Catalog of United States Government Publications*
- *Newsbank* (on microfiche or CD-ROM only)
- *InfoTrak* (on CD-ROM only)

In each of these look up your subject under as many headings as you can think of: alcohol, alcoholism, Alcoholics Anonymous. Look for cross-references and check them out. Make note of any books, articles, and publications that look and sound promising—one source for each 3 x 5 card.

Don't neglect the catalog of government publications. Few students take advantage of it, regrettably. Our government is the world's largest publisher, and it publishes quality work. Since you help pay for it, you might as well get the benefit of it.

Now that you've begun to narrow your focus, you may also want to make a list of potential primary sources. In researching Alcoholics Anonymous, you might call the local chapter, ask for any literature, and see if any members would be willing to talk to you about the history of the organization. Also you might look up articles in various newspapers about the founding of Alcoholics Anonymous.

SUMMARY OF SEARCHING STRATEGIES

1. Make a list of the sources that will help you develop answers to the questions raised by your preliminary inquiry about your subject.
2. Conduct interviews, examine available newspapers, use reference aids (including databases), find secondary sources, take notes using two sizes of notecards or a laptop word processor to keep records.

3. Examine secondary sources for credibility. Analyze these sources' use of facts, inferences, and judgments. Evaluate the writer's style and organization.

4. Keep eventual readers in mind as you search.

5. As answers emerge, see if there are other sources you need for further support and development. Don't hesitate to seek further information and to change your answers as your inquiry grows.

APPLICATIONS

1. Search any reference sources related to the campus feature you may be investigating following the directions for Application 1 on pages 53 and 57. Brochures may contain historical facts on this material, as well as the names of people who were or are involved. For purposes of comparison, consider also examining fact sources for similar situations on other campuses. Suppose, for example, you're looking into your school's successful CPA program. Through the card catalog, the *Reader's Guide,* and the monthly catalog of government publications, find material dealing with CPA programs across the country in order to learn about their structure and their policies and to determine their success.

2. Check several reference sources—dictionaries of biographies like *Who's Who,* for example—to find facts about the life of the public personality you may be researching following the directions for Application 2 on pages 53 and 57. Be sure to cross-check the dates of your subject's various landmark events, such as marriages, first public accomplishments, even birth and (if applicable) death. Keep careful notes.

3. Start a file list of quotations about the historical event you may be researching following the directions for Application 3 on pages 53 and 57. Use any quotation reference book, such as George Seldes' *The Great Quotations* or *Bartlett's Familiar Quotations.* Since your specific event may not be listed as a category, look at related headings. If you are investigating the bombing of Pearl Harbor, for example, look up *war.* Even if your subject is a listed category, such as *assassination,* look up related categories like *murder* and *killing.* On your larger note cards record the quotations that seem worth saving.

4. If you're working on the assignment in Application 4 on pages 53 and 57, look up the word *fashion* in any dictionary and note all the meanings. Also, go to the library and look up the word in the unabridged *Oxford English Dictionary,* and note the origins and history of the word. Also, check the entries for *fashion* in two or three encyclopedias—the *Britannica,* the *Americana,* and *Colliers,* for example. Take notes.

5. Survey reference aids for further information on the local issue you've been investigating. (See Application 5 on pages 53 and 57.) For example, if you've been examining athletic programs on campus, look up the original meanings of "athlete" in the *Oxford English Dictionary* and how the term has been used. Also look up the history of intercollegiate athletics in an encyclopedia, and search for newspaper and magazine articles on a database.

6. With members of your writing group, examine reference aids for further references to advertising. (See Application 6 on pages 54 and 58.) Be sure to look up the origins of the word, as well as current histories of advertising. Discuss your information.

A Brief Guide to Documenting Sources

Documenting means citing all appropriate sources you used to make or support your points. You need to document any idea or any expression of an idea that didn't originate with you. Documenting sources is important for several reasons:

- It gives credit where credit is due.
- It helps readers who want to know more.
- It helps readers judge the currency and reliability of sources.
- It enhances your own credibility by showing you've done your footwork.

Plagiarism is one of the worst transgressions for writers. Derived from a Latin term meaning "to kidnap," the word has been used for almost four centuries to mean stealing another's ideas. Whether you intend to plagiarize or not, the punishments for stealing ideas can be severe. They range from loss of a career to public ridicule and scorn (several candidates for public office have suffered this fate) to failing a course or being expelled from school. The least you can probably expect is to get an F on the paper.

There are only two situations when you're not required to document sources in academic writing. The first of these involves ideas and means of expressing ideas that are entirely your own. In personal writing, for example—autobiographical writing, journal/diary writing, exploratory freewriting and such—you would hardly ever use a citation. The second involves "common knowledge," factual material which virtually all readers know and for which they don't need a source. Examples of common knowledge include the terms of U.S. Presidents, the fact that the earth is a sphere, the dates of national holidays, the capitals of Canadian provinces, the meaning of words in common acronyms (such as ERA or NASA), and so on.

Whether something is common knowledge may sometimes be unclear, of course, and it may then be difficult to decide whether to include a citation or not. In such cases, consider your audience and purpose. For example, writing for a general academic audience, you would probably need to document your source for information about how the twelve-step Alcoholics Anonymous program has been applied to other addictions. For experts in the treatment of substance abuse, however, this information is common knowledge, and citing a source for it might tend to weaken your credibility, making you seem less than expert. A rule of thumb: when in doubt, cite your sources; it's better to overdocument than to be accused of plagiarism.

Remember, of course, that *whenever you use a direct quotation or paraphrase, you must document.* Ignorance is no excuse; many students have flunked a paper (or worse) because they "thought" they could paraphrase a source in their own words without documenting.

There are a variety of accepted formats for documenting sources: the one you use depends on your intended audience. Articles in newspapers and magazines tend to document written sources rather loosely, perhaps just indicating within the text the author and title of the work being cited. The formats required for documenting sources in academic and professional journals, however, are much more detailed and precise. And these are what will be expected of you in virtually any academic writing you do.

We'll concentrate here on the MLA (Modern Language Association) format, which applies to fields in the humanities, such as English, speech, and the fine arts. (If you need further guidance, we suggest that you consult the *MLA Handbook for Writers of Research Papers.*) For other fields, there are other formats, such as those detailed in the *Publication Manual of the American Psychology Association* (APA) and in the *Chicago Manual of Style.* If you're not sure which citation format to use, ask your instructor. In some cases you may use whatever format you prefer, as long as you follow it accurately and consistently.

The MLA format calls for a brief parenthetical reference to the source at the end of a sentence or quotation, with the full citation on a Works Cited page at the end of the paper. All citations on the Works Cited page are arranged alphabetically (usually by the authors' last names) and double-spaced. (Footnotes or endnotes, when used, supply only commentary that would be unnecessary or inappropriate in the text of the paper and are placed on a Notes page, just before the Works Cited page at the end.)

The key to the MLA citation format is simple: don't clutter sentences with information that can be placed on the Works Cited page, and be sure that readers can find all the information they might need to look up your source.

There are two ways to do this. One is to use the author's name in the sentence and to include the appropriate page number from the source in parentheses at the end of the sentence (but *before* the period):

> Atchity points out that writer's block is "a matter of not being in charge of your own mind" (40).

The second way is to put the author's name in the parentheses with the page number:

Sometimes writer's block is "a matter of not being in charge of your own mind" (Atchity 40).

Either way, readers can easily turn to the Works Cited page to find the full reference:

WORKS CITED

Atchity, Ken. *A Writer's Time*. New York: Norton, 1986.

If you have more than one source by an author, you need also to distinguish which work you're referring to in the text, either in your sentence or in your parenthetical reference.

Note that the MLA format does not use "p." before the page number, and the period for the sentence occurs *after* the citation. Note also, that this format uses abbreviations for publishers on the Works Cited page: "Norton" for "W. W. Norton and Company," "Harcourt" for "Harcourt Brace Jovanovich," and so forth. Page numbers need to be given on the Works Cited page only if the work is a portion of a larger work—say, an article in a journal or a chapter in a book.

Interviews are cited in this manner on the Works Cited page:

George, Samuel. Personal interview. 19 July 1991.

You need not give the interviewee's title or any other pertinent information on the Works Cited page, although this may be helpful in the text:

The head of the University Chemistry Department asserts that not all cures for campus pollution are created equal (George).

Do make a distinction between a personal interview and a telephone interview:

George, Samuel. Telephone interview. 19 July 1991.

Following are samples of other common Works Cited entries using the MLA citation format.

Interview cited in a periodical:

Sagan, Carl. Interview. *Playboy* Dec. 1991: 69–74+.

Book with one author:

Calkins, Lucy McCormick. *The Art of Teaching Writing*. Portsmouth, NH: Heinemann, 1986.

Anthology with an editor rather than an author:

McLeod, Susan H., ed. *Strengthening Programs for Writing Across the Curriculum*. San Francisco: Jossey-Bass, 1988.

Book with an author and an editor:

Robinson, E. A. *Selected Early Poems and Letters*. Ed. Charles T. Davis. New York: Holt, 1960.

A signed article from a daily newspaper:

Soth, Loren. "Ethanol Subsidy Isn't Best for World Trade." *Des Moines Register* 13 June 1992: 7A.

An unsigned article from a daily newspaper:

"Court: Man Being Illegally Detained." *Waterloo Courier* 19 May 1992: A10.

An article from a monthly or bimonthly periodical:

Gooding, Judson. "France: An Ambivalent War Against Smoking." *Atlantic* June 1992: 50–55.

An article from a weekly periodical:

Kilday, Gregg. "Dangerous Games." *Entertainment Weekly* 12 June 1992: 14–21.

To sum up: When you use sources well, it's as though you provide readers with a boat. Your sources provide the water—the river, lake, or ocean that must be navigated. But without your boat to give direction and meaning to your readers' voyage, there could be no trip at all.

Formulating

So far, you've learned that researching involves inquiring and searching: beginning with curiosity, seeking to find some real answers to real questions, and learning where you might go to find answers, including your own experiences, observations, and memories.

Now for the final step: *formulating*. It's not enough to raise questions and find answers. You wouldn't like a movie in which a man and a woman meet, fall in love, and never speak to one another again or a baseball game that ends before anyone scores or a planning session in which the participants go home without anything being resolved. We all need resolutions, closures, completions. That's what *formulating* is all about.

Let's say you've been investigating a question, and you've found sources that helped you discover some reasonable answers. Now's the time to formulate, that is, to decide which answer or answers are best and how to express them for maximum effectiveness. Sometimes you will have to return to the original question and look for new sources. If you do, don't despair. All investigators often have to start again, sometimes several times.

Recognize that formulating involves a good deal of intuition. Sometimes the answer will arise suddenly as an "Ah-Ha" in the middle of your research, in which case it can serve as a guiding principle. Other times it will unfold slowly as your investigation proceeds. Either way, you will often arrive at some definite point that you want to make: a hypothesis, or thesis, or major idea. Keep in mind, though, that sometimes it's enough just to explore your ideas without arriving at a single definite point, without putting all of your facts together in a simple report. You don't always have to have a thesis to prove to write an essay.

Here is some excellent advice on formulating from Donald Murray:

> Put your notes away before you begin a draft. What you remember is probably what should be remembered; what you forget is probably what should be forgotten. No matter, you'll have a chance to go back to your notes after the draft is completed. What is important is to achieve a draft which allows the writing to flow.

As a rule you will need to formulate a hypothesis or thesis first for yourself, then for your readers. The two are equally important.

Formulating for Yourself

While researching, keep your original question in mind. This will help you gauge whether you're getting any closer to an answer. It's easy to go off on a tangent without knowing it—even when writing about yourself. Suppose, for example, you began with the question "What was a significant event in my life, and how did it change me?" You search your memory and remember your Aunt Jane's funeral. You were just seven years old. When you were told of her death, you talked about it at length with your teddy bear, Floppy. You always talked about serious things with that bear. He was your best friend until you were ten, at least. What an amazing teddy bear he was, too—with the cutest little button eyes. . . .

Oops. What happened to Aunt Jane's funeral?

Or take the question of how *Gone with the Wind* was received at the time of its release. You locate several sources that discuss this, and find, interestingly enough, that several other actors and actresses were considered for the major roles. Think of that—Rhett Butler played by Cary Grant! How did they cast those older movies, anyway? How did they come to choose Clark Gable?

At this point, you might *want* to get into an entirely different question, such as the effect Floppy had on your childhood or how movies are cast, but remember that you have promises to keep. If you've already done a fair amount of research, you might be better off staying with the original question. You can, of course, change your mind, but sticking to your original question—assuming it still seems to you a good one—can save a good deal of time and help you avoid confusion and missed deadlines.

As you keep your question in mind, watch for patterns of evidence. You already do this, probably without paying much attention to the process. Suppose you arrive in an unfamiliar town with a car that's barely running and you're looking for a good mechanic. The clerk at the closest convenience store recommends Bob's Repair. You want a second opinion, so you try another convenience store where you're steered to Arlo's Auto. You mention you heard Bob's was a great place. "Who told you that?" the second clerk asks. When you tell him, he rolls his eyes; "Yeah, of course that's Bob's big brother." So you get yet another opinion—a third clerk. She says she's taken her car to Arlo's for a couple of years and isn't related to Arlo in any way. Based on this, you have detected enough of a pattern to choose Arlo's (or at least to look the place over).

Now consider a more complex question, one that you might actually want to answer for a research essay: "How does alcohol change people's perception of the world?" In your search, you keep finding sources that use phrases like "blurring," "softening," "toning down," "lessening of distinctions." You also notice that nearly every source mentions a suppressing of normal inhibitions, a "loosening-up" effect. You clearly have found points that you will want to use in formulating your answer. When several sources agree, you may be sure that you have found something worth noticing.

Next, *test* your answers as they emerge against your own common sense, as well as against what other sources say. Even given the two recommendations for Arlo's, would it make sense to go there once you learn that he works only two hours a night and sells vacuum cleaners the rest of the time? Or that there are junked cars all around the place? Maybe you had better get a fourth opinion, or try Bob's after all.

As you're researching, then, rely on your own experience, logic, and common sense to formulate the best answers. Finally, in formulating answers for yourself, it's most important to satisfy yourself that you've actually found the best answer. Have you really searched the relevant sources? Have you found answers that make sense? (If not, you won't take much pleasure in researching.) Do some of the answers raise more questions that demand further searching? Have you encountered evidence that contradicts your emerging point?

If you find counterevidence you *must* find ways either to refute it (showing how it is false or misleading) or to show that it doesn't damage your point in any substantial way. If you cannot counter such evidence, you may have to consider changing your point substantially. With research on alcohol, for example, you might find evidence and opinions that point toward the benefits of moderate alcohol use, while others insist that complete abstention is the only solution to problem drinking. What are you to think? "Experts" often disagree, leaving us unsure just whom to believe. When this happens, all you have to rely on is your sense of who has the best answer, a matter of intuition as much as logic. To evaluate the suggestion that moderate alcohol use makes sense, you would look at several features of the point being made:

- *When* was the judgment made? Was it before certain other researchers discovered that alcohol, even in moderation, can cause more problems than it solves?
- *Who* made it, and on what basis? Is the researcher widely respected? What method did he or she use to reach this conclusion? Was it a valid method, with enough samples to justify the conclusion?

- *What* is the recommendation, exactly? Is it a general recommendation for all people, or is it limited to people with high blood pressure? Does the writer qualify the recommendation (that alcohol be consumed with food, for example, or always with friends)?

Sometimes acknowledging qualifications can eliminate most of the disagreements between two positions.

Keep in mind that if you assert a position without taking into account counterevidence, you run the risk of losing credibility. Your reader may well be aware of such counterevidence and expect you either to refute or discount it. You cannot ignore counterevidence without putting your credibility on the line.

Formulating for Readers

Suppose that you've found an answer that seems clear to you. You've discovered several repeated patterns, and tested the answers against what you know. You've chosen among the best alternatives, and you're satisfied that your answer can be supported from the research. Now you have to decide, given what you know about your potential readers, the best way to explain your answer so they will agree.

There are three major considerations: your readers' *knowledge* of the subject; your readers' *attitude* toward the subject; and your readers' various *needs,* particularly their need, or obligation, to read your formulation.

Reader Knowledge The more your readers know, the less you need to explain; the less they know, the more you need to explain. The trick is to tell readers exactly as much as they need to know to understand your point—no more, no less. If you tell them too much, they'll think you're talking down to them; if you tell them too little, they won't know what you mean. So you must define your readers as precisely as you can and address them specifically.

Of course, sometimes you can't define your readers very precisely. Then you have two choices. The first is to acknowledge early in the piece that you're covering certain material some readers may already know. Those readers may skip particular sections if they wish, while others who are less familiar with the subject will want to read them closely. Your second choice is to make an educated guess about the level of your readers' knowledge. Ask yourself: What are my readers *likely* to know about this subject? Will they be familiar with the terms that I'm using? Will they know any of the facts? Will they have heard of the sources? If your answer for any of these is no, then plan on explanations, either in an appendix or a glossary or (more likely for informal writing) right in the paper.

Often, though, you know just who you're writing for. In fact, unless you're writing for a very general audience, you will probably know the boss for whom you're writing a report or recommendation, the colleagues for whom you're preparing a memo, the members of city council for whom you're writing a criticism of new leash laws, or your instructor and classmates for whom you're preparing an essay on alcohol in the dorms.

Indeed, in many writing classes, when your audience consists of classmates and instructor, you can simply ask what they know about this subject. Are they aware, for example, of dorm policies on parties with alcohol? Do they know the university policy on fines or other punishments for being caught drunk on campus? If they're quite knowledgeable, you need do little more than add reminders. If they're not, you should plan on more extended explanations. You might even consider attaching a "cover letter" briefly explaining dorm alcohol policies, especially if doing so in the piece itself would seem awkward.

Reader Attitudes Here's a rule of thumb concerning reader attitudes: if your readers are likely to be unfriendly to your ideas, arrange your explanations from least threatening or disagreeable to most threatening or disagreeable.

Suppose in a piece on campus alcohol policies you decide to push for a strong alcohol education program. In particular, you have found that several major universities require students who have been found guilty of violating alcohol rules to attend special classes and that in many cases students who have been so disciplined credit the requirement with saving their academic careers, if not their lives. Therefore, you want to recommend such a program in your school. You expect resistance, if not outright hostility, to your recommendation, which includes stiff punishments—including expulsion—for those who refuse to take the class.

So how should you proceed? You would do best to begin with "safe" areas where you can assume agreement. Discuss how much fun a good party can be, and the benefits, intellectual and social, of fellowship at a favorite bar. Then bring in some specific examples of the dark side of that fun—students (specific students, actual students) injured in car accidents, students beat up in brawls, students who were raped, students getting so hooked on the party scene they flunk out, students becoming alcoholics. At this point, even the most unfriendly readers would have to agree that alcohol can be a serious problem at college. Now is the time to begin developing your solution—not by setting it up as the single best solution to everyone's problems, but by showing that it is a solution that seems to be working at four major universities. Describe what it is, and how well it works.

Even though unfriendly readers might not like the solution, they will be forced to agree that it works—since you're citing facts, after all. *Now* you can make the point that such a program makes perfect sense at *your* university, because your university has the same problems with alcohol and therefore plenty of students who would benefit from a mandatory alcohol education class. Unfriendly readers will thus have a harder time refuting your points, since in effect you've caught them off guard. Your credibility is high, because you've already admitted how much fun alcohol can be and you've cited facts to show that a specific program actually works.

Reader Needs To address your readers effectively, you also need to anticipate their particular needs. Do they need information? Entertainment? Instructions? Supportive compliments and warm feelings? Fire and brimstone? Once you've decided what they need, you should formulate your approach accordingly. If they mainly need the facts, you should establish a businesslike tone, giving them the information as succinctly as possible and documenting your sources. If they need to be reassured, reassure them. If they need to be entertained before they are ready to get down to business, then open up with some entertaining anecdote that also defines your subject and your thesis. *Do what you have to do to get your readers' attention.*

In defining readers' needs, it helps to take into account whether they are obligated to read your piece. If they are assigned to read it—by their instructor, their fraternity or sorority, their coach—they will probably feel obliged to read it. Required reading doesn't happen only in school, by the way: supervisors often assign reading to staff—reports, instructions, journal articles, and books. The more obliged readers feel to read, the less obliged the writer is to entertain. If, for example, you are writing a report for your supervisor, you needn't entertain her with anecdotes and quips. She will be primarily interested in the business of your paper—the facts, the implications, and the recommendations—set forth as clearly, as credibly, and as quickly as possible.

Your writing instructor, on the other hand, may want you to practice writing entertaining introductions for readers who feel no obligation to read your paper, on the assumption that if you can learn to draw in non-obligated readers, you can probably also reach any obligated readers. This is, after all, your goal in writing: to reach readers by catching and holding their interest so that when they have finished, they feel as though your writing was well worth their time and energy.

SUMMARY OF FORMULATING

1. Formulate your point for yourself. Keep your question in mind, watch for patterns of evidence, test your answers against your own experience, and take into account any counterevidence.
2. Formulate your point for your readers. Keep in mind their knowledge, attitudes, and needs.

INVITATIONS FOR EXTENDED WRITING

As you gather material for these extended pieces of writing, remember to tune in to your yes voice. Without a strong yes voice, you run the risk of procrastinating, or worse, giving up altogether. Also if you found any concentrating or intuiting strategies helpful, employ them here.

1. Report on a Local Situation Write an extended report on the feature of your campus you've been investigating using Application 1 on pages 53, 57, and 62. If any readers outside your class might possibly be interested in your subject, write it for them. If you've been investigating the accounting program, you might want to write your piece for prospective accounting students; if you've been investigating campus neighborhoods, you might want to write it for city hall. Document sources consistently.

2. A Biographical Sketch Write an essay of five to seven pages on the celebrity you've been investigating using Application 2 on pages 53, 57, and 62. Focus on how your subject has been treated by the press, including writers of magazine articles and books as well as reporters and columnists. Write the essay for the students on your campus. Submit it to your campus newspaper for publication.

3. Reactions to a Historical Event Write an essay of seven to ten pages on the historical event you've been investigating for Application 3 on pages 53, 57, and 62. Don't just list various reactions; rather, put them together according to a particular perspective, to prove a particular point. You may have found, for instance, that a significant number of people still feel few regrets over the assassination of Martin Luther King, Jr., leading you to conclude that his goal has not yet been achieved. Or you may have found that a significant number of people care more about his assassination now than they did at the time, suggesting that his death did not put an end to his influence.

4. Fashion Write an essay of five to seven pages on that aspect of fashion you've been investigating for Application 4 on pages 53, 57, and 62. Write it specifically for the fashion section of your local newspaper or for a popular fashion magazine such as *Vogue* or *Mirabella*. (Read some articles in the magazine to get a sense of its style.) Get as much editorial assistance from your classmates and your instructor as you can. Polish it to a high shine and submit it for publication.

5. A Local Problem Examine all the information you've gathered about a local problem. (See Application 5 on pages 53, 57, and 63.) Decide what you'd like to explain about the problem and for whom. Settle on a definite point, and plan to write a piece that makes that point clear for some audience. Your audience could be one person (someone who chairs a committee, for example), a group, or general readers of the campus newspaper. Of course, your audience could also be members of your class and your instructor. You don't have to use all, or even most, of the material you've gathered; try to incorporate all that's relevant to your point, your audience, and your purpose.

6. A Collaborative Report on Advertising With members of your writing group, brainstorm what you've discovered about advertising following Application 6 on pages 54, 58, and 63. Then, with the guidance of your instructor, decide whether to write a single report, with contributions from all group members, or several different reports, with each member using the group's insights and research in whatever ways he or she prefers. If the group writes one report, decide together on an audience and purpose, and set up various writing tasks for each member: each member might write a section, or one member could be assigned to write the whole report, another to revise, another to illustrate, another to copyedit and proofread, and so forth. If each group member writes an individual report, make sure all members have copies of all the information gathered, with necessary citation information listed. Members should share drafts and offer comments for revision. (See Chapter 5 for more on collaborative writing.)

For Further Reading and Research

Biagi, Shirley. *Interviews that Work*. Belmont, CA: Wadsworth, 1986.

Gardner, John. *On Becoming a Novelist*. New York: Harper, 1983.

Gibaldi, Joseph, and Walter S. Achtert. *MLA Handbook for Writers of Research Papers*. 3rd ed. New York: MLA, 1988.

Gibson, Walker. *Tough, Sweet and Stuffy*. Bloomington: Indiana UP, 1966.

Hayakawa, S. I. *Language in Thought and Action*. San Diego: Harcourt, 1990.

Howarth, William, ed. *The John McPhee Reader*. New York: Vintage, 1977.

Murray, Donald. *Write to Learn*. New York: Holt, 1987.

___. *Expecting the Unexpected*. Portsmouth, NH: Heinemann, 1989.

Terkel, Studs. *The Good War*. New York: Pantheon, 1984.

Winokur, Jon. *Writers on Writing*. Philadelphia: Running Press, 1986.

Wolf, Naomi. *The Beauty Myth*. London: Vintage, 1990.

CHAPTER FOUR

Revising

I don't write easily or rapidly. My first draft usually has only a few elements worth keeping. I have to find what those are and build from them and throw out what doesn't work, or what is simply not alive.

—SUSAN SONTAG

I'll write a very rough first draft of every chapter, then I will rewrite every chapter. I try to get it down in the first rewrite, but some chapters I can't get quite right the third time. There are some I go over and over and over again.

—ROBERT STONE

In *The Craft of Revision* writer Donald Murray confesses that for years he didn't believe in rewriting. Instead, he "held firm to three beliefs":

- First draft was best. Good writing was spontaneous writing.
- Rewriting was punishment for failure. The editor or teacher who required revision was a bad reader who had no respect for my spontaneous writing.
- Revision was a matter of superficial correction that forced my natural style to conform to an old-fashioned, inferior style.

But Murray came to realize what all writers know. We don't revise just to polish an idea or to fix the mechanics of a draft for a critical editor or a teacher. Instead, revising helps us to develop our ideas in different directions, to generate new ideas, and to find the best way to express our thoughts. The word "revising" comes from *re-vision,* meaning to see again, to see further and more clearly. It involves gently introducing your no voice, not for destructive purposes but to motivate you to improve your writing, to take it as far as you can toward perfection.

Revising brings out facets that otherwise would remain obscure or invisible to the writer as well as to readers. Look, for example, at the three successive versions of a paragraph—the paragraph that states the thesis, in fact—of Ilene Kantrov's essay, "Women's Business":

(1) In the century that followed the first sales of Lydia E. Pinkham's Vegetable Compound in 1875, the handful of women entrepreneurs who emulated Pinkham's success frequently emulated her style of doing business as well.

(2) Lydia Pinkham is surely a special case in the annals of American business as well as women's history. Yet the ingredients that contributed to the phenomenal success of Pinkham's enterprise set a pattern for women entrepreneurs in the following century. The handful of women who emulated Pinkham's success likewise followed her in turning the limitations of traditional feminine stereotypes and roles to their benefit in the masculine world of commerce. In the process, they created an often effective, if sometimes uneasy, alliance between feminine ideals and the realities of the marketplace.

(3) Pinkham's introduction of feminine packaging to capitalist enterprise earned her a special place in the annals of American business as well as women's history. It also set a pattern for women entrepreneurs in the following century. The handful of women who emulated Pinkham's success likewise followed her in importing traditional feminine roles into the masculine world of commerce. When feminine ideals collided with the realities of the marketplace, however, the business-woman often bested the lady.

Much of the revision stems from Kantrov's effort to clarify her ideas, but in the process she re-viewed her subject—seeing, for example, that the alliance of feminine ideals and masculine commerce often involves conflict, and that commerce (it would seem) always triumphs, no matter which ideals one holds. By revising, Kantrov developed her point significantly.

In revising, you do four basic things to the text you're working on: cut, add, rearrange, and reword. You don't revise in a vacuum, however: you revise in anticipation of your readers' response, so they will find your writing readable and, more important, credible. In this chapter we will show you how to work with these three aspects of writing—revising the text, anticipating reader response, and establishing credibility.

Four Fundamentals of Revising

Cutting

I believe in the scissors more than I do in the pencil.
—TRUMAN CAPOTE

Richard Lanham estimates that most prose written by nonprofessional writers contains a thirty to fifty percent "lard factor," which is to say, that up to half the words in any given sentence can be cut out, like lard. The simplest form of revision, then, involves turning the no voice loose to cut out words, phrases, even whole sentences that add nothing to a piece of writing but useless fat.

Some professional writers compose complete drafts, then go back through to cut out the irrelevant and excessive. Others cut as they draft, even while writing a first draft. However they do it, almost all professionals cut out a good deal of what they originally write, to make their prose as tight and lean and focused as a well-conditioned athlete.

Here's an example of freewriting and cutting. The writer lives near a midwestern county park that authorities had been ignoring for years. After being asked to sign a petition encouraging the county to put the park back in working order, he decided to write an article for the newspaper to help the cause. He began with a nonstop twenty-minute focused freewrite, putting down anything and everything about the park that came to mind. Then he went back through and, without changing a word, simply cut lard, drawing lines through the sentences he found unnecessary:

> It's such a great park there, with all those paths. But right now no one really uses it. It's a bit like a paradise lost, with all those tree branches down, those smashed electrical outlets. They probably figure no one uses it, so why fix it up. Naturally no one uses it—it's so crummy. That's called a vicious circle, or maybe Catch-22, whatever. ~~Maybe I shouldn't worry about it so much. If none go there, I get it all to myself. No that's selfish. When you have a nice park, people should use it. I wonder what it takes to get a park board interested in supporting a park.~~ I know what they will say too—it's a flood plain, and they can't maintain a flood plain very well. ~~Hmmm, I wonder if anybody pays any attention to petitions? Will that petition do any good? Do they ever really pay any attention to petitions? Or letters, for that matter. Maybe a short signed piece, a column is best. That way I can get their attention and list all the problems.~~ All right, what are they? Tree branches; pathways that aren't marked or mowed; electrical outlets that are unsafe; outhouses that have holes in them and that are unmaintained. Also that opening board-thing, a registration booth or something like that. It's all just a shell. No one's touched it for five or six years, anyway. Also there used to be more space, but now it's just grassy swampy muck—probably because they didn't fill it in, or take care of it after those floods. ~~What a mess. I wonder how many acres it really is? Probably seventy or eighty anyway, counting both sides. Also I wonder how many people really do use that park—if they make enough from camping fees to pay for any upkeep? That's another problem, I just remembered.~~ No barrels for trash, and no picnic tables for probably half of the park. So people who do use the park often just throw their trash on the ground—I've often picked up other people's trash and carried it over to a distant barrel. That creates another mess for visitors, and it's no wonder that people drive in, then drive right back out. I would too. ~~Well, maybe a letter that details all this stuff would help. I had better think about who will be reading it. They're a group of citizens, either appointed or elected to the county conservation board, who have the job of~~

~~overseeing the county park system. They will want to do a good job, I would think, and will be sensitive to complaints about a park gone bad.~~ I'll try to remind them that it's their duty to pay attention to those parks, that even Adam and Eve had to dress and keep the garden, and that was *before* the fall! Say, that might not be a bad opener. ~~Also that they ought to drive out there and look it over, get a sense of what a nice park it could be. They ought to make a choice — either maintain a park right, and keep it up, or scrap it — leave it alone, maybe even sell it for private development. It shouldn't be left to just look sorry, like nobody cares.~~

The writer scrapped about half the original—everything that was not directly about the park but about potential readers, his own questions, and so on. From this beginning he added material, rearranged and rewrote sentences until he wound up with the following article on the opinion page of his local newspaper:

MAINTAINING PARADISE

The lesson for today is simple yet profound: as Adam and Eve had to dress and keep the garden, there in paradise *before* the fall, so we need to maintain our little paradises, the public parks that provide many people a great deal of pleasure.

That's why, when a formerly nice park is allowed to run down, it becomes a sad reminder of our fallen state—not a place to play in, but a spot to mourn.

Which brings me to a grand little park on the far northwest edge of the county: Thunderwoman. Named after a real Indian woman who is buried near the park, it's unusual in several respects.

A sand-bottomed, clear-running stream divides the north and south sides. This stream, the West Fork, provides perfect wading and tubing in the summer. A county-built swinging footbridge connects the north and south sides. It's probably the most quiet, unspoiled, idyllic park in the county, if not Northeast Iowa.

And it's a mess. On the south side, there's a large tree branch down. There are holes in the south outhouse, and a privacy fence has disappeared. There is one trash can for the whole park, north and south. The electrical outlets on the north side are unsafe, and the registration "booth" on the north side looks as though it hasn't been touched in years.

Worse: ten years ago there were several marked trails on the north side. Trees were labeled, and it was a fine Sunday walk among old hardwoods. There are no more trails in Thunderwoman.

I know, the park floods regularly, and upkeep of a flood plain is expensive. But if we could afford to maintain the park before, we can afford to now.

It has been argued that the condition of the park has deteriorated because the number of people using it has declined. But that argument, it seems to me, puts the effect before the cause. After all, who would want to visit a large park with four beat-up picnic tables, one grill, one trash barrel, and unusable bathroom facilities? No wonder so few visitors bother with Thunderwoman. The park turns people away, just as a rundown business turns away potential customers.

There may be a happy ending in the works, though. Just last week a nearby resident took time to circulate a petition about the park. It details the problems and pointedly suggests that "Black Hawk County tax dollars allotted for the care and maintenance of the parks (such as Thunderwoman) are not being used properly. We hope that Thunderwoman is not an example of the future stewardship of the County Park system."

The petition suggests that "direct action be taken to make necessary improvements" and that possibly a "resident Park Attendant/Custodian" be hired to care for the park.

Nearly everyone in the area has signed the petition, and with any luck it will help us regain a small lost paradise.

It's long overdue.

Starting with a twenty-minute focused freewrite, then revising by cutting, adding, rearranging, and rewording, the writer finished the article in two hours. (The park board, by the way, agreed to fix the park.)

APPLICATIONS

1. Take a paper (or any section of it) that you are working on for another class and see if you can cut it by 25 percent without sacrificing precision or clarity.

2. Take a paper (or any section of it) that a member of your writing group is working on and see if you can cut it by 25 percent without sacrificing precision or clarity.

3. Take a short article from a magazine or newspaper and see how much you can cut without sacrificing precision or clarity.

4. Look over a paper you've already written (for any class), then do a twenty-minute focused freewrite on the subject. See how much of the freewrite you can use to improve the paper, cutting out what is of no use.

Adding

In revising, it's often as necessary to add as it is to cut material—not to pad the piece, but to make it clearer, more precise. Student writers often need to add details, partly because they don't have much confidence in their ability to use detail, and partly because they don't spell out their logic as extensively as necessary.

To see how adding material can improve a piece, compare the freewrite of "Maintaining Paradise" with the finished article. The purpose of the article was to persuade people that Thunderwoman Park was worth the expense and trouble of rehabilitating. Two kinds of detail were therefore in order: illustrations of the park's disrepair and illustrations of its particular virtues.

As for its disrepair, in the freewrite the writer cited tree branches down, smashed electrical outlets, unmarked and unmowed pathways, unmaintained out-houses, a dilapidated registration booth, no trash barrels, no picnic tables for half the park. In the final article he added details and made others more precise: a missing privacy fence, smashed outlets on the north side, one trash can for the whole park, once-marked trails that no longer existed, four beat-up picnic tables, one grill. By adding such precise detail, the writer makes certain no one can quibble with his facts and undermine his credibility.

In finishing the article, the writer also added details to illustrate the park's particular charms: the fact that it is named after a real woman buried nearby (suggesting its unusual historical value), a sand-bottomed, clear-running stream for wading and tubing, a swinging footbridge, its quiet, unspoiled atmosphere. Such detail makes the park look like a place worth restoring.

The writer didn't just include new details, however. He also elaborated the logic of his position, focusing on the county's ability to afford maintaining the park and the cause-effect relation between the park's condition and its popularity.

Here's another example of revision by addition, by essayist Susan Allen Toth. In its original version the conclusion of her essay "Cinematypes" consisted of one sentence: "Most of the time I go to movies by myself." Toth's editor asked her to do more with it, noting that while the sentence might mean a great deal to her, it wouldn't mean much to her readers. It was catchy but oblique. Toth agreed and elaborated on her point considerably:

> I go to some movies by myself. On rainy Sunday afternoons I often sneak into a revival house or a college auditorium for old Technicolor musicals, *Kiss Me Kate, Seven Brides for Seven Brothers, Calamity Jane,* even, once, *The Sound of Music.* Wearing saggy jeans so I can prop my feet on the seat in front, I sit toward the rear where no one will see me. I eat large handfuls of popcorn with double butter. Once the movie starts, I feel completely at home.

And she wrote more, an entire page in fact, adding detail and elaborating logic. In the process of explaining what her sentence meant, we would wager that Toth not only developed her idea about going to movies alone, she also discovered that movies served as a comfort center for her, as a home away from home. That's just what writers often do when revising: they explore and discover as much as they refine and clarify.

APPLICATIONS

1. Look up Toth's essay, "Cinematypes" (it is commonly anthologized) and compare the entire last part to its one-sentence original: "Most of the time I go to movies by myself." Note Toth's additions of detail and of logic. Write a paragraph explaining what her revision enables you to understand that her original doesn't.

2. Look over a paper you have recently written (for any class) and note where you could have used more showing (detail) and more telling (logic). Look over a paper in progress to the same end, and make the necessary additions.

3. Look over a friend's paper in progress to see if it needs more showing and/or telling. If it does, indicate to your friend exactly where and, to the extent possible, how and what.

Rearranging

Rearranging means examining every part of a draft in relation to every other part, deciding on their best order and arranging them accordingly, adding and omitting passages where necessary.

Let's look at "Maintaining Paradise" as a case in point. In the freewrite, we find the following order (or disorder, as the case may be):

1. park unused because of disrepair: paradise lost
2. cause and effect of disuse and disrepair
3. speculation about personal involvement
4. flood plain
5. speculation about petitions and letters
6. list of things wrong: branches, pathways, outlets, outhouses, booth, swamp
7. speculation about size of park and number of people who use it and fees
8. list of things wrong: trash, picnic tables
9. speculation about writing a letter and about the authorities in charge
10. Adam and Eve dressing and keeping the garden
11. the authorities' choice: maintain the park or get rid of it

Here's the rearranged order of the finished article:

1. Adam and Eve dressing and keeping the garden: paradise lost
2. Thunderwoman: list of things right about it
3. list of things wrong with it
4. flood plain
5. cause and effect of disuse and disrepair
6. petition to save the park

In the freewrite there is no order to speak of, making it very difficult even to list the items without breaking the passage down into a sentence-by-sentence paraphrase. There is also a great deal of repetition. In the article itself the smaller points are neatly subsumed into larger categories that follow one another with a clear, progressive logic: statement of need for parks, description of the park itself (positive, then negative), arguments against fixing the park refuted, proposal to fix the park defined.

In rearranging your material, always look for the simplest, clearest order you can find that makes sense of the subject. There are, basically, five strategies for deciding on an effective arrangement.

First, *group similar material.* If you're dealing with causes and effects, put causes in one group, effects in another. If big and little are your concern, put all the bigs in one group, all the littles in another. (Then decide the best order for presenting them.) If you're discussing city government, group your details according to department (police, fire, street, parks). If you're dealing with Thunderwoman Park, put all the things right about it in one group, all the things wrong in another, arguments against restoring it in another, and so on.

Second, *get chronological sequences straight.* If you are describing a series of events, put those events in the order of their actual occurrence. It is especially important to get the order straight in long, complex sequences, to avoid backtracking and jumping ahead, repeating yourself and losing the reader:

> My brothers, friends, and I walked north on the railroad tracks after leaving our home on Butterworth every morning for Union High School which was on Broadway three blocks beyond Orsulowitz Funeral Home and St. Mary's Catholic Church. Along the way we walked through skid row after passing deserted store fronts and small businesses that inevitably failed on Bridge Street. Before skid row we had to go through the hobo jungle near the railroad tracks we followed through the switching yard past the Kent Foundry and furniture factories. . . .

Confusing, isn't it? Getting the sequence straight gets rid of the confusion:

> Each morning my brothers, friends, and I left our home on Butterworth for Union High School on Broadway three blocks away. We walked north on the railroad tracks that ran by the Kent Foundry, through the hobo jungle, past furniture factories, and through the railroad switching yard, stepping over the intricate network of steel veins. Then we turned east on Bridge Street, passing the deserted store fronts and small businesses that inevitably failed. . . .

For the sake of emphasis you may sometimes depart from strict chronological sequence, but make sure that you do so for a definable purpose. Otherwise, put events in the order they occurred.

Third, *consider using a 2-3-1 arrangement.* When you have several points or specifics and you're not sure what order to put them in, try starting with the second most important, then using the least important, and winding up with the most important. This structure works as well for sentences and paragraphs as for entire essays.

To illustrate, consider these four points:

a. Television-watching children seem bent on wearing the latest designer shoes, eating the most sugary cereals, and owning all kinds of expensive electronic toys.

b. If parents would watch more Saturday morning television, they would be shocked at how skillfully and effectively their children are manipulated.

c. Children's programming may even incite some children to commit serious violence.

d. Saturday morning television advertising incessantly sells candy-like cereals, expensive toys, brand-name shoes and jeans, not to mention modes of behavior.

In this order, the points don't connect very well. In order to make them more connected, the 2-3-1 pattern can be used. Decide which point seems most important (1), which seems least important (3), and which fall in the middle (2). Then, arrange the points (adding appropriate connecting words) in a 2-3-1 pattern. Suppose you decide that the most important point is point c, the notion that television might incite children to violence. The next is point b, that parents would be shocked to see how skillfully their children are being manipulated. Points a and d can be placed in the middle. Here is the paragraph rearranged using the 2-3-1 principle:

> If parents watched more Saturday morning television, they would be shocked at how skillfully and effectively their children are manipulated. Saturday morning television advertising incessantly sells candy-like cereals, expensive toys, brand-name shoes and jeans, not to mention modes of behavior. Thus television-watching children seem bent on wearing the latest designer shoes, eating the most sugary cereals, and owning all kinds of expensive electronic toys. Children's programming may even incite some children to commit serious violence.

Of course, you must exercise your judgment as to which points are most important, and add any needed connecting words. But considering this structure forces you to rearrange (and possibly rethink) your position to make it as effective as possible, given your audience and purpose.

The 2-3-1 structure also helps you discover whether you need more evidence: if a point seems weak because you haven't supported it, yet you rank it number 1, you would know you need more support.

Fourth, *visualize the structure.* Look at your material with the idea of shaping it according to a visual pattern. Here are some possibilities:

Small points to large points, like a pyramid:

Large points to small, like an inverted pyramid:

Large points to small, then back out to large (this is one way of visualizing the 2-3-1 pattern, described earlier):

Circles within circles:

A snaking pattern that returns to the same place:

A tree pattern:

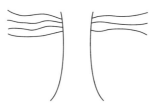

Many writers find that if they can visualize the structure, they have an arrangement that works. Or (just as likely) they have an arrangement they can make work by cutting, adding, and rearranging.

Fifth, *reconsider your point, your purpose, and your likely readers.* Often, when you get stuck, you need a quick reassessment of what you are doing: the point you are making, your purpose in making it, the audience you're making it to. This reassessment should be in writing (so you're forced to do it fully). We suggest you use headings:

Point:	*Purpose:*	*Likely Reader(s):*
Campus parking problem is now far more dangerous than last year	To motivate officials to find solutions to parking problems	Campus parking committee— students and faculty

Having reestablished your point, purpose, and readers, you can make a list of possible formats:

- a letter to the committee detailing the problem and suggesting solutions
- a letter to campus newspaper and the committee detailing the problem and suggesting solutions
- an article for the campus newspaper consisting of interviews with students and faculty concerning the parking problem
- a petition to change parking policies

Considering your purpose and readers, you then decide which format will probably work best.

APPLICATIONS

1. Take any draft you're writing for another class and examine the arrangement. See if you can group like items together or use the 2-3-1 pattern or visualize another structure. If none of these help, define your point, purpose, and audience and the format most likely to succeed. Then see what kind of arrangement you can come up with.

2. Read a short essay or a news or feature story, and examine the arrangement. Is it the 2-3-1 pattern or some variation? Can you visualize it? Does the arrangement make sense? Would you change it? Write a paragraph explaining what you discover.

3. Have members of your writing group bring drafts of their current writing. Examine their writing for arrangement, either individually or as a group.

Where appropriate, encourage writers to make discoveries by reconsidering how they've arranged their points, and suggest other arrangement options.

Rewording

> The difference between the right word and the almost-right
> word is the difference between lightning and a lightning bug.
> —MARK TWAIN

While the difference between the right word and the almost-right word may be as large as Twain claims, the fact remains that one can say pretty much the same thing in a number of ways—though there will, of course, be different nuances in each:

- Tina bought George a red carnation for his birthday.
- For his birthday, Tina bought George a red carnation.
- George received a red carnation for his birthday from Tina.
- For his birthday, George received a red carnation from Tina.
- George received a red carnation from Tina for his birthday.
- A red carnation was bought for George by Tina for his birthday.
- A red carnation was bought for George for his birthday by Tina.
- A red carnation was Tina's birthday gift for George.
- Tina's birthday gift for George was a red carnation.

And so on. Given so many possibilities for every sentence, you need certain principles to be able to choose the best one. Fortunately, you need only a few, and they are easily mastered.

One, *make your topic the subject of the sentence.* If you want to emphasize George, make George the subject of the sentence: "George received a red carnation. . . ." If you want to emphasize Tina, make Tina the subject: "Tina bought a red carnation. . . ." If carnations deserve emphasis, make that the subject: "A red carnation was the gift Tina bought. . . ."

Two, *give the subjects of your sentences active verbs.* The verb is the heart of the sentence, the muscle that pumps the life-blood into all its members. Active verbs mean vigorous sentences, sentences that make readers take notice. Even so, a strong tendency exists, especially in bureaucratic circles, to omit responsibility by casting sentences in the passive voice. Instead of "Tina bought George a red carnation," which identifies who did what to whom, we get "A red carnation was bought." Instead of a clear admission of responsibility, we get the all-absolving "Mistakes were made." Who purchased the red carnation and for whom? Who made mistakes and whom did they affect? Passive constructions allow writers to avoid assigning responsibility to anyone.

In general, use the passive voice only when you want to emphasize the "done to" rather than the "doer":

> George was run over [by a runaway truck].

If, however, your point is the random, arbitrary violence of life, you should turn the sentence around:

> A runaway truck ran over George.

Linking verbs are those formed out of *to be:* am, are, is, was, were. They link the subject with the complement that follows (I *am* hungry), but they provide none of the vigor of strong active verbs. You should make them the main verb only when that linkage is the point of a sentence.

Three, *put coordinate items in coordinate structures.* Commonly known as parallelism, this technique gives your style grace and balance. Here's an example where sentence elements are not parallel:

> George and Tina went to the Dairy Queen, then bought groceries at the 7-Eleven, and finally they went over to the Five Screens Cinema.

The sentence feels awkward, doesn't it? Even though it's gramatically correct, it might read better if the items were listed in the same manner. Revised for parallelism, the sentence reads:

> George and Tina went to the Dairy Queen, then to the 7-Eleven, and finally to the Five Screens Cinema.

Of course whether you actually revise your sentence in this manner would depend upon your audience and purpose. If you want to give the impression of someone talking, strict parallelism may seem too formal.

Parallelism works with larger sentence units as well. Let us look again at the quotation from Mark Twain at the beginning of this section:

> The difference between the right word and the almost-right word is the difference between lightning and a lightning bug.

The parallelism is precise: "The difference between A and B is the difference between X and Y." Look what happens when we trash that structure:

> The difference between the right word and one that is almost-right is the disparity you find comparing lightning with a lightning bug.

Parallelism is to grace what the active verb is to vigor: indispensable.

Four, *put modifiers next to the things they modify.* In other words, avoid dangling modifiers, like the following:

> Barking and yelping, the mail carrier ran from the dog.

Unless the mail carrier was in fact barking and yelping, the modifier here is misplaced. Such mistakes are common because knowing what you mean, you don't always see what you literally say. Once you spot them, though, dangling modifiers are easy to correct:

> The mail carrier ran from the barking, yelping dog.

or

     Barking and yelping, the dog chased the mail carrier.

Five, *use the simplest words that do the job.* This rule is relative. There are times when you may have to use a five-syllable technical term, or even a bunch of them. But if your readers are not experts in the field, be sure to define such terms. And be sure they're necessary: often nonprofessional writers use big words because they want their prose to look impressive and because they are afraid that simple words will make them look simple-minded. Ironically, the truth is that simplicity and clarity are far more impressive than a string of pretentious ten-dollar words. So, when you find you have written something like "We proceeded to traverse the thoroughfare," change it (depending, as always, on audience and purpose) to "We crossed the street."

Using precise words also means avoiding clichés. Clichés are worn-out figures of speech: dead as a doornail, a rotten apple in every barrel, a rolling stone gathers no moss, and the like. Comb your work for clichés, and replace them with your own words and figures.

Six, *use the fewest words possible.* This rule is also relative: the point is to use the fewest words possible to say what you have to say. But cut as much as possible. Eliminate all filler. "In the event that" means "in case," so say "in case." "In order to" means "to," so say "to." "Proceed to take our departure" means "go," so say "go."

Seven, *make clear transitions.* At the beginning of each sentence and at the beginning of a series of related sentences, let your readers know where they are. Let us look again at a piece of "Maintaining Paradise" to show you what we mean.

     The lesson for today [*the reader knows a lesson is coming*] is simple yet profound: as Adam and Eve had to dress and keep the garden, there in paradise before the fall, so we need to maintain our little paradises, the public parks that provide many people a great deal of pleasure.

     That's why, when a formerly nice park [*the reader knows that the opposite principle is about to be defined*] is allowed to run down, it becomes a sad reminder of our fallen state—not a place to play in, but a spot to mourn.

     Which brings me to a grand little park [*the reader now knows the writer is getting to the specific case*] on the far northwest edge of the county: Thunderwoman. Named after a real Indian woman who is buried near the park, it's unusual in several respects [*the reader knows a list of features is coming*].

     A sand-bottomed, clear-running stream [*the first feature is identified*] divides the north and south sides. This stream [*the reader knows more information is coming on this particular stream*], the West Fork, provides perfect wading and tubing in the summer. A county-built swinging footbridge [*a new feature is introduced*] connects the north and south sides. Thunderwoman is probably the most [*the reader is prepared for an overall assessment of the park*] quiet, unspoiled, idyllic park in the county, if not Northeast Iowa.

     And it's a mess [*the reader knows another list of features is coming*]. . . .

When revising, check to make sure you let the reader know exactly where you are and where you are going.

1. Go through a short published essay you particularly like and note the following: use of active voice (check out the percentage), parallel structures, location of modifiers, and use of transitions. See if the writer uses any unnecessarily big words. Notice words and phrases you especially like. See if there are any words or phrases you would change. What would you replace them with?

2. Go through a draft you're writing (for this class or for another) and note everything that seems to need changing. Then, using the six principles defined above, change it in any way you think is appropriate, given your audience and purpose.

Anticipating Reader Response

When we talk face to face, we usually have a good idea how our words affect our listeners because we can see their response. We know whether we're being understood or not and whether we need to explain in greater detail or clear up a misunderstanding. And we revise as necessary.

When we write, however, we cannot see how our words affect our readers. We have to anticipate their responses in advance, and, based on what we anticipate, revise to get the responses we want. In short, we have to put ourselves in our readers' place.

To anticipate effectively, we need to have a sense of who our readers will be, of their knowledge, their attitudes, and their needs. When writing for friends and family, anticipation is not a problem: we know all we need to know. The problem arises when we write for people we don't know. What do we do then?

First, we need to recognize that readers fall into three basic groups: (1) general readers, who have no particular expertise in the subject we're writing about; (2) experts, who do have expertise in the subject; and (3) executives, who have the power to do something about the subject. Sometimes we write for one specific group, sometimes for a combination of the three.

Anticipating experts and executives is relatively easy; anticipating general readers is considerably more difficult; anticipating a mixed readership is very difficult, but not impossible. In this section we will consider what revising for each group and for mixed groups entails.

General Readers

When you write for your classmates, for your student newspaper, or for any of the mass media, you are addressing general readers. As a rule, general readers are not required to read what you write, much less to feel interested in it. Your task—in fact, your challenge—is to get them interested and to hold their interest all the way through by addressing their knowledge, attitudes, and needs.

Knowledge Think of general readers' knowledge in relative terms: most of us know a good deal about some things, know less about many things more, and know nothing about a lot. The difficulty is, general readers don't know about the same things. So we need to keep this guideline in mind: *The more familiar and common the subject, the more you can expect general readers to know, and the less you have to explain. Likewise, the more technical and remote the subject, the less you can expect general readers to know, and the more you have to explain.*

Suppose you're writing about baseball for American readers. You shouldn't have to explain such terms as home plate, base, mound, dugout, bunt, single, home-run, double play. While a few Americans might not be familiar with these terms, explaining them would waste the time and forfeit the interest of a vast majority of your readers. Better to lose a few readers than many. If you were writing about baseball for British readers, however, you would have to explain every one of those terms, plus every other term you used, because baseball is as remote to most Britons as cricket is to most of us.

If you're writing about something technical or scientific, you have to discuss concepts in terms most general readers will understand. Among themselves, physicists discuss atomic size in the language of their trade. For general readers, physicists must use the common tongue. It is not nearly as precise—it is so imprecise, in fact, that physicists cannot do the real work of physics with it—but it is intelligible to nonexperts. That way we get at least a rough idea of the entities and events they study. Here's an example, from Fritjof Capra's best-seller *The Tao of Physics,* written for the general reader:

> An atom . . . is extremely small compared to macroscopic objects, but it is huge compared to the nucleus in its center. . . . If we blew up the atom to the size of a football, or even to room size, the nucleus would still be too small to be seen by the naked eye. To see the nucleus, we would have to blow up the atom to the size of the biggest dome in the world, the dome of St. Peter's Cathedral in Rome. In an atom of that size, the nucleus would have the size of a grain of salt! A grain of salt in the middle of the dome of St. Peter's, and specks of dust whirling around it in the vast space of the dome—this is how we can picture the nucleus and electrons of an atom.

Sometimes when you must make a technical point, you need to use jargon—the lingo of the trade—because everyday language won't do the job. In his book *Physics as Metaphor,* for example, Roger S. Jones explains for general readers how René Descartes' analytical geometry accounts for space in totally nonspatial terms:

Analytical geometry is a correlation of algebra with geometry. By means of a simple and elegant representation, the now famous graph-grid with its perpendicular "X" and "Y" axes, Descartes was able to show that any algebraic equation in two variables (x and y, for instance) is a precise description of a figure in plane geometry. For example, a circle of radius r is given by the equation $x^2 + y^2 = r^2$. In this equation, x represents the distance along the X-axis and similarly for y. Thus any figure in two-dimensional plane geometry can be transformed into a mathematical or logical statement, and vice versa.

If he were writing for fellow physicists, Jones would dispense with much of that explanation because he would assume they know it. Writing for general readers, he assumes far less, but he cannot dispense with the mathematics altogether because it is the very point he is making. Even so, he holds the math to a minimum, making Descartes' graph-grid as accessible to general readers as possible.

In his essay "Politics and the English Language" George Orwell formulated a rule we recommend when writing for general readers: never use a scientific, technical, or jargon word if an ordinary English word will do. Note the proviso —*if* an ordinary English word will do. If one will not do—if ordinary English misleads rather than informs—then you must use the unordinary language of the trade. But when you do, define it. Explain the unfamiliar in terms familiar enough to general readers that the point will be clear. The juxtaposition may be odd—comparing an atom to the dome of St. Peter's, for instance—but the familiar term makes for comprehensibility, the oddness for interest.

A question suggests itself: what do you do to create interest when you're writing about the *familiar*? General readers know plenty about domestic life, for instance, so how can you say anything about it that will make them want to read what you have to say? The answer: by putting it in unexpected terms. The terms themselves should be familiar, but the combination (or combinations) should be surprising. In her essay "Very Basic Housekeeping," for instance, Suzanne Britt writes about "the art of doing the minimum amount of housework to produce the maximum effect." She lists a number of specific tips, of which the following is first:

> Never change your sheets except when company is coming. If this idea disgusts you, consider the times you've stretched out on the living room rug, the un-reupholstered sofa or the dirty old ground without thinking a thing about it. Why does the only thing clean that ever touches your body have to be sheets? You don't wash off the toilet seat every time you use it. I suggest that you just take a shower every morning, on the theory that it's easier to wash yourself than to wash a big load of sheets. Also, be sure to use only dark patterned or navy sheets. You would be a fool to use white.

By coming at this utterly familiar subject with consistently surprising specifics, not to mention a strong voice and sense of humor, Britt keeps at least some of us reading.

Attitudes In addition to anticipating what general readers know, you need to anticipate how they think and feel about various matters—their attitudes—whether you want to change those attitudes, stir them up, or simply avoid trespassing against them.

As we've said, general readers do not comprise a single homogeneous group. Politically, for example, some are conservative and some liberal; spiritually, some are religious and some secular; on any given issue—abortion, disarmament, affirmative action—some are pro and some con and some fall in the middle. Depending on the occasion, you may address one end of this spectrum or the other end or even the entire range of general readers. You must, therefore, decide as specifically as possible whom you are addressing and anticipate their attitudes accordingly.

This paragraph from Walker Percy's essay "A View of Abortion, With Something to Offend Everybody" shows anticipation at work:

> True legalized abortion—a million and a half fetuses flushed down the Disposal every year in this country—is yet another banal atrocity in a century where atrocities have become commonplace. This statement will probably offend one side in this already superheated debate, so I hasten in the interests of fairness and truth to offend the other side. What else can you do when some of your allies give you as big a pain as your opponents? I notice this about many so-called pro-lifers. They seem pro-life only on this one perfervid and politicized issue. The Reagan Administration, for example, professes to be anti-abortion but has just recently decided, in the interests of business, that it is proper for infant formula manufacturers to continue their hard-sell in the third world despite thousands of deaths from bottle feeding. And Senator Jesse Helms and the Moral Majority, who profess a reverence for unborn life, don't seem to care much about born life: poor women who don't get abortions, have their babies, and can't feed them.

As Percy knows, abortion rights advocates don't think of themselves as indifferent to human life, but as vitally concerned, especially in terms of quality. That is why they are likely to find such phrases as "flushed down the Disposal" intensely offensive, and that is why Percy uses such phrases—deliberately to offend them, in the belief they need offending. Likewise, opponents of abortion don't think of themselves as callous about the down and out, but as vitally concerned for the physical and spiritual welfare of all people, including the unborn. That is why they will find it offensive to be told bluntly they "don't seem to care much about born life," and that again is why Percy does so—because, in his opinion, they need offending. In both cases he is anticipating and attacking his readers' cherished attitudes toward themselves as well as their position.

Let's suppose Percy had decided to say something about abortion without offending either side—if that is possible. How could he have tried to make the same points diplomatically? The following is one possibility for addressing one end of the spectrum:

Pro-choicers are not callous, indifferent people. Indeed, they usually support a woman's right to have an abortion precisely because they care about human life. They see the number of children born into abject poverty, into disease, into intellectual and physical deformity, into hateful, violent homes, and they want to reduce the damage these conditions cause. But I would ask them to consider for a moment some implications of abortion—that the fetus would have been a human being like them; that poor and diseased and deformed people have a right to live, too, and most are glad to be alive, including those in hateful homes; that we are aborting a million and a half fetuses a year, a sum greater than the population of many major cities.

We are not suggesting, by the way, that the diplomatic approach is better than Percy's broadside. We are only showing you that it is possible to anticipate readers' attitudes in different ways, depending on the reaction you want.

Needs As a writer you must take into account your readers' needs. You cannot, of course, satisfy all their needs: you cannot give them food, shelter, clothes, transportation, and the like. But you can satisfy more needs than you may realize. Just consider how many newspaper and magazine articles deal with food, shelter, clothes, and transportation, telling readers how to buy, how to prepare, how to fix, how to sell. On any subject you can think of, literature is available to inform, to interpret, and to entertain.

Writing fulfills these three basic needs: the need for *knowledge,* the need for *understanding,* and the need for *pleasure.* These needs are not mutually exclusive; in fact, they are often indistinguishable. To understand something, we need to know about it, and learning can be one of our greatest pleasures. These introductory paragraphs from an essay by Nat Hentoff demonstrate how the three needs come together:

WHEN NICE PEOPLE BURN BOOKS

It happened one splendid Sunday morning in a church. Not Jerry Falwell's Baptist sanctuary in Lynchburg, Virginia, but rather the First Unitarian Church in Baltimore. On October 4, 1981, midway through the 11 A.M. service, pernicious ideas were burned at the altar.

As reported by Frank P. L. Somerville, religion editor of the *Baltimore Sun,* "Centuries of Jewish, Christian, Islamic, and Hindu writings were 'expurgated'—because of sections described as 'sexist.' "

Touched off by a candle and consumed in a pot on a table in front of the altar were slips of paper containing "patriarchal" excerpts from Martin Luther, Thomas Aquinas, the Koran, St. Augustine, St. Ambrose, St. John Chrysostom, the Hindu Code of Manu V, an anonymous Chinese author, and the Old Testament. Also hurled into the purifying fire were works by Kierkegaard and Karl Barth.

The congregation was much exalted: "As the last flame died in the pot, and the organ pealed, there was applause," Somerville wrote.

I reported this news of the singed holy spirit to a group of American Civil Liberties Union members in California, and one woman was furious. At me.

"We did the same thing at our church two Sundays ago," she said. "And long past time, too. Don't you understand it's just *symbolic?*"

I told this ACLU member that when the school board in Drake, North Dakota, threw thirty-four copies of Kurt Vonnegut's *Slaughterhouse Five* into the furnace in 1973, it wasn't because the school was low on fuel. That burning was symbolic, too. Indeed, the two pyres—in North Dakota and in Baltimore—were witnessing to the same lack of faith in the free exchange of ideas.

What an inspiring homily for the children attending services at a liberated church: They now know that the way to handle ideas they don't like is to set them on fire.

The stirring ceremony in Baltimore is just one more illustration that the spirit of the First Amendment is not being savaged only by malign forces of the Right, whether private or governmental. Campaigns to purge school libraries, for example, have been conducted by feminists as well as by Phyllis Schlafly. Yet, most liberal watchdogs of our freedom remain fixed on the right as *the* enemy of free expression. . . .

Hentoff provides us information—about a book burning at a Unitarian church service, an ACLU meeting in California, a book burning in a school in North Dakota. He provides us interpretation—mainly his own interpretation of the events he describes (although he does include an opposing interpretation from the woman in California). And what about pleasure? It may sound odd to say that we find pleasure in reading Hentoff's article about book burning, that we find it entertaining, but, in fact, we do, because we find it interesting. And we find it interesting because we find it consistently *surprising,* in ways both large and small.

It is surprising in large ways because Hentoff shows us book burning by people from whom we don't expect it. It is surprising in small ways because Hentoff keeps dropping facts we don't expect: the authors and books that the Unitarian congregation chose to burn, the anger expressed by the ACLU member toward Hentoff.

His interpretation also surprises: his linkage of the North Dakota school board's burning of *Slaughterhouse Five* with the actions of the Baltimore Unitarian church, his assertion that the lesson for children is to burn books whose ideas they can't handle. Hentoff consistently states his interpretation in unusual terms, from unexpected angles. The terms, moreover, are precise and specific, never merely general and abstract.

To satisfy general readers' needs, then, keep those needs in mind as you revise. Give them details and facts to satisfy their need for knowledge. Give your interpretation of the details and facts to satisfy their need for understanding. And to satisfy their need for pleasure, find the most interesting details and facts, arrange them as much as possible in an order of surprise, and state your interpretations in the most unusual yet precise terms you can.

Experts

Experts are those who know a great deal about a subject, the structure and dynamics of its various elements, and the jargon used to discuss it.

But expertise is relative. Compared to the layman, a physician is an expert in medicine. But physicians have their own specialties: allergies, anesthesiology, cardiovascular diseases, dermatology, endocrinology, gynecology, hematology, and so on. A couple of hematologists could have a conversation about blood that a dermatologist could hardly understand. On the other hand, a hematologist and a dermatologist could have a conversation about blood (or any medical issue, for that matter) that laypeople would find incomprehensible.

Students often find the idea of expertise intimidating, as if it were reserved for an elite few. This is a misconception. While there are degrees of expertise, all people are experts in something: they can comfortably talk to other experts in terms nonexperts would hardly understand, and they are intensely interested in finding out what other experts have to say about their subject. We know students who are experts in rock music, in science fiction, in judging livestock, in chess, in photography, in tennis, basketball, and synchronized swimming—the list is virtually endless. These students may not be as expert as others who have been involved in the subject longer, but they are certainly experts according to our two criteria above.

In college, you will often write in your major classes as an apprentice expert. That is, you won't be expected to impress your professor with the depth and breadth of your knowledge; however, you will be expected to write about ideas in such a way as to show that you're learning how experts in your field discuss issues and ideas. This will mean paying attention to the conventions and formats of lab reports if you're a biology major, to literary criticism if you're an English major, to case studies if you're in law, and so on.

Writing for experts means by definition writing about their particular field of expertise. (If you should speak to an audience of physicians on zoning laws, you would not address them as experts.) It means, moreover, writing as an authority on the subject, having something to say that readers haven't heard before. Writing for experts involves, then, specific considerations in anticipating their knowledge, attitudes, and needs.

Knowledge In writing for experts, use the terms of the trade when such terms enable you to have your say more succinctly than would otherwise be possible. Jargon is a kind of professional shorthand that relieves you (and your readers) of the burden involved in describing a concept every time you use it. Instead of saying "words that begin with the same sound," you say "alliteration." It's simply easier. And if your readers are in the literature business, you don't need to define the term because you can assume they know it. Journalists regularly use terms such as "put to bed," "bullets," "dupe," "stringer," "sidebar," and "top-off." If they were to read a piece in which the writer defines these terms, they would quickly infer the piece was not written for them.

A word of caution. You should not use jargon merely to prove your credentials or to sound scientific or impressive. In the hard sciences—in mathematics, chemistry, physics, biology—specialized language often is indispensable. Without it, as we have observed, work in a field cannot be done. Of course, superfluous jargon does occur in the hard sciences as well as in professional fields such as education, psychology, sociology, literary criticism. That is why we say to use jargon *when it makes communication quicker and easier.* Even when addressing experts, remember Orwell's rule: if an ordinary English word does the job as well as a jargon word, go with the ordinary English word.

In addressing experts you don't need to provide extensive background information. They know the background—that's why they're experts. You may have to catch them up on a recent development, a newly erupted controversy, some breaking research; but do so quickly, just enough so they can understand whatever it is you have to say. (For a detailed account of any new developments, they'll go to the primary sources.)

Experts want to know more about the subject than they already know. If you have figured out a way to remove bicycle tires with no special tools, *Bike World* would be interested in publishing an account of it. If you have found a mnemonic device for remembering scale positions on a guitar, a system that other guitar players would find useful, *Frets* magazine would probably like to share your discovery with its readers. If you have discovered that the Beatles found many of their tunes in the works of Mozart, *Rolling Stone* would want to know about it. If you have nothing new, don't feel discouraged—someday you may. Besides, there are other audiences to address, other tasks to perform.

Attitudes Experts are impatient with the hype of advertising—endorsements of cars by athletes and movie stars, nameless ingredients that doctors recommend most, mini-dramas about the romance a mouthwash can induce. Experts want facts and (if they are appropriate) figures, and they want interpretations based squarely on those facts and figures. Sound technicians, for instance, in considering equipment to buy, may be interested in testimonials by knowledgeable people, but they demand accurate technical data. A judge doesn't want mere assertions that the driver was drunk, he wants facts ("According to breathalyzer data administered on the scene, his blood alcohol was .17, which in this state is .07 over the legal limit that defines intoxication.") that warrant the interpretation that the driver was drunk.

Whether you are informing experts or trying to persuade them of some argument or other, you may be sure that whatever their position on any particular issue, they value facts above all else.

Needs Experts need to learn more about their subject, and they do so in two ways: through facts about the subject they hadn't known before, and through interpretations that point to ways of understanding the subject they hadn't considered before. Thus, while they value facts above all else, they are vitally interested in what various experts make of the facts. Facts come first—they dismiss out of hand an interpretation that slights the facts—but facts alone are not enough.

You should not get the impression, by the way, that experts like only technical literature about their subject. Every fly fisherperson we know loves Norman MacLean's novel *A River Runs through It* for the beauty of its fly fishing descriptions, just as aviation experts enjoy the novel *Night Flight,* about the early days of flying, by French writer Antoine de Saint-Exupéry. Like all other readers, in other words, experts also need pleasure. In writing for them, you should pay the same attention to aesthetic considerations as for any other type of reader: to arresting detail, to unusual angles, to surprise.

Executives

By "executives" we don't necessarily mean people who sit behind big desks in large offices. We mean, rather, people who are in a position, permanent or temporary, to make some decision regarding the issue at hand.

Thus for students, teachers are executives because they make decisions about grades. If you are trying to get your spouse or friends to clean up their act, you are treating them as executives because they can choose to follow or ignore your recommendation. If you are running for President of the United States, you are addressing the entire public as executives because they can vote for or against you. If, on the other hand, you happen to be regaling the board of General Motors with a joke, you are not addressing the members as executives because you are presenting them with nothing to decide.

As a rule, then, you usually write for executives in the institutional worlds of business, government, and academia, in the form of memos, papers, and reports to specific people who have the wherewithal to act upon whatever it is you have to say. Such writing, therefore, usually concentrates on information, evaluations, implications, conclusions, and recommendations. To make it effective, you must of course take into account the executives' knowledge, attitudes, and needs.

Knowledge Generally, executives are expert in their particular field, but not necessarily in all the areas under their charge. Consider, for instance, the dean of the college of arts and sciences on your campus. He or she is an economist, perhaps, or a chemist yet has to make decisions affecting the entire college, which includes departments of physics, biology, history, political science, English, philosophy, math. However learned and multifaceted a dean may be, he or she cannot have anything approaching expertise in all the disciplines included in the college.

In writing for executives, therefore, unless you know your subject falls in the area of their expertise, address them as general readers.

Attitudes In general, executives place a premium on clarity and the "bottom line." They want essential facts clearly spelled out, basic alternatives sharply delineated, the implications fully acknowledged, conclusions and recommendations defined and supported. They appreciate any visual aids—tables, graphs, charts, pictures—that will help them see your points quickly and coherently. (Be careful, however, of throwing in superfluous visual aids—they serve only as a nuisance and will undercut the result you're after.)

In writing for executives, keep in mind that their basic attitude is practical: they want information that will help them make the best decision they can, though, of course, they may be just as influenced by emotional appeals as anyone else.

Needs Executives not only want the best information; they need the best information. They need clarity in the presentation of facts, of arguments on both sides, of implications, of the conclusion, of any recommendation. Each of these elements, therefore, should be clearly labeled as such. If you have information you regard as important but not essential to understanding the basics of the case, put it in a labeled attachment or appendix. For the convenience of busy readers, provide summaries and, when such papers are long enough, abstracts—the whole case in a nutshell. Make certain you make every sentence and every word as simple and precise as possible, so executives can read it quickly without any chance of misunderstanding or confusion.

Mixed Readership

Now for the hard part: those occasions when, like it or not, you must write for more than one group of readers. Often the memo you write for your department head as an expert will be forwarded to higher-ups, to executives in marketing and accounting and personnel who are not experts, yet who need to be able to understand what you have written. Sometimes what you write for general readers will also be read by experts hoping to learn something new, if only a little. How do you handle the conflicting requirements of different kinds of readers?

First, if among your mixed readers one group dominates, write primarily to that group. Write as best you can so that the others can understand and enjoy your work, but aim for the dominant group. If your dominant group is composed mainly of experts, don't oversimplify your subject for the benefit of nonexpert readers. Consider, for example, defining specialized vocabulary in an appendix so the experts don't get bogged down with definitions they don't need.

Second, when addressing a mix of readers, try to divide your paper into specifically labeled parts so different readers can pick and choose what to read. You can suggest that certain parts are intended for experts, that certain parts are intended primarily for general readers and executives, and so on. This list of parts that follows is intended as a guide. You need not use all of these in a paper, unless it is long and complex enough to require them all. To decide which to use, make function your guide: choose those which will help make your paper as accessible to as many readers as possible.

- *Preface:* a brief explanation at the beginning of the purpose and scope of the work.
- *Directions for Reading:* in a preface, or as the preface, an explanation of which sections are intended for which types of readers.

- *Abstract:* a quick preliminary overview of the work as an orientation and as a means of review.
- *Table of Contents:* if the work is long enough, a list of the parts by title and page number.
- *Illustrations, Tables, Graphs, Charts,* and *Calculations:* visual aids that help specific readers see, quickly and clearly, what you're saying.
- *Summaries:* quick distillations or reviews of what you've just said at much greater length.
- *Appendices:* supplementary pages at the end presenting supporting material for the benefit of those who want to examine the subject under consideration in greater detail.
- *Index:* for longer pieces, an alphabetical list of crucial names and terms with the pages on which they appear.

Revising effectively requires anticipating probable readers' knowledge, attitudes, and needs, and knowing whether they're experts, executives, general readers, or some combination. Paying attention to readers helps you rethink your own ideas, possibly discovering aspects you wouldn't otherwise have considered.

APPLICATIONS

1. Examine an area about which you are an expert, one whose lingo you understand and that you keep up with through reading and conversation. Think of people you know who are not experts in this area—some classmates, for example—and make a list of words, phrases, and concepts that you would have to define for them if you were to write an essay for them on the subject.

2. Find and bring to class three pieces on a similar topic, each written for a different kind of reader—general, expert, executive. Write a page or so explaining for your classmates and instructor the distinctions among them. Note whether there are any provisions for a mixed readership, and, if there are, whether the piece is aimed at one group more than the others. Analyze each piece for flaws and failures in reaching its intended readership.

3. Ask members of your writing group to bring letters they don't mind sharing from friends and relatives. Have each member make a list of all the words and phrases in these letters that only the reader (and maybe a select few others) would understand. Then, write a one-page explanation of what the words and phrases mean and how they came to be a part of the letter writer's and reader's private vocabulary.

4. Find a piece written either above or beneath your level of expertise—an article from a medical journal if you've never studied medicine, a junior-high biology text if you're a biology major, a high-school American history text if you're an American history buff. Read a portion of it closely and make a list of what bothered you—the inaccuracies, the inanities, the obscurities, the murky waters, the dry deserts. Also make a list of what you liked—the illustrations, the descriptions, whatever. Write a page describing your experience for your classmates and teacher.

5. What could you write about right now that would interest general readers in terms of information or entertainment? That would interest expert readers? That would interest executives? List three topics for each kind of reader and explain to your instructor why you chose them.

6. Think back over the writing you've done in the past year. Include all of your writing—letters, essays, class papers, lab reports, and so on. Did you write mostly for general readers, experts, executives, or mixed? Write a page explaining your most common readership.

7. Take any brief piece (no more than 500 words) that you've written lately, and adjust it for a different kind of reader. Take your last class essay, for example, and adjust a page of it so elementary-school students could understand. Or take a letter you wrote a friend and adjust it for your parents. Note the sorts of changes you have to make.

8. What kind of reader are you most of the time—general, expert, or executive? Has this changed in the past? Do you see it changing again in the future? Briefly trace your personal reading history for your writing group.

Credibility

One aspect of revision involves remembering how readers will judge your writing. This affects nearly everything else, from how your evidence is received to the effect on your readers of careless typos, if any. Remember, readers have only your written words in front of them; even if they know you, their task is to try to understand your ideas through your writing. Aristotle pointed out that to win the day, orators must make their case not only with logic and feelings, but also with credibility. Aristotle called this "ethos," or the ethical appeal.

Suppose someone tries to convince you to vote for a particular candidate solely on the basis of the issues, and you discover that he stands to get a job if the candidate wins. He consequently loses his credibility, which is to say his believ-ability and authority. You could no longer find his arguments trustworthy. Why? Because (1) you discovered something about him he didn't tell you himself and (2) he stands to gain personally from his candidate's victory. If he himself had pointed out that he had something to gain, he might have been able to persuade you anyway. And, of course, if he had nothing personal to gain, you'd have no reason not to trust him. We commonly assume that a person who is honest and selfless is also trustworthy, but that we can't trust someone who's selfish.

But however honest and selfless, if a person appears to be a jerk, smelling like a locker room, telling dumb jokes, and picking his nose, he will go down in your estimation. Credibility is not just a matter of morality—it is also a matter of manners. That is why trial lawyers, who make their living being persuasive, observe all the elaborate decorum of the court: a breach of manners could mean a loss of credibility with the judge and the jury.

To write effectively, you must establish credibility, by generating and developing an image of yourself that your readers will trust and respect. This image (whatever its form) is usually called the *persona,* a theater term referring to the mask worn by actors in antiquity. You may think of the persona as an act you put on, as long as you keep in mind that it should be an honest act.

This may strike you as a paradox—"putting on an act," after all, usually means trying to fool people—but we actually put on honest acts all the time. We behave differently around different people—we have a certain behavior for our parents, another for our teachers, yet another for friends, still another for formal occasions among strangers, and so on. The purpose of these "acts" is not to perpetrate fraud, but to relate to others effectively.

To establish a credible persona, you must pay particular attention to accuracy, to your use of sources, to appropriate formats, to your tone, and to your style.

Accuracy

A misstatement of fact, however minor, seriously erodes credibility. We once read a piece in which the writer stated that some handball players had hands so tough they didn't wear gloves. But the primary purpose of handball gloves is not to protect the hands; it's to keep the ball dry. So you never find handball players who don't wear gloves. The writer's error was hardly serious—it's no big deal whether handball players wear gloves or not—but it made us wonder how many other items were also in error. The writer lost some credibility.

The lesson is obvious: in your writing, state as facts only those items that you know are facts. Be especially wary of assuming something is so, simply because everyone else assumes it's so. After the 1986 Chernobyl nuclear plant disaster, the western media, one after another, reported that 20,000 Soviet citizens had died. All of the reporters assumed it was so since all of them were saying so. Several days later, when the fact emerged that the death toll was actually quite small, the media had to eat crow.

A newspaper editor we know calls the process of verifying facts "bulletproofing." If you verify your facts, he points out, then readers can't "shoot holes" in your work, at least in terms of accuracy.

Factual accuracy also means qualifying your statements when necessary. "Students never study on Saturday nights" may be true of most students, but not all. Few things are always or never, and if you say they are and readers know of exceptions, they will discount your credibility. To keep your statements in the realm of fact, then, qualify them: "Most students don't study on Saturday night." Such a statement lacks the impact of a screaming headline, to be sure, but it does something of far greater value: it keeps the readers' trust.

Accuracy also involves matters of interpretation and judgment. Be careful, for example, not to confuse inferences and facts. If you notice several dead fish floating in a backwater downriver from your city's sewage treatment plant and you write a letter to the newspaper stating that the sewage treatment plant is killing fish in the river, you've confused an inference with a fact. You don't know that the treatment plant is killing the fish. You only know that some dead fish are floating around downstream from the plant, and you have inferred (perhaps correctly, perhaps not) that the plant is responsible. To verify your inference you must investigate further.

You can, however, still write a letter stating the facts and pointing out that the plant *could* be responsible and that it *should* therefore be investigated. By making the distinction yourself between fact and inference, you enhance your credibility.

In addition, be careful not to exaggerate the importance of your facts. Two teenage suicides do not an epidemic make; one politician taking bribes does not mean the system is corrupt. Readers distrust writers who insist on making too much of too little, and with good reason. To be credible, maintain perspective.

Perspective also requires giving facts reasonable emphasis. Emphasis is more subtle than fact, but it is crucial to credibility. Not all facts are of equal value. If you treat them as if they are, or deemphasize some that are of vital importance, or overemphasize those of marginal importance, your readers will dismiss your work as lacking judgment. We read a review of a musical performance, for example, in which the reviewer spent most of the article complaining about the expressions on the performer's face rather than considering the music she played and the way she played it. So we dismissed the reviewer, and his review, as silly.

Concentrate on emphasizing items in accordance with their real value. If you find you must emphasize something that won't seem worth such a fuss, then explain why it is worth it. A few dead fish may not seem like much, you may say, but pollution starts small and is much cheaper to clean up now than later, when millions of fish downstream have died.

Use of Sources

Just as your readers will consider your credibility, so should you consider the credibility of your sources. While you shouldn't regard credentials as an infallible guide, you can't ignore them, either: by and large, people with credentials have them for a reason—they've proven themselves. So, consider whether the authorities you rely on are respected in the field, whether they have contributed original and important research, whether their statements are informed by recent events that might have a bearing on the subject. As for sources by people who are not well-known in the field, use them if they make sense and you can show they tell the truth, pointing out that while an author may not have the credentials of an authority, he or she has come up with something significant to consider.

Finally, remember to verify information when necessary. Reporters know, for example, that a politician's accusations about his or her opponent should not be printed as truth until carefully verified. (The accusation could be published as a statement by the politician, deflecting the issue of credibility from the reporter to the accuser who has something to gain.)

By checking your sources scrupulously and citing them accurately, you will go a long way in establishing your credibility.

Appropriate Formats

For many types of writing—memos, formal letters, research papers, and so on—you are expected to follow conventional formats. *Format* refers to a specific layout or form on the page; when something is *conventional,* it is done a certain way mostly because of a tradition that has proven useful. It's easy to find fault with convention—and sometimes it's necessary—but you should keep in mind that, like it or not, conventions are one means by which people judge each other. All of us behave according to certain conventions, and we examine each other according to the conventions we choose to follow and those we choose to ignore. Theater and film, for example, have specific formats for scripts. If you submit a movie or a play for consideration and your script does not follow the format, chances are very good that the first reader to see it will, without going past page one, assume you don't know how to write a movie or a play because you don't even know the proper format. You will have lost your credibility before you got started.

Whenever you have a writing task to do, then, check with your instructor or boss to see if there is a format you are expected to follow. If there is, follow it consistently.

Tone

Tone refers to the attitude you convey toward your subject by your choice of diction, sentence structure, rhythm, pace, figures of speech, details, and emphasis. Credibility requires that your tone be appropriate to the occasion and to your point. An inappropriate tone can result in a lost audience. Consider this funeral eulogy:

> You probably think I'm going to sing poor old George's praises. But we didn't come here to praise the guy. We came here to bury him. After all, he's dead. Deader than prohibition, deader than the gold standard, deader than a joke by Milton Berle, deader than the marriage of his recently divorced daughter.

A tone inappropriate to your point can undermine everything you're trying to accomplish:

> I believe I can say with unqualified enthusiasm that we probably should adopt this proposal. It seems to offer everything that, so far at least, we have agreed would be in our best interest, at least in the short term.

Expressed like this, a recommendation is likely to be passed over since it is hedged with so many tentatives it sounds like the writer doesn't want the proposal adopted.

Sometimes writers rely on tone to make a point beyond their literal words. Look at the following, for example, from the letters section of a local newspaper:

> To the editor:
> I can't for the life of me understand why some people persist in letting their dogs run free. My husband and I have had to clean up our yard nine times this week, and if we have to do it again, my husband swears he'll start shooting. The owners, not the dogs.

Obviously, the writer's husband is not going to start shooting either the owners or the dogs. The witty tone of the final sentence cleverly suggests the real point: that this couple has had it with careless dog owners and wants them to be more responsible.

Irony is a tone writers use then they mean just the opposite of what they are literally saying. This infamous passage from 18th-century satirist Jonathan Swift's "A Modest Proposal" is a case in point:

> I have been assured by a very knowing American of my acquaintance in London; that a young healthy child, well nursed, is, at a year old, a most delicious, nourishing, and wholesome food; whether stewed, roasted, baked, or broiled; and I make no doubt, that it will equally serve in a fracasee, or ragout.
> I do therefore humbly offer it to public consideration, that of the hundred and twenty thousand children, already computed, twenty thousand may be reserved for breed; . . . A child will make two dishes at an entertainment for friends; and when the family dines alone, the fore or hind quarters will make a reasonable dish; and seasoned with a little pepper or salt, will be very good boiled on the fourth day, especially in winter.

Taken out of context, this passage seems simply monstrous, the proposal of a cannibalistic madman. In the context of the whole essay, however, this proposed "solution" is Swift's attempt to expose England's economic stranglehold on 18th-century Ireland. The notion that raising children for food would solve Ireland's poverty is not meant to be taken seriously but as an indictment of England's treatment of the Irish. Irony was Swift's main weapon in his war against England's injustices.

Irony can be very effective, but it can also backfire. Used with too heavy a touch, it makes the writer seem merely sarcastic, and sarcasm undermines credibility.

Whatever you're writing about, whomever you're writing to, make certain that (1) your tone expresses how you actually feel and (2) your tone is appropriate for the occasion. Among friends, for instance, you may be able to express anger effectively by swearing. In a court of law you must express your anger within the bounds of conventional decorum; otherwise you may be held in contempt.

A final word. While revising, listen to the tone that seems to naturally emerge. That way, you may well *discover* how you actually feel about a subject. Like every other aspect of writing, attention to tone is also a means of generating and developing ideas.

Style

Careless writing quickly destroys credibility. Clumsy constructions, needless repetitions, awkward or mixed metaphors, clichés, dangling modifiers, unnecessary jargon, unvarying sentence length and structure, incorrect punctuation, misspellings—all these say you don't care enough to take the trouble to do the job right. Your readers will respond exactly in kind: if you don't care, neither do I.

> Its very important to get rid of collegate athletes because they don't do good and they actuly do harm because they get alot of injurys playing athletics.

Such writing doesn't have a chance, even though the writer may have a good point. Most readers respond to such a sentence with disbelief. How could anyone writing like that be capable of making a reasonable assertion?

Style means far more than correct grammar, usage, and mechanics, however. It means a certain form of behavior in words, and different occasions call for different styles. For practical purposes, we will divide style into two basic categories, informal and formal, and define the characteristics of each. These are not absolutes, but the opposite ends of a graduated scale: we write more or less informally or formally depending on the occasion.

Informal Style The more familiar the occasion, the more informal you can be. In notes and letters to family and friends, you can be absolutely colloquial—that is, conversational—using all the fragments and slang and street grammar you wish. In essays and business letters and memos, you should be colloquial but avoid slang, careless fragments, and nonstandard grammar. In all informal writing, the basic idea is to write as you would talk to your readers if you were face-to-face. A few techniques will help you catch this colloquial note.

First, *use contractions.* In ordinary talk, we seldom say "I will not go," "He would not agree," "She would not either." As a rule, we say "I won't go, "He wouldn't agree," "She wouldn't either." In informal pieces, use contractions as you would when talking. Contractions give your style the rhythm and pace and emphasis of conversation, and readers respond accordingly, as if in a person-to-person exchange.

Second, *leave out "that" and "which" whenever possible.* Those little relative pronouns are quite formal, usually unnecessary, and, in clusters, invariably awkward: "I think that Joan said that she would go." Such stilted awkwardness is, happily, very easy to fix: "I think Joan said she would go," or, better yet, "I think Joan said she'd go."

In an informal style, use "that" only when its absence creates ambiguity: "Most immigrants understand at least a rudimentary grasp of English is necessary to get a job." Here we must read the sentence twice to see that "rudimentary grasp" is not the object of "understand," but the subject of the verb "is." Including "that" in the sentence makes the meaning immediately clear: "Most immigrants understand that at least a rudimentary grasp of English is necessary to get a job."

Third, *use personal pronouns.* You may have been taught never to use first or second person pronouns in writing, but talking to someone person-to-person you say "I" and "we" and "you" all the time. So we suggest the same when you're writing. It sounds natural, and it's to the point.

Fourth, *feel free to put prepositions at the end of sentences.* You may have also been taught never to end a sentence with a preposition. To see how ridiculous that rule is, consider what Winston Churchill had to say about it: "This is the sort of English up with which I will not put." Sentences such as "Who are you going with?" and "What is that for?" make perfect sense in English. You shouldn't put prepositions at the end of every sentence as a matter of principle, but feel free to put them at the end when they sound right there.

Fifth, *write short to-the-point sentences.* When a sentence goes beyond twenty words, see if you can break it up into two (or more). Look to vary the length of your sentences, to spare your readers monotony, but make the structure of your sentences as simple as possible.

Simplicity is relative, of course. Clarity is the primary consideration. If you're dealing with a complicated topic, you may have to write some complicated sentences. The point is to make them as simple as you can without over-simplifying the topic.

Sixth, *feel free to use fragments.* Fragments—phrases without either a subject or a verb that are nevertheless punctuated as if they were complete sentences— are another common no-no. Inadvertent fragments that get in the way of a reader's understanding should, of course, be avoided. But used consciously, fragments can be pithier than a complete sentence. More emphatic. Colloquial. That's why professional writers use them a great deal. So use a fragment when (but only when) it says what you want more effectively than a complete sentence.

Formal Style The tendency among Americans is to write as informally as possible under the circumstances. For example, business writing, which was once decidedly formal, has taken a definite turn toward the informal. But certain occasions demand a degree of formality: term papers, academic papers, conference reports, doctoral dissertations, formal presentations to executives, and the like. What you need to do is find out the degree of formality required—it varies from occasion to occasion, from academic discipline to academic discipline, from firm to firm—and to adjust your style accordingly.

Such adjustment involves certain techniques:

Use fewer contractions than in informal writing. Contractions make your style more colloquial. Verb forms completely spelled out make your style more formal. So, instead of "He didn't agree" at least consider writing "He did not agree."

Use "that" if its absence sounds breezy. You can be formal and conversational at the same time, but not formal and breezy. "Mr. Porter said he would" might sound too chatty, whereas "Mr. Porter said that he would" is entirely proper. This rule requires you to listen and to make a subjective judgment about what you hear. For a rule of thumb, try this: if in doubt, use the relative pronoun "that" when writing formal prose.

Use personal pronouns sparingly. You may have no choice: certain disciplines discourage the use of "I" and "you" (engineering and the hard sciences), and that's all there is to it. If there is some leeway, the writer should use personal pronouns only when not doing so creates awkward or unclear sentences. If in doubt, read professional journal articles in the field and see how writers handle personal pronouns.

Put prepositions at the end sparingly. In a formal style, you should put the preposition at the end only if putting it elsewhere means winding up with a ridiculous sentence like Churchill's: "This is the sort of English up with which I will not put." Otherwise, put the prepositions before their objects.

Avoid fragments. Fragments are too colloquial for readers expecting formality. They well may assume a fragment is inadvertent, a mistake. In their eyes, consequently, the writer will lose credibility.

To make sure you don't make mistakes that would damage your credibility, have two books at your side as you write: a handbook of writing and a dictionary. Check the handbook for grammar, punctuation, and other usages. Check the dictionary for definitions and spellings. Check not only items you don't know, but also items you only think you know. At this point in the stage of revising, you're making productive use of your no voice, allowing it to help you create effective writing rather than slow you down.

Finally, when you've finished your final draft, proofread it! Examine it inch by inch for mistakes, typos, goofs. Readers prefer corrections, even if they don't look good, to mistakes.

On a superficial level, revising for credibility may seem like little more than polishing—making sure your facts are accurate, your sources are in order, the format is proper, the tone appropriate, and the style finished. Do remember that revision also often involves discovery; don't be afraid to start new ideas, set aside sections for later development, develop a line of thought that you now find interesting. Revising, after all, means re-seeing, seeing anew.

Checklists for Revision

Writing involves so many considerations that it is easy to overlook some of them when revising. With checklists you have a means of making yourself consider your subject in ways you otherwise might not have. Asking yourself questions about drafts, in fact, offers an ideal means of gently introducing your no voice, your critical referee, without getting into general, unfocused negative feelings.

Revision checklists work best after you've let your writing "cool" awhile. In that time you've acquired sufficient distance to be able to see it better, to see *it* rather than what you had in mind when you wrote it. Only when you're able to see what you've actually written, rather than what you think you've written, are you ready to use a checklist. As an obvious corollary, you should not wait until the last minute to write. Writing usually requires rewriting, which requires time. So do yourself a favor—give yourself the time you need to do the best job you can, a job that your readers will enjoy and appreciate.

Following are six checklists for various kinds of writing tasks. The first is a comprehensive checklist you can use for nearly any kind of writing. The rest are geared to specific kinds of writing: personal writing, expository writing, argumentation, report/research writing, and business communications.

THE TWENTY-QUESTION CHECKLIST

Purpose

1. Where in the piece do I make my purpose clear?
2. In a few words, what is my purpose in this piece?
3. Would my purpose be clear from one reading, or would it require more readings? Is this a problem for my intended readers?

Quality of the Writing

4. Where do I stumble when I read it aloud, and how can I make those passages flow?
5. Does the subject unfold clearly, as signaled by transitions and connective words?
6. Are there any repeated words or phrases that run through the piece, tying it together? Should there be?
7. Which passages seem especially well written and why?
8. Which passages seem weak, and how can I improve them?
9. Are there places where I could *show* instead of *tell* my points, using details, anecdotes, or examples? If so, should I change them?

Effect on the Reader

10. What questions does this piece answer for readers?
11. Where in the piece is my attitude toward the subject not as clear as it could be for my intended readers?
12. Would readers find my attitude appropriate?
13. Will the writing make readers think more seriously about the subject? See it more clearly? Want to know more? Want to take action? Make them mad? Depressed? Happy? Thoughtful?
14. Will any passages probably confuse the readers? If so, how can I clarify those passages?

15. What advice might readers want to give me upon reading this piece?
16. What aspects of this piece might be needlessly offensive?

Credibility

17. Are my facts accurate?
18. Did I use and cite sources appropriately?
19. Does the format fit the needs of my audience and purpose?
20. Have I fixed the mechanical errors?

CHECKLIST FOR PERSONAL, EXPLORATORY WRITING

1. In a sentence or phrase, what would I like a reader to think or feel immediately upon reading this piece?
2. How would I describe the voice in this piece? Strong and assertive? Angry? Rational? Emotional? Sarcastic? Questioning?
3. What would my ideal reader feel or think after reading this piece?
4. What parts please me the most? Where might I continue to rewrite?
5. Where might I try to have this published?

CHECKLIST FOR EXPOSITORY, THESIS-ORIENTED WRITING

1. Do I need a single thesis sentence? If so, what and where is that sentence?
2. Are the supporting subpoints for the thesis clear, without obvious overlap?
3. How have I supported each of my subpoints?
4. Does the order of elements make sense? Have I arranged the material to make my point effectively? If some specific order is needed (a logical sequence, left to right, top to bottom, first to last) does my organization follow that sequence?
5. Have I documented sources that are not common knowledge or that do not come from personal observation and experience?

CHECKLIST FOR ARGUMENTATION

1. Is this piece a genuine argument concerning a real issue, or is it essentially a matter of opinion or taste?
2. Have I considered the other side of the issue, specifically citing (or implying) its main arguments?
3. Have I effectively refuted opposing arguments with facts and/or logic?
4. If I couldn't refute an argument, have I conceded that the other side has a good point?
5. Have I used facts to make my case as much as possible?
6. Have I used credible sources to help make my case and documented them consistently according to some standard format?

CHECKLIST FOR REPORT/RESEARCH WRITING

1. Have I used headings and graphics effectively?

2. Have I added important information in an appendix, a preface, or a foreword?
3. Does the piece need a table of contents?
4. Is the documentation appropriate?
5. Is the tone appropriate and consistent?

CHECKLIST FOR BUSINESS COMMUNICATIONS

1. Have I followed appropriate formats?
2. Have I triple-checked for proofreading errors?
3. Would every sentence be clear on a first reading?
4. Does this contain all the information the reader needs in order to call or write me?
5. Does this answer the reader's probable questions?

APPLICATIONS

When you work through any of the following applications, examine your writing from the point of view of the readers, to see if, on the basis of what's on the page, they should believe you. This deliberate shift in perspective will enable you to discover aspects of your writing and your subject that you may not have realized before.

1. Examine the list of terms you would probably have to define for your classmates if you were to write a piece for them as an expert. (See Application 1 on page 98.) For each term write definitions that your readers would find not only clear but convincingly credible—that is, make them sound authoritative without being pompous, so that they truly convey your expertise.

2. Reread the three pieces you chose that were geared for three different kinds of readers. (See Application 2 on page 98.) Now, in one page or less for each, comment specifically on the credibility of each piece for its intended readers. Take into account the items we've just examined: accuracy, use of sources, appropriateness of format, tone, and style.

3. Reexamine the letters you read to members of your writing group from their friends or relatives (see Application 3 on page 98). Would any passages in these letters pose a problem for other readers in terms of credibility? Write a brief comment on this issue of credibility in personal letters for members of your group.

4. Return to the passage you commented on for Application 4 on pages 98–99. Write a one-page critique of the piece for your writing group in which you judge the credibility of the writer, taking into account accuracy, use of sources, appropriateness of format, tone, and style.

5. Go back to the subjects for various readers you listed for Application 5 on page 99. With which would you have the least amount of trouble establishing credibility for yourself as a writer? The most trouble? Explain for your classmates in one page.

6. As an expert on credibility, write a short piece explaining in your own words the concept of credibility to general readers—that is, people who haven't studied the concept. What is it? How does one go about establishing it? Use supporting examples from either speakers, writers, or both.

7. Look at the letters to the editor in your local newspaper. Choose one that is credible and one that is not, and compare and contrast them briefly for your writing group. Be sure to specify what each writer does—or doesn't do—to establish or lose credibility.

INVITATIONS FOR EXTENDED WRITING

As with all pieces of extended writing, use any of the concentrating, intuiting, and gathering strategies you find useful, and other strategies as well. Try to listen to your yes voice as you draft, then your no voice as you revise and edit.

1. Your Revising Process   Write an exploration of your own revising processes. Include your experiences with revising, whether your attitudes toward revising have changed, and what advice you would give student writers who don't revise much.

2. A Revised Paper   Find a paper you wrote for any class in the last year (or earlier) and read carefully for ways to revise it. Write an essay of two or three pages that explains what you would do and why. If you wish, actually revise the paper and compare the two drafts.

3. A Report on Revision   Write a report of five to seven pages on what professional writers think of revising, and how they revise. Use published interviews (there are plenty), and try to interview working writers—journalists, technical writers, poets, novelists, instructors. Draw whatever conclusions on revision that seem appropriate.

4. An Article About Revising   Find seven or eight feature articles in newspapers or magazines and consider whether they could use revision. If so, write a paper of three to five pages describing the kinds of revisions the articles need, citing examples wherever possible. Write this as a feature article for the publications where the original articles appeared.

5. A How-To Essay   Write a how-to essay for student writers on revision. Use whatever strategies you think work, and provide examples whenever you can to illustrate those strategies. The bibliography at the end of this chapter suggests some resource books on revision you may find useful for this assignment.

For Further Reading and Research

Cheney, Theodore A. Rees. *Getting the Words Right: How to Revise, Edit, and Rewrite.* Cincinnati: Writer's Digest Books, 1983.

Kuriloff, Pesche C. *Rethinking Writing.* New York: St. Martin's, 1989.

Lanham, Richard A. *Revising Prose.* New York: Scribner's, 1979.

Murray, Donald M. *The Craft of Revision.* New York: Holt, 1991.

Williams, Joseph. *Style: Toward Clarity and Grace.* Chicago: Univ. of Chicago Press, 1990.

CHAPTER FIVE

Collaborating

Like the legend of the lone alchemist, the legend of the lone creator
is also wrong. In recent years, investigators have begun to appreciate
that creators collaborate in all sorts of ways in order to do their work.
In fact collaboration is one of the best kept secrets of creativity.

—JOHN BRIGGS, *creativity theorist*

[Collaboration] can result in some of the best work of your career, if
you and your collaborator can produce, together, something beyond
the ability of either of you alone. After all, the great works of film
and theater, dance and music are usually collaborations of writer/
director/choreographer/composer and many performers who together create what no one of them could possibly produce alone.

—ORSON SCOTT CARD, *science fiction writer*

All writers—especially the pros—seek the help of others. This is precisely
why we consider collaborating to be a foundation strategy for writers. The common image of writers working alone and then sending their works forth finished
and shining like a fine sword is only partly true, and then only to a point. Often
writers do work alone, and when they send their work out, it does have a fine
finish to it. But then begins the process of collaboration, of working with others—
friends, colleagues, editors—to make the final adjustments that the writer alone
would not have thought of making.

A good deal of writing, moreover, is done collaboratively from the outset.
People often find themselves, for example, on a committee charged with preparing a report. The committee considers the subject, divides up the writing chores
in some manner or other, and then puts the results together for the final product.
Much of the actual writing is still done alone, because composing sentences and
paragraphs by committee is a very cumbersome procedure. But when you take

into account the planning, the research, and the polishing, a great deal of the writing amounts to a group activity.

So collaborating—getting input from others on your own writing and sometimes working with others to produce a piece of writing—is virtually inevitable. In this chapter, we explore two forms of collaboration: (1) formal writing groups and (2) informal collaboration. We also provide some concluding checklists to help readers and writers in informal collaboration.

Formal Writing Groups

In formal writing groups members all share at least partial responsibility for the creation of a document, whether by brainstorming, researching, drafting, creating graphics, or revising. Each member of the group contributes something— ideally, about the same amount of energy and material.

Much writing in business, government, and academia is done by formal groups: members of a committee, a task force, or an *ad hoc* group generate material together, share either their drafts of the whole or their portions of the whole (depending on the length of the work), then as a group revise and polish. They then submit the final draft as their official report. The Declaration of Independence is such a collaborative document, as are various contemporary government reports and studies published by private foundations, industries, and corporations. As writing collaborators and theorists Lisa Ede and Andrea Lunsford point out, "people in a range of professions regularly write as part of teams or groups, and . . . their ability to participate successfully in such collaborative writing efforts is essential both to their productivity and job satisfaction." Our own experience in collaborating on this text supports the notion that people writing together can successfully and enjoyably create writing that they would not create (or even attempt!) alone.

Members of formal writing groups can collaborate effectively in five ways: brainstorming, researching, drafting, creating graphics, and revising.

Brainstorming

A common strategy, brainstorming can be both organized and productive, especially if it proceeds step-by-step. Often, brainstorming groups are formed to tackle some issue or other; then they pass their ideas to another group or an administrator to develop or act upon. The end result may be a report, a set of recommendations, even a piece of legislation.

Here are the five steps of a brainstorming strategy called the Nominal Group Technique, or NGT. A detailed description of this strategy can be found in *Group Techniques for Program Planning* by A. L. Delbecq and colleagues.

Step 1: Generating. The group (five to seven people) defines a question. The question should not be answerable with yes or no ("Do you favor building a new concert hall on campus?"). Rather, it should be open-ended ("What do you see as the major roadblocks to building a concert hall on campus?"). Then each member lists, without prior discussion, as many answers to the question as possible. The answers need not sound profound or important; anything that pops into mind should go down on the page.

Step 2: Sharing. One at a time, each group member reads his or her answers aloud. A leader selected by the group records each answer on a chalkboard or a flip-chart so that everyone can see them all. Only answers that obviously repeat a previous one are not recorded. At this point, group members should refrain from comments or questions about the answers going up on the board or flip-chart.

Step 3: Clarifying. Now, it's time to talk. The group examines each answer one by one, seeing if any clarification is necessary: definition, detail, rephrasing. If new ideas pop up in the discussion, they too are recorded and discussed in their turn. The writer of the particular question under discussion need not explain or defend; the meeting is not a debate, but a process for getting ideas.

Step 4: Ranking. Having gone through all the answers, group members now weed out the less from the more important answers by consensus. It is often helpful for the group to agree upon criteria before ranking and to decide how many final answers are desirable (a manageable number might be five). Each member then lists what he or she sees as the five most important answers and ranks them. The most important gets five points, the least important gets one. The leader tallies up the votes to see which five came out on top and in which order. If it is necessary (as it often is), the voting is repeated until there is a clear consensus on the top five answers and their rankings.

Step 5: Debriefing. The group now decides what action will be taken on its results. Assuming the group's purpose is to write some sort of report, the members now determine how to do so. It may be that each member will write an entire draft and the various drafts be put together, culling out the best of each. Or each member may be assigned a part, all of which will be combined into an eventual whole.

Our experience is that NGT yields an enormous amount of useful information in a very short time—far more than any single group member could generate. With a bit of effort, the group can discover priorities, hierarchies of material, or just areas of interest to be explored further.

Researching

Much writing, particularly of the sort done by formal groups, requires research. The group may choose one or two members to do all the research, or each member may be assigned an area of research, divided up so that members don't duplicate each other's work. Whatever the group decides, those doing the research should copy material and keep notes to bring to the group. We suggest that group members who volunteer for research be conversant with database searches, and take advantage of printouts to bring material back to the group for discussion.

Drafting

Having gathered the material, the group now begins putting together a first draft. Members may decide to parcel out writing to all members, each taking a section, or they may prefer to find the best writers, and let them write the whole early draft. How the job is allocated depends upon the size of the job and the composition of the group. If the job is large, it should be shared, obviously. If one or two group members are especially adept at synthesizing large amounts of material and writing it up quickly, the group should take advantage of their talent.

Another common approach to collaborative drafting involves writing and rewriting with members' suggestions. This textbook, for example, was written in just this manner. One of us would write a chapter and send it to the other. The other would then rewrite the chapter and return it, adding material, deleting passages, changing passages to make it read more smoothly or consistently. The rewritten chapters were usually accompanied by a letter explaining the changes, which had often already been discussed in a phone call. Then, the first writer would examine the changes, making further additions, deletions, and rewriting various passages again. Ultimately, we would mail the whole section to an editor, who would make further suggestions and revisions. Depending on the editor's suggestions, we would consider the section more or less complete, or we would rewrite again—and sometimes again.

All in all, this can be an arduous process, and certainly discouraging at times, but both of us are convinced we have written a much stronger text because of our collaboration.

Graphics

If the report needs graphics, the group decides what they should be and who will prepare them. One of the great advantages of collaborative writing should now be apparent: different members will have different interests and talents that the group as a whole can take advantage of.

Revising, Editing, and Proofreading

Although some members may be especially gifted at revising, editing, and proofreading, the entire group should be involved in these activities. Each member should have a copy of the draft to work with separately. Then the members should meet to compare their revisions and to work together on a final draft. The group may find it necessary to revise separately and together several times before the draft is complete. The same process should be used to edit the piece for sentence problems, muddy passages, poor transitions, and so on. And everyone should proofread the final version to ensure the credibility of the report that is submitted.

Advantages and Disadvantages of Formal Collaboration

Collaborative writing in formal groups has distinct advantages, one of which we have mentioned: enlarging the pool of talent with which to put a paper together. Group brainstorming produces more ideas than one person can dream up. With several people there is the benefit of several perspectives, reducing the chances of oversight and distortion.

Collaboration has disadvantages, too, that you must guard against. Writing by committee too often destroys an effective voice, producing in its place the faceless voice of an automaton, affording readers no variety, no surprise, no delight. Such a result may not be inevitable, though. Depending on the audience and purpose for a particular piece, the group can take advantage of the distinctive style of the writer with the clearest voice, doing everything possible to preserve and enhance that style.

Another disadvantage is the possibility that some members of the group will end up doing considerably more work than others. If that happens, there's little to be done (except to remember the shirkers and avoid working with them in the future). Do make certain that you perform at least your own part in the project.

Finally, there is the possibility that the more aggressive members of the group will dominate, taking it over and maybe even leading it astray. To prevent this, the group should consciously select a leader who will maintain a balance among the members, checking those who lack self-restraint, encouraging those who lack assertiveness.

Collaboration in a formal group setting can be especially effective for projects requiring research. Scientists and scholars often collaborate, as do people in business and government engaged in putting together reports based on market or social research. Formal collaboration is not particularly effective however, for writing of a personal nature—essays, poetry, fiction, and the like. Don't try to make it yield results where it doesn't fit. But don't hesitate to put it to work where it has a strong record of effectiveness.

Informal Collaboration

Whether assigned to or not, you can form a writing group to read and comment on your work—as long, of course, as you're willing to do the same with other members' work. Such groups should be small, three to six members. They should meet regularly but not too frequently—say, every two weeks. (A variation: meet during class and discuss drafts on certain "draft due" days. If your instructor allows class time for this activity, so much the better.) Well before each meeting, members should exchange what they plan to discuss—don't waste precious group time reading!

Some groups work best when sharing one piece from every member every time. Other groups work best when focusing on one member's work each time, on a revolving basis. You can imagine gradations between. Your group may find checklists a help—such as those at the end of this chapter—or it may find them an impediment. Different groups have different dynamics, so don't try to impose a pattern. Rather, find out how your group works best, then stay with that pattern.

Whatever the dynamic turns out to be, at the beginning group members will benefit from the five following ground rules:

First, during the first few meetings members should establish an atmosphere of trust and goodwill by allowing mostly praise and support, even if some members insist they want their work treated with hatchet-like honesty. Chopping prose means chopping egos; until positive rapport is established, damaged egos can destroy a group's ability to work together. (In our experience, even members who insist on criticism don't want criticism that cuts deep. The best criticism grows out of a genuine concern for helping group members create the best possible draft. The Golden Rule of comments: give the kind you yourself would like to receive.)

Second, writers whose work is being discussed should simply listen, speaking only to answer questions addressed specifically to them. If they begin challenging comments and defending their writing, the group will quickly turn into a debating society—and that's an ordeal for everyone. Should this begin to happen, someone should gently remind the group that the purpose is to respond and learn, not to garner praise and refute criticism.

Third, approach the work under consideration in one of two ways. Offer a play-by-play account of your immediate thoughts and feelings as you read, or evaluate the work according to certain criteria you regard as important (clarity, development, logic, sentence structure, voice, credibility). Whereas the first approach can help a writer learn his or her words' very first effect on a reader, the second is based on considered judgment. Obviously a writer can benefit from both approaches, so some members of the group should follow the first, others the second.

Fourth, while reading drafts, it helps to concentrate on one of the following three questions. (The first in each set is for immediate responses; the bracketed question considers specific criteria.)

1. What moved you and how? That is, what made you think, made you laugh, made you angry, made you feel curious, enlightened, appalled? [What are the effects of various parts—the details, the ideas, the people, the actions, the style, word choice?]
2. What did you have questions about? [Comment on matters of taste, coherence, logic, tone, diction, organization, and so on.]

3. What would make the piece work better for you? [What recommendations do you have for improved organization, deletions, additions, revising logical flaws, adding facts or details?]

Fifth, all members of the group should bring their essays back for more readings. One of the most exciting aspects of a writing group is seeing the members improve their drafts. Unless a member no longer wants to work on a specific draft, try to plan at least a couple of discussions for each.

Nothing works perfectly—not even the best writing groups. Here are three cautions that may head off problems:

One, while informal group work is useful for any type of writing, try to form groups of people interested in the same kind of writing, and let that kind of writing determine the focus of the group. Someone interested in poetry and someone interested in technical writing may simply not be able to critique one another's work effectively. For a group to work well together, there should be a common writing focus.

Two, since working in a group means extensive and frequent revision, members may well benefit from drafting on a word processor. Though word processing doesn't work for everything, drafting by hand or on a typewriter makes rewriting a genuine burden; with a computer the work is almost pleasant, since word processors eliminate the tedium of redoing the whole draft just to move a paragraph or to fix an editing problem.

Three, whenever possible, readers should make comments in writing, directly on the manuscript or on a separate paper, for the writer to take home. Readers will define their points more clearly this way than they otherwise might, and the writer has a record to rely on rather than just memory. A variation is for writers to attach a set of questions to their drafts for readers to answer before the meeting, which can then be read and discussed. The checklists in the next section can help.

Checklists for Collaborative Revision

Few writers can be entirely objective about their own writing. Professional writers of all kinds rely on editors, because outsiders can often see a piece of writing more clearly and thus help the writer see it more clearly too.

You may think it a trifle pushy to ask someone to go to the trouble of criticizing your work. Most people, however, are flattered and glad to help, especially when you can return the favor.

A word of caution. Don't pick just anybody to criticize your work. Make sure your reader has the energy and time to do a good job, along with the integrity to be honest. Likewise, let it be known that you are seeking not praise but an honest appraisal. There is a big difference.

Just as the writer needs help, readers need help, too. Here are some checklists that you can give to potential collaborators to help guide them in responding to your writing.

Checklists should be short (a long one *would* be pushy). Here is a brief comprehensive checklist that works for many kinds of writing, followed by more specific checklists for personal, expository, argumentative, research/report, and business writing.

COMPREHENSIVE CHECKLIST FOR COLLABORATIVE READING

1. What is the best aspect of this essay? Please be specific—mention items like the subject, the organization, the basic points, the detail used to support points, and so on.
2. Does it raise important unanswered questions? Again, please be specific: cite specific questions this essay raises that I do not answer.
3. Does anything injure my credibility as a writer? For example, are there any errors of fact and/or logic, mistakes in grammar and/or punctuation, misspellings, problems in citing sources? Please note anything that makes you wonder whether you can believe what I am saying.
4. Please make any suggestions for improving this piece. Mention anything, however large or small—from redefining the subject to reorganizing to finding better detail to adding some commas—that might help me make this a better product.

READER'S CHECKLIST FOR PERSONAL, EXPLORATORY WRITING

1. What do you understand or care about as a result of reading this essay?
2. Do you sense a "voice" that's unique and appealing in some way? Point to examples that help you define that voice. Are there any places where the voice seems too bland or inappropriate for the subject?
3. What aspects of the subject does this essay clarify for you? Do any aspects need further clarification?
4. Do any of the metaphors or similes help you understand the subject? Are there any that need further development?
5. Were you aware of some overall pattern as you read? If so, was it distracting or helpful? If not, did you wish you had one to follow?

READER'S CHECKLIST FOR EXPOSITORY, THESIS-ORIENTED WRITING

1. Is the thesis of the essay obvious? Can you state it in your own words?
2. Is each point supported with enough specific, concrete facts and details? Which details work best? Which points need further support?
3. How would you describe the organization? Is it clear and effective?
4. Does the documentation (if any) provide all the necessary information—author, source, date?

READER'S CHECKLIST FOR ARGUMENTATION

1. Is the argument about a valid issue that has at least two sides? If not, can you point out why?
2. Does the essay define and refute the opposition's key points? Can you think of any such points that aren't defined?
3. Are the facts used effectively?
4. Are the sources (if any) credible? Should there be more?
5. Do I seem to have the best interests of all involved at heart?

READER'S CHECKLIST FOR REPORT/RESEARCH WRITING

1. Are the graphics (if any) and headings appropriately placed and clear?
2. Is the documentation appropriate and clear?
3. Is more supporting material needed—in an appendix, in tables, in references?
4. Have I established a consistent objective attitude toward the subject?
5. Are the sections complete and ordered in a meaningful way?

READER'S CHECKLIST FOR BUSINESS COMMUNICATIONS

1. Would you be pleased or impressed with this if you were to receive it in a business context?
2. Does the format seem appropriate?
3. Did you understand it the first time through, or did you have to reread some of it?
4. Are there any mechanical errors—grammar, punctuation, spelling?
5. Does it answer the important questions it raised in your mind?

APPLICATIONS

1. Interview any professional writers (journalists, novelists, academicians who publish regularly) about how, why, and when they collaborate on their writing. Write a brief summary of what you discover for your classmates.

2. Write about your own experiences collaborating: repairing a car, making a dinner, writing a paper, any time when you worked with others to produce a product or complete an activity. How well did it work? Could you have done it better alone? Do you look forward to collaborating again? Are there certain activities for which you think collaborating is more useful than others? In an essay of two to three pages, discuss your experiences and ideas on collaborating for your classmates.

3. If you found that collaborating on your writing helped you, write a brief argument for collaboration, addressed to an instructor who normally doesn't encourage writing groups of any kind. See if you can persuade him or her to allow or encourage students to form writing groups. If you think your letter may make a difference, send it off.

4. If you used any of the checklists in the last part of this chapter, write a brief evaluation of how well the checklist worked. Does it need any other questions? Did some of the questions work better than others? Are there other checklists that might work better, or that need to be added? Answer all these questions and send them to us!

5. Find an essay or report you've written for another class. Have the members of an informal writing group comment on it, using one of the checklists in the last part of this chapter. Then, revise it according to the results. When you're finished, return it to your reading group for further comments. Then, discuss whether you might want to submit the piece to a journal (local, regional, national), a newspaper, or a magazine.

INVITATIONS FOR EXTENDED WRITING

As you write drafts for these invitations, be sure to listen to your yes voice, introducing your no voice only as you revise and edit.

1. Collaborative Report on Textbook Writing You may not know it, but you're probably an expert on textbook quality. That is, you've read dozens of textbooks in your life, and you know which ones work and which ones you find dull or daunting. Form a group of four to six students, and investigate any of these questions:

- What are the features of good textbook writing?
- How do textbook writers establish their credibility?
- When you read a textbook you find effective, what specific qualities are you responding to?

After finding and ranking your responses as a group, divide up to find examples. Report the findings back to the group. After each member reports his or her findings, come to a consensus on what constitutes good textbook writing. Then, collaborate in writing up a report on your findings. (The group should determine how it wants to split the labor of putting the report together.)

2. Argue For or Against Collaboration

> I've always believed in writing without a collaborator, because where two people are writing the same book, each believes he gets all the worries and only half the royalties.
>
> —AGATHA CHRISTIE

What points might be made for or against writers collaborating? Use your own experience—as well as interviews with other writers, if you wish—to make a list of all the pros and cons of collaboration. Remember to distinguish between writing fiction and writing more technical, nonfiction prose.

Then write a report about collaboration or an argument for or against collaboration. If you write a report, summarize the various points of view on collaboration, and make a recommendation about which point of view you agree with, given your own experience. Address your piece to composition teachers who regularly ask students to form writing groups.

3. Collaboration on a Campus Problem Form a task force specifically to collaborate on a campus issue or problem that is not being addressed. Begin with a brainstorming session to find out group members' areas of concern and to come up with possible solutions. Divide up, and have some members research the areas you've agreed on, others use that research to put together a draft, and others work on appropriate graphics. Then, as a group revise and edit the draft for a specific group of readers (your student government, the student body as a whole, certain members of the administration, certain faculty). When complete, submit the piece to those readers.

For Further Reading and Research

Briggs, John. *Fire in the Crucible.* Los Angeles: Tarcher, 1990.

Delbecq, A. L., et al. *Group Techniques for Program Planning.* Glenview, Illinois: Scott, 1975.

Ede, Lisa, and Andrea Lunsford. *Singular Texts/Plural Authors: Perspectives on Collaborative Writing.* Carbondale: Southern Illinois UP, 1990.

PART TWO

FURTHER DISCOVERY STRATEGIES

CHAPTER SIX

Questioning

Why do people always expect authors to answer questions? I am an author because I want to *ask* questions. If I had answers I'd be a politician.

—EUGENE IONESCO

[A writer is] the unsatisfied child who dares to ask the difficult question which arises from the schoolmaster's answer to his simple question, and then the still more difficult question which arises from that.

—ROBERT GRAVES

As reporters, scientists, artists, lawyers, politicians, and writers know, questions contribute mightily to results. Everything we do, everything we know and believe, is the result of someone having asked and answered questions—about the food we eat, the clothes we wear, the buildings we live in, the business we do, the gardens we keep, the games we play, the society and economy we're part of, the science and religion we practice.

Questions occur constantly: When shall I get up? What shall I wear? What do I think? What do you think? What do you want to do? How do logarithms work? What does this movie mean? Should I sell or buy? Do we need more missiles? Is war a rational exercise of foreign policy? How can we simplify the tax system? Will the price of peaches rise or fall? Is it raining out? Hot? Cold?

Questions are quite literally endless.

In this chapter we introduce you to three sets of questions that can help you approach a subject systematically, from a number of angles. They are the *reporters' questions* (along with the related questions of Kenneth Burke's *pentad*), *cubing* questions, and *gridding* questions. With such sets to guide your curiosity, you are far less likely to leave stones unturned, considerations unconsidered, possibilities untried. Good writing requires understanding. If you don't know what you're talking about, how can the reader? And if you don't ask, how will you ever know? Understanding requires getting to know the subject as broadly and deeply as time and energy allow.

Indeed, using these questions, you will often have so much material at your disposal that you will ask how you can possibly manage to cram it into one little essay. You will learn first-hand the meaning of "a wealth of riches," for you will probably have more to say than space to say it.

Reporters' Questions and Burke's Pentad

Imagine you are Roger Watkins, a chemistry major in your junior year at State University. You've just finished a long, difficult lab. To unwind, you drive out to a woods and take a walk, alone. In the slant of the late afternoon sun, you suddenly see what looks to be a man overhead—a very old man with long hair and a short gray beard wearing a blue plaid shirt and green trousers. Instead of arms, he seems to have wings, and he flies over a hill and out of sight.

You're stunned, of course—amazed. You know it was a man. It had a man's face, a man's clothes, and—except for wings—a man's body. You're trembling all over.

Then it—he?—soars back, glides overhead, and looks directly at you. You think you catch a smile. You're certain now—this is a real man with real wings, which he moves with power and grace. He swings up and away, disappearing in the distance.

Deeply shaken, you have to sit down and try to take it in. You're a student of the sciences, not a wild-eyed mystic or visionary, and you just saw something outside the parameters of scientific knowledge. As you brood on this, your amazement turns into excitement, too much excitement to contain. You must share the news with someone—with everyone! The old man must be caught and studied! He is a phenomenon worthy of world scientific attention!

You rush back to town and call the *City News*. Breathlessly, you tell the editor your story. After hesitating a moment, he puts a reporter on the line. Her first question: "Exactly *what* did you see, Mr. Watkins?" After you answer as best you can, she goes on to other questions: "*When* did you see it?" "*Where* did you see it?" "*Who* are you?" "*How* do you think this could have happened?" You answer her questions one after another. Then she asks: "*Why* would you make up a story like this?"

Irritated by her skepticism, you hang up without answering. The next morning you pick up the *News* and see your story in a box on the bottom of the front page:

STUDENT THINKS HE SEES FLYING MAN

Roger Watkins, a student at State University, claims to have seen a man with large wings flying north of town.

Watkins was walking near Meyer's pasture late Tuesday afternoon when he says the creature flew overhead. According to Watkins, it disappeared behind a hill, then returned to fly directly over him. The creature smiled at him, Watkins insisted in an interview.

No explanation has been offered for the sighting, and no other sightings have been reported.

A junior at State University, Watkins is a chemistry major with a B plus grade average and no history of psychiatric episodes.

All day you catch plenty of kidding from your friends, and that night you get phone calls from two more reporters, representing the major wire services. They ask almost the same questions as the first reporter, and seeing your chance to set the record straight, you answer them in greater detail. The next afternoon a couple of friends call your attention to articles in the *Capitol Times,* a major state newspaper, and in *USA Today,* a national newspaper. The *Times* article appears in the middle of page three:

FLYING CREATURE STARTLES STUDENT

COLLEGETOWN (UP) A young male student, Roger Watkins, was startled to look up and see a man who seemed to be flying over him.

Watkins said that instead of arms the man had large wings which enabled him to soar overhead like an eagle.

The sighting occurred late in the afternoon of April 17, as Watkins was taking a walk in the woods north of Collegetown. The "winged man" disappeared without a trace, Watkins said. No other sightings were reported.

Watkins was not injured in the incident.

You find the *USA Today* story near the bottom of page four:

WINGED CREATURES TO REPLACE UFOs

COLLEGETOWN (API) A new fad in extraterrestrial sightings may be about to replace UFOs.

Instead of the whirring, flashing discs that were so popular in the fifties and sixties, flying men with wings may soon become the rage.

One such creature was sighted yesterday near Collegetown. Roger Watkins, a junior at State University, claims to have been walking north of town in the late afternoon when a normal-sized old man flew overhead. "He smiled at me," said Watkins, a chemistry major who is regarded by his teachers as a serious student.

No other sightings of the alien flying creature—which flies without the aid of flashing lights—have been reported in the Collegetown area.

"We're sure to have more sightings now that one has been spotted," said Dr. James Whitman, a psychiatrist on the staff of State University Medical School. "These hysterical sightings occur in clusters."

Watkins has not requested psychiatric evaluation.

Now, what did you as Roger Watkins learn from being at the center of a minor journalistic event? First, you learned that reporters usually probe their subject by asking what?, where?, when?, how?, why?, and who?

Second, you saw that even though reporters ask the same questions and get the same answers, they write different stories because they quite naturally arrange and emphasize information according to their own sense of the truth. This is inevitable; all news stories contain large elements of subjectivity, no matter how objective they seem.

Third, you learned that writers can only make sense of an event if they place it in some context. A man with wings doesn't fit any context other than "hysterical" or "hallucinatory" or "crazy," so that was the context implied in each reporter's story.

In dealing with *any* event, ranging from the silly to the sublime, the six reporters' questions will serve you admirably. They force you to examine all aspects of an event, and to place it in some context. Further, they yield quick results, enabling you to put together an account of an event in a hurry.

The very convenience of the journalistic formula, however, implies its danger: because it can get results so quickly, it can lead to superficial conclusions or unwarranted judgments. (There really was an old man flying around, after all, explainable or not.) Use the formula, then, but don't allow it to rush you to false judgments. You cannot deal honestly with any subject by shortchanging it.

To protect against snap judgments, to look thoroughly as well as quickly at an event, you may use the same six questions in a different way. This approach was developed in detail by literary philosopher Kenneth Burke. Burke points out that every event has a dramatic structure, like a play. Something happens; hence, there is an *act*. The act takes place at some time and some place; hence, it has a *scene*. Something—human or otherwise—must perform the act; hence, it has an *agent*. The agent commits the act by some means or other; hence, the act requires *agency*. To perform the act the agent must have some motive; hence, the act involves *purpose*.

After their fashion, the five parts of Burke's pentad approximate the reporters' questions:

Act = What?
Scene = Where and When?
Agent = Who?
Agency = How?
Purpose = Why?

The reporters' questions tend to emphasize the event more than the people involved; Burke's formula places more emphasis on people. That is, using the pentad you may listen more carefully to the agents' accounts of the event, asking questions to discover a context that does more than reflect your own point of view.

Thus you may find the reporters' questions more suitable when your primary interest is in the event itself, while Burke's pentad works better when your focus is primarily on the people involved. Or you may simply find one set of questions more congenial to the way your mind characteristically works. Used responsibly, either set can help you understand an event and write about it in detail.

APPLICATIONS

1. Find three brief news articles (four to six paragraphs) that cover the same event. (The articles should be from three different newspapers; use the library if necessary.) Label each article to show where the reporters' questions are answered. Notice whether any of the questions are not answered and which are given most emphasis in each story. Write one or two pages reflecting on how the treatment of the event differs from story to story.

2. Find a news story based on an event you are familiar with—a sporting event you saw, a wreck, a parade—anything you happened to witness either directly or on television. Examine how the reporter wrote the story. Are there any obvious omissions? Do you agree with the emphasis? Write a brief reflection on the strengths and weaknesses of the news story, given your own perspective on the event.

3. Consider an experience you were involved in, either as participant or witness—something that changed you in some way. From your memory, write out answers to either the reporters' six questions or to Burke's pentad. Write at least a complete paragraph for every question for your classmates to read. Try to make it as complete an explanation of the event as you can.

4. Attend an event you think will be interesting—a performance, a concert, a workshop, a support group meeting, a church service, a dance, a party, a fight—anything you can understand through questioning. Afterwards, ply the event with the reporters' set of questions, writing a paragraph for each. Do the same with the parts of Burke's pentad. Write a one-page reflection on the differences between the reporters' questions and the pentad.

A variation: attend an event with members of your writing group, and discuss the event among yourselves using both the reporters' questions and the pentad. Separately, write a one-page reflection on the differences between the two approaches to share with the group.

5. To see how the elements of a story hang together, take a well-known historical event with which you have some acquaintance and briefly list answers to the six reporters' questions. Change one of the answers. For example, for the 1941 bombing of Pearl Harbor, you might change the main agents from Japan and America to Switzerland and America. Note how changing only one item necessarily changes all the others: in this case the original why and how become completely mysterious (especially since Switzerland always remains neutral in wars). With this and all the other necessary alterations, write a brief news story on the event.

Cubing

Imagine a large cube. On each of its six sides you see a word:

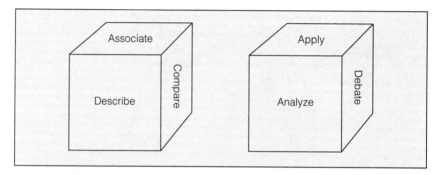

Cubing means asking questions derived from each of the words in sequence: describe, associate, compare, analyze, apply, and debate. You can use these activities for writing about people, places, and objects, generating the kind of detail to allow you to write about any of these in great depth. And cubing can be indispensible for writing about aesthetic creations—movies, plays, television shows, novels, musical compositions and performances, paintings, sculpture, and so on. For such works the "analysis" and "debate" sides of the cube are particularly helpful as you move from understanding to evaluation, ultimately trying to persuade readers that your understanding and appraisal make sense.

Let's examine each side of the cube in detail.

Describe

"He was a neat, thin young man who wore light suits with lintless pockets." So goes a sentence in the short story "I Look Out for Ed Wolfe" by Stanley Elkin. That's a quick description of Ed Wolfe, a picture in words that goes beyond what's visible (we can't, after all, see into someone's pockets) to show us not only the way he looks, but the way he *is*: well-groomed, wrinkle-free, abstemious, fastidious to a fault.

To describe means to create an image in words—a visual image, usually, but not necessarily and not exclusively. The image may well include sound, smell, taste, and touch, and it may exclude appearance. "He came in like a loud crash in a briar patch" says nothing about what the subject looked like, but offers a strong image of what he sounded like. Moreover, it expresses an opinion as to his nature, his identity. Description always involves such interpretation. The purpose of description is to *see* the thing described in the deepest sense—to understand it with the mind's eye, with insight.

To see with insight requires seeing first with the senses, then finding the right words to describe what you see (or hear or smell or taste or touch). To see well, you *must* describe: putting your perceptions into symbols—words, pictures, musical phrases—forces you to consider and reconsider those perceptions, and to keep perceiving, to make sure you get it right. Scientists observe, then *record* their observations, not only to communicate but also to observe precisely.

To describe something accurately, then, you need to identify its distinguishing traits: its size, shape, structure, color, texture, sound, smell, taste. Let's take for an example a peanut, described with such precision that a reader could find it in a bunch of other peanuts, just from reading the description.

First, we'll consider size, which can be described using both measurements and comparisons. The degree of precision depends on the occasion: for purposes of quick identification, you may need only a rough approximation; for purposes of science you may need a precision far beyond that which you can perceive through your unaided senses. Whatever the purpose, measurement and comparison can often be combined: "This peanut is about one and a half inches long, or about the length of the tip of the first finger to just before the first knuckle."

Next, shape. You can describe shape geometrically: round, square, rectangular, oblong, triangular. You can describe shape comparatively: like a star, a ball, a table, a record, a box, a can. Or you can combine the two: "This peanut is an oblong composed of two rounded parts, like a figure eight or a long balloon cinched in the middle."

Considerations of shape lead to considerations of structure, the underlying pattern that articulates the relationships between the parts forming the whole. The human body, for example, is composed of a particular arrangement of soft organs, surrounded by an arrangement of hard bones, surrounded in turn by elastic layers of muscle, fat, and skin. The structure of the peanut is simpler: "The peanut has a fragile, fiber-like shell that encapsulates two individual, roundish seeds."

Color is one of the first things we notice about anything: rooms, cars, clothes, water, flowers—whatever you can think of. Police investigators always want to know the color of a suspect's hair and eyes and car—color is one of the most important criteria by which we distinguish an object or person from similar objects. Describing something, then, involves paying attention to its color or colors: "The shell of this peanut has the coloring of a lion or a shag carpet—tawny to dark yellow with light brown specks and mottling."

Texture means touch, actual or imaginary—how does or would the object feel? Rough? Smooth? Ridged? Sharp? Furry? Slick? Like half-dried paint? Like corduroy? Like granite? A combination of descriptive words and comparisons is often appropriate: "This peanut shell has a rough, ridged texture, much like burlap in miniature."

Sound, smell, and taste are different from the other characteristics we've considered. First, whereas the others are always relevant, these are often not. You well might describe the sound of a piano, but not its smell and taste; with peanuts, on the other hand, it's just the opposite. Second, whereas you can describe the other characteristics with relative precision, you can describe these three with only rough approximation, and you must do it by way of comparison: "Except when you eat it, a peanut doesn't make any noise. It smells like . . . well, a little bit like red dirt, and a little bit like olive oil, and a little bit like broiled eggplant. Roasted, a peanut tastes somewhat like a pistachio minus the sweet. Raw, it tastes sort of like a chewy pellet of pancake batter."

Finally, when describing something, you want to understand it, to identify what makes it unique as well as what it shares with its class. You need to describe your peanut as peanut—that is, by pointing out the features it has in common with all other peanuts—but you also want to describe it as a particular peanut just as you might describe *that* dog or *your* room. To that end, you need to find a feature or a combination of features that distinguishes your object from all others: "This particular peanut is a somewhat flattened figure eight with a slight twist in the indented area, like the waist of someone turning the upper body hard left or right. At one end this peanut has a little twirl, like the tail of a piglet or the swirl on a Dairy Queen ice cream cone."

Describe aesthetic creations is obviously different from describing objects or people. For narrative works you generally offer a brief summary of the plot; for poems you might summarize the central idea. In both cases, your description should include mention of imagery, style, and whatever else is necessary to provide a brief overview description of the creation from your perspective.

Associate

Many items in our vocabulary almost never come alone, but have a sidekick or companion that pops into mind almost automatically. Associations can be loose, based on common use or mere proximity: bacon and eggs, salt and pepper, knife and fork, bread and butter. Some are based on cause and effect (fire and smoke) even when we customarily put them in the wrong order (thunder and lightning). Some are based on the principle of opposites attracting: hot and cold, wet and dry, north and south, east and west, black and white, yin and yang. Others are based on the principle of birds of a feather flocking together: ma and pa, aunt and uncle. Sometimes associations derive from custom reinforced by advertising, like pure and white. Sometimes they just occur together, like singing and dancing. However they come about, associations involve a connection of at least two items, and the connection is worth examining because it says something we otherwise might not hear about the items.

In considering a subject, then, you should see what associations come to mind—in a focused freewrite, perhaps, or some form of meditation. Then, you should examine those associations for insight into the subject, your perception of the subject, or both. Peanuts, for example, might bring to mind peanut butter, George Washington Carver, baseball games, a nutritious but high-calorie snack, parties and bars, former president Jimmy Carter, and a host of other associations. Let's think about a couple of these in a bit more detail. (For reasons of space, we'll keep these brief. We urge you to work out your own associations much more fully.)

> *Peanuts and peanut butter.* Consider all the associations of peanut butter with childhood. Consider the various foods people put peanut butter on: bread, crackers, bananas, celery, apples, chocolate. Consider the food value of peanut butter and the importance of peanut butter in the American diet. Consider other products derived from the peanut—if you don't know of any, consult an encyclopedia.

> *Peanuts and George Washington Carver.* Consider how one man found so much in so little. Consult your encyclopedia again and find out the status of the peanut in American culture before and after Carver. Think about what all Carver saw in the peanut and what he did with his perception.

If we followed up on these various leads, taking notes—and did the same with the other associations that seemed productive—we would have far more information than we could use. That's exactly where we would want to be: the more we have to choose from, the better our chances of coming up with surprises and discoveries.

If your subject is a place, ask what other places it reminds you of, and why. Then explore the answers that pop into your mind. If you're writing about a person, think of other people you're reminded of or people who are friends with the person. What do they have in common? Any surprises? Are there any outstanding differences? If so, what do they suggest about the person who is the subject of your writing?

In considering aesthetic objects and performances, associations will arise naturally. Anytime we read a novel, watch a movie, see a play, or hear a concert, we think of other novels, movies, plays, or concerts. We even group such things according to common traits—war movies, for example, and detective movies, musicals, science fiction, horror.

An important point: when associating deliberately, always keep an eye out for the odd association that says a great deal about the subject. In writing, you often need to surprise readers with revelation, insight, clarification, understanding—whatever will lead them to think "Ah Ha!" Associating can help you with those sorts of surprises.

Compare and Contrast

With associations in mind, you first examine why the association exists. But you can also *compare and contrast* the items associated, looking specifically for similarities and differences. Why? Comparing and contrasting give us a better sense of just what it is we are considering and how we think and feel about it.

When you buy a car, you usually compare and contrast various models, examining in detail how the cars you look at are alike and how they're different.

Comparing and contrasting gives you a better sense of each model than you'd have if you only considered them individually. You examine similarities and differences among any subjects for the same reason that you do so with cars: comparing and contrasting yields clarity.

Thus, if you were reviewing the sequel to *Batman*, for example, you might compare it to its predecessor, to the television series, to the comic books, to other superhero movies, to other movies directed by Tim Burton. If you were writing about a coming-of-age novel like *The Catcher in the Rye,* you might do well to compare and contrast it with, say, *Lord of the Flies.* Should you choose to write about Disneyworld, you could have some fun comparing and contrasting it with a local carnival.

Comparison and contrast come naturally, and for a good reason: they teach us much about our subjects. Go with nature, then—in examining a subject, always compare and contrast it with something else, or with several things.

Analyze

Perhaps you're the sort who has to take things apart and put them back together again—a clock, a bicycle, a motor, a piece of music, a play, a football game, a dance, a business structure, a love letter. Everyone takes something apart now and then: The act of understanding requires it. If you take golf lessons, for example, your instructor will show you every part of the swing—otherwise you will never understand it—then show you how to put the parts together into a good swing. With understanding (and practice), you will be able to develop what you've been taught for yourself.

When you do what we've described—when you take something apart— you are *analyzing.* When you put the parts back together again, you are *synthesizing.* If you don't synthesize, you have a a mess of disconnected parts on the floor rather than a motor that runs. Synthesis, then, is a close associate of analysis, as close as inhaling to exhaling, and just as indispensable.

Let's perform an operation on a ballpoint pen. It's composed of a number of parts:

- a plastic two-part barrel that screws together and apart and that holds the cartridge;
- the cartridge, a slender, hollow tube tipped with a small stainless steel ball;
- a spring that allows the cartridge to be snapped out and back in;
- a gizmo at the top that depresses the cartridge, pushing the tip out at the bottom of the barrel, and that releases the spring, allowing the cartridge tip to snap back into the barrel;
- a clip fastened on the barrel with which the user can hang the pen on a pocket.

Now that we have taken the pen apart and seen all of its parts, we can put it back together again, apply it to a piece of paper, and begin writing. But it still may not work: the cartridge may be out of ink, in which case we have, for all practical purposes, a useless synthesis of parts—a non-functioning pen. In anything well designed, no part can be omitted because every part has a purpose.

The more complicated the object, the more complicated the analysis. A ten-speed bicycle makes a ballpoint pen seem as simple as a paper clip. Many legal contracts make a ten-speed bike seem as simple as a toenail clipper. Many works of art make a legal contract seem simpler than, well, a ballpoint pen. In a play, for instance, the characters must be considered in relation to the setting (both time and place), to the other characters, to their own motives and predispositions, to their society and religion and world view, to the plot as it affects them and as they affect it. To understand such a complex whole, the analyst often needs to concentrate only on parts, since it is virtually impossible to analyze the whole completely. (We know a man who, for his doctoral dissertation, undertook to analyze all of Shakespeare's *Othello:* the dissertation came to over 2,000 pages and he still hadn't fully examined the whole play.)

Analyzing anything complex requires selecting a piece of it for close study. To understand the way a plant performs photosynthesis, botanists must analyze the behavior of certain cells; even so, they must always keep in mind the whole of which those cells are a part, because the organism as a whole determines their peculiar operation, just as they help determine the health and fate of the organism.

Thus, analysis of complex objects involves a back-and-forth movement between part and whole, whole and part, as each affects the other. If you analyze a part without considering the whole, you may get some interesting close-ups, but you will miss the big picture and thus the point.

Apply

Imagine an airplane that carries neither passengers nor cargo nor weaponry. Imagine a stadium in which no events are held. Imagine a leadless, eraser-less pencil. Imagine a typewriter with no keys, a computer with no memory, a radio with no speaker, a stove with no heat, a filing cabinet with no drawers, a fork with no tines. Imagine, in other words, these objects in such a way that they have no function, no *application* to the world, and you begin to realize the importance of application in understanding something.

In examining a subject, then, you may wish to consider its use—past, present, and future. Further, you should consider the contexts of its applications: something may be used for one thing in certain contexts and for something else in other contexts. Keep in mind that application takes different forms depending on whether your subject is an object, a place, a person, or an aesthetic work.

You will find it relatively easy to consider the applications of objects, because most have a fairly clear history of use. You will often find surprises, however. In England and western Europe, animal urine has been applied in various ways in the woolen industry, in indigo extraction, in engineering, in iron and steel hardening, in tanning, in the alum industry, in alchemy, in medicine, in art and early photography. At present urine is used to detect diabetes, pregnancy, and yeast infections. It is used in medical research. It is also used in various forms of witchcraft. With a little looking you may find that it is applied in other ways. As for the future—who knows? Weed killer? Cottage industry fabrics? Cosmetics? Kitchen and bathroom cleansers?

In thinking about places, think of application in terms of *effects*. How did such and such a place affect the rest of the world? How does it affect the world now, and how is it likely to in the future? That is, what difference did, does, and will it make to people? Massachusetts, a state long known for its institutions of higher education, was once the educational, religious, textile, shipping, and publishing headquarters of the colonies and the United States. In the future it is likely to continue being important in higher education and technology, including robotics, and also, perhaps, in the space program, in medicine, and in finance (among other things).

When dealing with people, think of application in terms of *activities* that have made a significant difference to themselves and to others, activities that define who and what they are (or were). What have they done? What do they do now? What are they likely to do? If the person you are sketching is no longer living, you will, of course, have no present and future to reckon with. But the principle remains valid: to sketch a character, you need to consider as much as possible an entire life of activity and its ongoing effects. What did he or she do that made or continues to make or is likely to make a difference? Note that you use these criteria in describing *any* person, famous or obscure.

As for aesthetic objects and performances, consider how they were originally received and the influence they had, how they are viewed now and their contemporary influence, how you think they will be viewed in the future and the influence they may have then. Orson Welles' *Citizen Kane*, for example, was largely shunned when first shown in 1941. Audiences thought it was dark, overly complex, and troubling, and it barely broke even at the box office. Gradually, however, as film audiences grew more sophisticated, the film's reputation grew. Finally, when colleges and universities began serious film studies in the late 1960s, *Citizen Kane* became a touchstone film for a generation of film students. Undoubtedly, filmmakers worldwide will continue to be influenced by Welles' groundbreaking use of camera angles, lighting, flashbacks, and shifting perspectives; even now the film has a surprisingly contemporary look.

Debate

By *debate* we don't mean making a case for or against something in a formal argument. At this point, that would be like buying pre-wrapped meat at the supermarket—making a decision after looking at only one side. We mean, rather, weighing pros and cons, seeing for yourself what can be said both for *and* against the subject. For by looking at the subject from both sides, you get to know it intimately, from A to Z.

You can make a case for something or someone based on a number of criteria. Some of the common ones are:

- It has a worthy purpose (Literacy Volunteers, for example)
- It fulfills its purpose (a reliable engine)
- It serves people in some way (dental care)
- It is valuable in and of itself (a fine movie)
- It is needed as part of a larger whole (the liver)
- It has been overlooked and deserves recognition (bureaucracy as a social stabilizer)
- It is true to itself and to its origins (the blues)
- It augments some existing good (senior citizen discounts)
- It is favored by an expert (a particular brand of tennis shoes endorsed by your coach)
- It is like something else that is good, and so is probably good itself (packaged cookies that "taste like homemade")

You can make a case against something or someone for the same reasons turned inside out:

- It has a bad purpose (people who hand out poisoned Halloween candy)
- It does not fulfill its purpose (a corrupt police department)
- It harms people (tobacco)
- It has no value in and of itself (a bad horror movie)
- It hinders or interferes with a larger whole (cancer)
- It received recognition it didn't deserve (an Olympic champion who was later found to have used steroids)
- It is false to itself and to its origins (most of the music on Muzak)
- It diminishes or damages some existing good (racial prejudice)
- Experts hold little or no credence in it (astrology)
- It is unlike other things of value in several important ways (mosquitoes as compared to bees)

These criteria of value are not mutually exclusive. A corrupt police department is bad not only because it does not fulfill its purpose, but also because it harms people, it is false to itself and to its origins, and it damages some existing good, namely, the trust necessary for a decent society.

To prepare to make a case for or against your subject, examine the pros and cons closely using these criteria. Ideally, you should know the other side's case as well as you know your own. At the very least, you may discover where you can concede the other side's strengths. (You can always concede points instead of refuting them!) You will probably also discover the full complexity of the case, which is one of the purposes of examining pros and cons in the first place. And should you discover that the other side has a stronger case than you, you can always change your mind.

APPLICATIONS

1. Examine your list of answers to the reporters' questions about a significant experience in your life. (See Application 3 on page 129.) Pay particular attention to the answers to the *who, what,* and *where* questions. From one of those answers choose a person, place, or object important to that event. (It could be a comic book, a teddy bear, a catcher's mitt, a doll house, a tree house, a swing, Fort Lauderdale, your first car, anything.) Examine this subject from the six sides of the cube. If you select your sister, for example, first visualize, then *describe* her. Next, see what turns up by *association.* Then, *compare* her with other people you know, *analyze* her significance to the event and to your life, and *apply* her activities (past, present, and future) to defining her identity, who and what she is. Finally, *debate* the pros and cons of her relationship to you. Make complete notes of all you turn up.

2. Using the same event you interrogated like a reporter for Application 4 on page 129, cube it as an aesthetic work (a story or movie), even though it was a piece of history. *Describe/summarize* it in detail. *Associate* it with movies, novels, short stories, plays. *Compare* it to similar works. *Analyze* its parts. Consider its *Applications. Debate* its aesthetic value—would you recommend it to friends or not, and why? Keep notes. If you attended the event with your writing group, cube it together and keep notes about each member's responses.

3. Recall the historical event you revised for Application 5 on page 129. Cube it as an aesthetic work (a movie or a novel). Share the results with classmates.

4. Choose an object, a person, a place, or an aesthetic work you find interesting and know very well. (Avoid subjects like a star you know only from performances and interviews or an exotic place where you've never been.) Cube your subject carefully, taking notes.

5. Look up an article in a professional journal related to your major or to a discipline that interests you. Take extended notes by cubing it. Save the notes.

6. Persuade a friend outside of this class to let you teach him or her the strategy of cubing. Together, cube something or someone of mutual interest. (You may think of this exercise as structured brainstorming.) Keep notes on how it worked.

Gridding

In painting, perspective is the representation of three-dimensional space on a flat canvas. When the concept of linear perspective was first formulated in the fifteenth century, artists placed grids—large-mesh screens, much like transparent checker boards or graph paper—between themselves and the scenes they were painting. These grids made the ratio of distance and size as exact as a blueprint. In fact, our word *perspective* comes from the Latin word for *looking through*. By looking at a subject through a grid we see it better, because we force ourselves to see it precisely, both part by part and as a whole.

In this section we will be concerned with looking at a subject through a three-cell grid taken loosely from physics: particle, wave, and field. This grid will help you examine a subject from three perspectives or vantage points, as the following diagram suggests:

	1. Particle	2. Wave	3. Field
Subject	(static)	(dynamic)	(contextual)

When you examine a subject through the particle cell of the grid, you ask yourself "What is the nature of the individual subject apart from any changes it has undergone or is undergoing, and apart from its context?" From this perspective you are taking a *static* view of the subject.

Suppose you are examining the concept of freedom, a dense and difficult abstraction with which philosophers and politicians have struggled for centuries. How to approach such a daunting issue? The grid can provide a way. Starting with the particle or static perspective, look at "freedom" apart from any changes it may have undergone and apart from any particular philosopher's viewpoint. In so looking, you might come up with something like a dictionary definition: "freedom means being able to make and act upon choices without worrying about coercion, though consequences may still be a problem. You are free to jump off your classroom building, but you are limited as to what you do next. You are free to vote, provided you meet certain conditions of age and citizenship."

Then, moving to the wave cell of the grid, you ask "What changes have occurred in the subject over time? What changes are occurring now?" These questions require you to view the subject from a *dynamic* perspective.

Regarding "freedom," you might note that in the United States freedom has not always been considered an inalienable right of every adult. African American men were not free to vote until the close of the Civil War. American women were denied the right to vote until a constitutional amendment in 1920, while many states discouraged people of color—both men and women—from voting until 1964.

Changing attitudes toward the right to vote is only one way of looking at the concept of freedom. Other wave perspectives on freedom might lead to explorations of civil rights laws and how they have changed or to the various laws designed to limit individual choice, ranging from prohibition laws to abortion regulations. With some research you would find plenty of information concerning any of these ideas relating to freedom and how points of view changed over the years.

From the third cell, the field perspective, you ask "What sort of area does the subject inhabit or occupy?" Or to put the question another way, "What sort of group does the subject belong to, and how does it relate to other members of the group?" These questions point to the *contextual* view, requiring that you look at the subject in terms of its context or setting. When a subject has more than one context, you consider the subject in several settings.

For the concept of freedom, you might consider how the right to vote fits into the broader context of the history of the United States. You might also consider it in relation to other Constitutional rights, such as the right to worship freely and the right to bear arms. Or you might consider voting rights in the United States in relation to voting rights in other democratic societies. You might even go further and explore the concept of freedom in its economic and philosophical senses, rather than just its political sense.

Changing perspectives can make a radical difference in your treatment of any subject, guaranteeing a rich yield of material. And you can apply the three-cell grid just as effectively to a person, a place, a thing. Take an old building in town, say a fine old house. Viewed from a particle (static) perspective, the house may now be a restaurant. As such, it might be examined in terms of the food it serves, the patronage it encourages, its decor. From a wave (dynamic) perspective, you might find that the house was built as a private residence and subsequently served a variety of purposes: rooming house, library, law office, funeral home, beauty parlor, massage parlor, health food store, and now a restaurant. Such a history provides you with a lot of interesting information. When you view the house from the field (contextual) perspective, you have some choices. You can concentrate on the restaurant in the context of other restaurants in town or in the context of its immediate neighborhood. You might consider the structure itself in the context of other fine old houses in town or in the context of urban renewal projects in other towns. By now you may be wondering how you can write about this building in anything less than a book, and that's good: as we keep reminding you, to write about something well, you need to have far more to say than room in which to say it.

SUMMARY OF QUESTIONING
When your subject is an event:

1. Use the reporters' questions: ask who, what, where, when, why, and how; *or*
2. Use Burke's pentad: examine the event's act, scene, agents (who were the major characters?), agency (who or what was most responsible for its occurrence?), and purpose (why did it occur?).

When your subject is a concept, an object, a person, a place, or an aesthetic work:

1. Try Burke's pentad; *or*
2. Try cubing: describe, associate, compare, analyze, apply, and debate the subject; *or*
3. Try gridding: examine the subject from the particle, wave, and field perspectives.

APPLICATIONS

1. Take any subject that you know something about and apply the three-cell grid to it. Make notes as you go, and note where you need to do research in order to answer the questions.

2. Look at your notes concerning the significant experience you examined with the reporters' questions (see Application 3 on page 129) and with cubing (see Application 1 on page 138). Using the three-cell grid, examine your attitude and how it has changed as a result of that event. That is, examine what your attitude is now (particle perspective), how it has changed (wave perspective), and how it compares to your attitudes about other experiences you have had (field perspective).

3. Look at your notes concerning the event you explored for Application 4 on page 129 and Application 2 on page 138. Reexamine that experience with the grid, and see if any further insights emerge. Keep notes on what you discover. If you have been discussing the event with your writing group, continue discussing it using the grid. Again, keep notes on each member's responses.

4. Examine the journal article you cubed for Application 5 on page 138. See whether the author shifted his or her perspective in any way that accords with gridding. That is, did the author attempt in some way to apply a wave perspective, seeing how the subject changed over time? Did he or she look at the subject in the context of similar subjects, thus applying a field perspective? Note everything in the article that fits the grid format. (Bear in mind that the author need not have deliberately gridded the subject to have asked the same basic questions.)

5. Take a problem in your life that you've been trying, without much luck, to solve. Summarize the problem in a sentence: "I need to get motivated to study but can't." "I want to try out for a play but am too frightened." "I want to ask that interesting classmate out for lunch but haven't the nerve." Now grid the problem in detail using the particle, wave, and field perspectives. See if you learn anything about the problem and yourself from shifting perspectives.

6. Explain gridding to a friend. (One of the best ways to learn something is to teach it.) Together, grid a subject of mutual interest and concern.

INVITATIONS FOR EXTENDED WRITING

As you develop these essays, be sure to call on any strategies you have found useful, particularly concentrating and intuiting strategies. Also use your yes voice for support; set aside your no voice until you revise and edit.

1. Significant Experience   Take the significant experience that you have been exploring. (See Application 3 on page 129, Application 1 on page 138, and Application 2 on page 141.) Write an essay of three to five pages explaining what happened, how it affected you, what you learned from it, and how it has changed you.

2. Argument for or against an Event   Consider the event you've been exploring. (See Application 4 on page 129, Application 3 on page 138, and Application 3 on page 141.) Would you make a case for it or against it—that is, would you recommend it to others, or would you warn others to stay away? Write an argument expressing your views. Consider using one of the following four formats:

- A letter of thanks to those responsible for the event, pointing out what was good about it and why and suggesting possible improvements.
- A letter of protest to those responsible, pointing out what was wrong with it and why and explaining why it shouldn't take place again.
- A letter to the editor of your local city newspaper, making a case for or against the event in terms of public welfare. (Be brief: editors usually cut letters over 200 words long.)
- A letter for or against the event addressed to the editor of your campus newspaper.

Remember to anticipate in your letter the position of those who might disagree. Show them, firmly but nicely, the error of their ways as well as the truth of yours.

If you've been exploring the event with members of your writing group, group members should be well prepared to undertake any of these. Using notes taken during your discussions, have each group member choose one of the four suggested formats as a writing task.

3. The "New" Historical Event   Go back to the historical event you changed for Application 5 on page 129 and Application 3 on page 138. In a feature article for your local city or campus newspaper, explore that changed event. Consider in detail how altering that single fact would have changed our view of the event and, indeed, have changed history itself.

4. Reviewing the Professional Journal Article   Take the article you've cubed (see Application 5 on page 138) and gridded (see Application 4 on page 141). Write an extended review of it. In your review include a brief summary of the article; the strong points of the article; its limitations; the overall value of the article to you and to other readers. Occasionally, you might use direct quotes from the article to support your points.

5. Term Paper Apply the appropriate techniques you have been learning to the subject of one of your term papers in another class. If the subject is an event, use the reporters' questions or Burke's pentad. If the subject is something else, use either cubing or gridding. Look for a focus or center of gravity as the organizing principle, the thesis, of the term paper itself. To define a focus and thesis, you may find it helpful to use one of the freewriting or concentrating and intuiting techniques discussed in Chapters 1 and 2 in conjunction with the questioning procedure you've adopted.

6. Explain a Questioning Procedure Write an article for your peers explaining the questioning strategy you found most useful. Be specific. Tell them how it works in general, and how it worked for you in particular. Explain also how it can work for students in other fields—in political science, history, economics, geography, or whatever. In other words, explain not only its relevance to writing an essay, but its general relevance as a tool of thought. Submit this as a brief feature for your campus newspaper.

For Further Reading and Research

Stock, Gregory. *The Book of Questions.* New York: Workman, 1985.
Ward, Hiley. *Professional Newswriting.* New York: Harcourt, 1985.
Young, Richard E., Alton L. Becker and Kenneth L. Pike. *Rhetoric: Discovery and Change.* New York: Harcourt, 1970.

CHAPTER SEVEN

Mapping

There is an outline or a plan in my head. I don't write it down because that sets it. But I have to have a plan because there has to be
something that can be changed. You can't start out with nothing,
and have nothing changed into something. But if you start with a
plan, then there's something that can be changed.

—MADELEINE L'ENGLE

When you hear the word *map*, you may automatically think of place maps,
of two-dimensional geographical representations of cities, states, countries. But
we want to introduce you to another sort of map. "Mapping" in this sense doesn't
mean cartography—drawing a representation of physical space—but rather
"ideography" (to coin a word), drawing a representation of *ideas*. Just as geographical maps help us negotiate the complexities of a place, so idea maps help us
negotiate the complexities of a *concept* and its various causes, implications, applications, processes, consequences—everything that makes it worth knowing.

Why map a concept? Because it is easier to get lost in an idea than in a literal wilderness. A concept like "love" has few familiar markers; it's full of side issues like "obsession" and "attraction" and of qualifiers like "brotherly," "erotic,"
"parental." It's possible to get lost forever—wandering through concepts that
don't connect, that loop back on themselves, that repeat through endless variations—without even realizing it. Maps help us start idea-journeys with a strong
sense of our destination. They also help us see information in useful ways. Many
professionals use idea maps specific to their specialties: sociologists use sociograms; economists use graphs and charts; physicians use X-rays, drawings, and
photographs; engineers and architects use blueprints. And although writers commonly use idea maps as private aids to understanding a concept, they are also frequently used as reader aids: what is a table of contents, after all, but a map of
a book?

Idea maps and geographical maps differ in one significant way. Geographical maps connect to the physical world and can be corroborated and valued accordingly. Conceptual maps, however, do not necessarily connect to the physical world outside your mind at all. Hence, you may (and indeed should) change your maps as your ideas change. An idea map is only a guide, and needs adjusting and refining when your emerging ideas take a different turn. You should never feel as though you must follow your early maps. When they don't help clarify and extend your ideas, they are no longer useful.

Here are four mapping strategies that will guide you on your idea-journeys:

Clustering amounts to visual brainstorming. But instead of listing ideas at random, you develop them by doodling with circles and lines in response to a central word or phrase. This doodling yields "clusters" of connected circles, like bunches of grapes, that indicate how ideas relate to one another. Clustering is most useful when you have a subject in mind but no clear sense of direction.

Outlining is the venerable strategy for representing all the major points of an essay in an orderly list. Although students often dismiss outlining as overrated and essentially useless (because they depart so often from their outlines while writing), it does work. This is especially true if you understand that you're not tied to one kind of outline, and that outlines work best when they serve as guides for the writer's convenience.

Flow charts offer a striking means of understanding a process or a sequence of events that requires several decisions, each with multiple potential outcomes. Flow charts have long been used for computer programming and organizational overhauling, but they are helpful as well for understanding and explaining all sorts of complex processes, from university registration to buying a car to planning a major building project.

Ranking tables help clarify any situation or problem composed of items that need to be placed in some hierarchical order. Such tables might result in a list of one's favorite movies or most important life priorities, or in a ranking of a series of processes from least to most complex.

Clustering

The directions for clustering are amazingly simple—so simple, in fact, that some students want at first to dismiss the process as childish doodling. If they're not writing words in sentences, one line after another, they fear they're just messing around. So keep in mind that clustering sometimes takes practice before it yields genuine revelations and insights. Those who work with it regularly, however, find that it evokes associations, ideas, and insights they can't get any other way. If you invest some time and good-faith effort in the process, it can pay rich dividends.

Try it now, step by step. All you need is a blank, *unlined* sheet of paper and a pencil or erasable ink pen—something that makes lines you can rub out and try again. In the middle of the page draw a circle and inside it write "Friends." From the first circle draw a line to a second circle in which you write "Present." From that circle draw several more lines, each with a circle at the end. In these circles write the names of people you presently consider to be friends. This group of lines, circles, and names—which amounts to your first cluster—should look something like Figure 7.1.

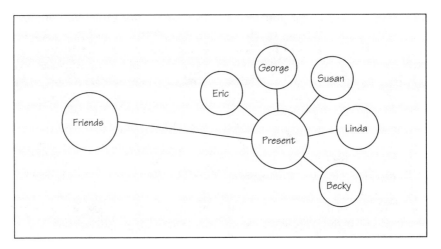

Figure 7.1   Sample of Clustering: First Step

Look your cluster over to see if you've included everyone worth including. If not, keep adding lines and circles until the cluster is complete.

Now, draw a second line from the center circle to a new circle in which you write the word "Past." Cluster around that circle people you used to be friends with but are now permanently separated from, who moved away (or perhaps died). Your cluster will now probably look something like Figure 7.2.

Next, draw a line for "former" friends—people who are no longer friends though you still run into each other occasionally. And make another for "almost" friends, those people with whom you occasionally chat but have never deliberately gotten together with—the guy in your English class who's on the debate team, the woman down the hall majoring in dance, the neighbor who likes to pump baskets and talk about sports, the lady you always see on the bus who talks about her grandkids. You may not know the names of these "almost" friends, but include them anyway, using short-hand descriptions. You might include a cluster of "would be" friends, people you would like to know better but never seem to find the nerve or the time to call—the cashier at the dining commons or the book store, the student who always has interesting things to say in western civ— or even "famous would be" friends—celebrities with whom, given the chance, you think you would hit it off. When it comes to clustering, your wishes, dreams, and imagination are the only limits.

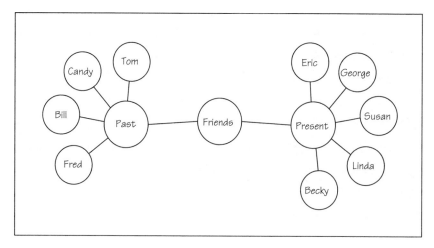

Figure 7.2 Sample of Clustering: Second Step

You may have noticed by now that in clustering one thing leads to another. You'll probably think of people who haven't crossed your mind in years, and who wouldn't have if you hadn't been doodling with lines and circles. The longer you continue to doodle, the more you'll remember. Figure 7.3 shows how one student's complete "friends" cluster came out.

The value of clustering is that it generates more ideas than simply thinking or listing what you know about a topic. Clustering amounts to much more than a list: clustering about friends, for example, can give you a *map* of your relationships with people, so you can see where you are, where you've been, and where you'd like to go—all in a few minutes.

But how do you get from a cluster to an essay? For starters, as you cluster notice where your mind seems to take off, to generate material in a spontaneous rush, a flow so fast it's all you can do to keep up. When that happens, you may have discovered a solid area of concern that could well become an essay. You may even want to stop at that point and begin a freewrite to cultivate that mass of connections.

If you don't immediately discover any flow but only stiffness and a suspicion that your mind will never take off, don't be discouraged or impatient. Maybe, instead of a rush or a flash, you will experience something more subtle—a felt sense, a little click like the tumblers in a combination lock falling finally into place. However your mind works, it is capable of memory and connection and discovery. If no such rush of attention or felt sense occurs *while* you're clustering, continue to make as many connections as you can, then stop and examine the cluster. Let your mind wander over it freely, noticing any connections or memories you hadn't seen before. Anything that draws your interest may be another place to start. Begin a freewrite at that point and see where it leads. Clustering and

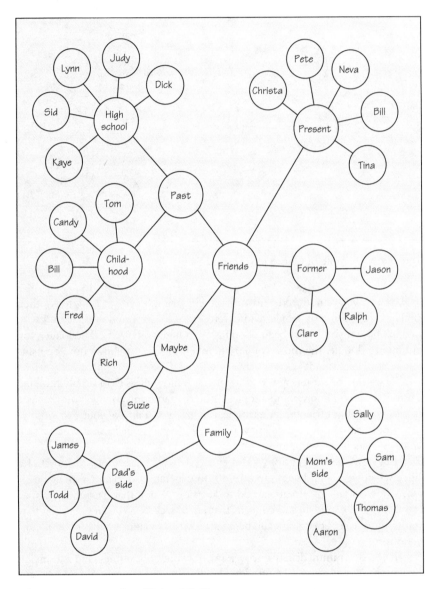

Figure 7.3   Complete "Friends" Cluster

freewriting offer a powerful combination, allowing you to work with both *pictures* and *words*, unleashing the pattern-making side of your brain along with the linear side.

To get the knack of finding and recognizing the buried treasure of your consciousness, try this: cluster either "mother" or "father." Whenever and wherever your mind takes off in a rush or settles down with a click, stop clustering and start writing. Take down everything that your mind connects with, without any regard to style or content, correctness or form. Just let the words flow, whether nimbly and quickly or deliberately and slowly. To get you started, here's an example of an older student's freewritten response to his cluster on "father" in Figure 7.4.

> So many fathers in my life. I seem to have five, besides my real father. My real father stopped being "fatherly" some years ago, when I became a full-time and serious student. He tried hard, but not having gone to college,

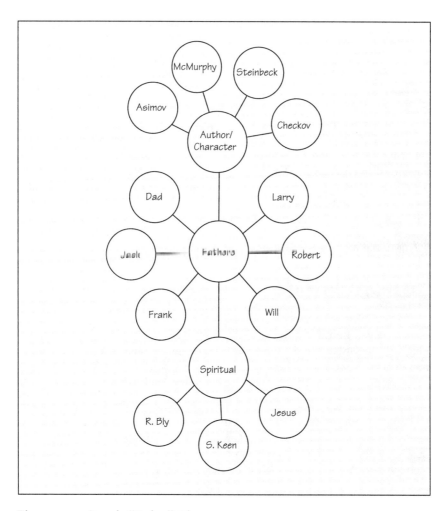

Figure 7.4 Sample "Father" Cluster

couldn't help me much with what I was going through. Then there was Larry, my oldest friend, who for so many years provided various kinds of guidance and role-modeling; his advice helped me through many a tough situation. He served as a kind of father, actually, until he died. I never saw him as my father until now. No wonder I grieved so long for him.

Of course there's old Will, my wife's father. Not exciting, but extraordinarily loving, kind, willing to do anything for us. And crazy Jack, my first wife's father-in-law who probably just developed some kind of chemical imbalance in his middle years and grew crazier and crazier. Not a pleasant end.

And Frank, my best friend in high school. He always seemed to know what to say. I always admired that in him, and tried to imitate him, though I'm ashamed to admit it now.

This all makes me wonder if others sense how much "fathering" they may have gotten from others besides their "real" father?

This is very private writing, of course, but it does reveal a concentrated mind, focused by the act of clustering. And as a direct result of clustering, that mind discovered an extremely important insight: that the concept of "father" might transcend the biological.

The next step is to explore that insight with more clustering, possibly by making "surrogate fathers" the center to see how many men fit the bill, then clustering these individuals one by one to find their important similarities and differences. In order to develop the subject in more general and objective terms, one might cluster the various "qualities" of fatherhood that emerge: role model, disciplinarian, buddy, and so on. One could then supplement all that information with some research on fathers and fatherhood, just to see what others have discovered and shared. As simple as it seems, clustering can take you a long way into any subject.

APPLICATIONS

1. If you find clustering valuable, explain how it works to a small group, using a blackboard as you demonstrate. Have the group then pick a topic of common concern—no matter how trivial—for each person to cluster individually. Compare the results to see what you can learn from and about each other.

2. Choose an emotionally charged issue about which you have a strong opinion (the stronger the better): abortion, gun control, pornography, censorship, the drinking age. Now, instead of expressing your usual conviction, cluster the subject, trying honestly to understand it from every angle. When you have finished, write down any new insights you may have gained.

3. Cluster the word "priorities." Make as complete a map of your personal priorities as you can, ranging from day-to-day activities to long-term life goals. If you learn anything new about yourself, explore this in a paragraph or two for your writing group.

4. Cluster your best friend. Use the major associations that come to mind—including things you've done and like to do together—as centers for the separate webs. If any insights occur, write them out in a brief biographical sketch. If you like the result, share it with your friend.

5. Cluster an upcoming test subject. Use your cluster to help clarify your strengths and weaknesses in the subject. If you have a writing assignment coming up in any class, get started on it by clustering.

6. Read a newspaper or magazine article—one of some length and importance—then cluster it. Use the article's main idea as the center word. Try to re-create the associations the writer seemed to make. Do any areas occur to you that should have been covered but weren't? Were any areas covered too little or too much? Using what your clustering turned up, write a paragraph critiquing the article.

7. Cluster your favorite novel, short story, movie, or television program, using its name as the center word. Write up the results in a paragraph or two for your writing group.

Outlining

> I don't see how anybody starts a novel without knowing how it's going to end. I usually make detailed outlines: how many chapters it will be and so forth.
>
> —JOHN BARTH

> Anytime I do outline something, I never consider it sacrosanct. I am quite willing to junk the outline if something better occurs to me.
>
> —ROGER ZELAZNY

To our knowledge, no student has ever exclaimed to another, "You've got to try *outlining*—you'll just love it!" But textbooks and teachers have traditionally claimed that the formal outline—with main headings designated by Roman numerals, and subheadings neatly indented and designated by capital letters, and sub-subheadings further indented and designated by Arabic numerals, and so on, and so on—will cure most of what ails one's prose. Such outlines look like this:

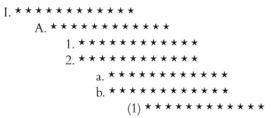

```
        (2) ★ ★ ★ ★ ★ ★ ★ ★ ★ ★ ★ ★
    3. ★ ★ ★ ★ ★ ★ ★ ★ ★ ★ ★ ★
  B. ★ ★ ★ ★ ★ ★ ★ ★ ★ ★ ★ ★
II. ★ ★ ★ ★ ★ ★ ★ ★ ★ ★ ★
```

You've seen this outline format, we're sure. In fact, you may have put one together—not to help you as you wrote but after you had finished writing, in order to satisfy a teacher's demand for an outline. If that happened, you probably concluded that outlines serve no purpose other than meeting a classroom requirement.

To persuade you that outlining can serve legitimate and useful purposes, let us start by pointing out that there are actually two kinds: outlines for *readers,* which are formal and finished after the fact, and outlines for *writers,* which are usually informal to the point of remaining messy all during the writing process. The formal, finished outline is a table of contents; the informal, working outline is a set of notes. To insist on a finished outline before the work is finished tends to breed confusion. It's more a nuisance than a necessity, as Roger Zelazny points out.

At the same time, writing requires organizing, and except for the very simplest of subjects, organizing means putting items in hierarchical order, in categories and subcategories and sub-subcategories. Organizing is one of the ways we make sense of a subject, for ourselves and for our readers. The great value of the outline, formal and informal, is that as a visual aid it enables both writer and reader to *see* hierarchies, the relation of major part to minor part, of greater to lesser. It also enables the writer in the process of writing to see any *lack* of relation, and thus the need to do more work.

Remember that a working outline is provisional, an aid to use in organizing your material, not a prescription to follow. When it indicates that changes need to be made in your essay, make the changes. When you find that you need to change the outline, don't hesitate for a second to do so.

The nice thing about working outlines is that you can make them just as you please. As with clustering, it's impossible to do a working outline wrong: it's simply a visual and verbal aid to concentration. If you are happier observing every formal protocol in your working outline, then do so, by all means; if you are happier making a mess, do that. Use any kind of outline that helps you make sense of the subject.

An alternative to a standard outline is a tree diagram. Instead of lining up different items down a page using indents, with a tree diagram you set up headings and subgroups, and draw diagonal lines from headings to each subgroup to show the connections. You can create quick tree diagrams about almost anything, from a television program (Figure 7.5) to an idea you want to develop (Figure 7.6). As our examples show, tree diagrams can be built either from the top down or from the bottom up.

Like clustering, outlining and tree diagrams help you see connections among ideas both before and as you write. They're also helpful strategies for ex-

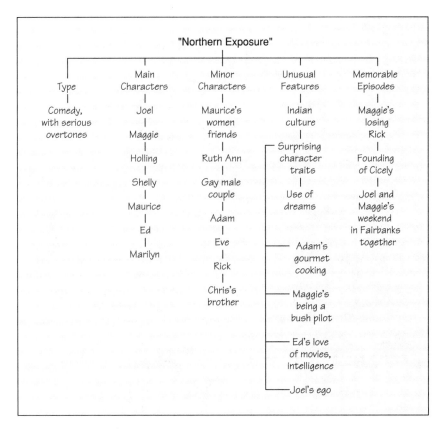

Figure 7.5 Sample Tree Diagram

amining writing; you can use them to analyze connections writers make in finished drafts.

When you write, you will use your purpose to help determine how to organize your material, and try different organizations to help you refine your purpose. But you don't need to try to hold all these alternatives in your mind. It helps to *see*—to make tracks on paper, however private and messy, that represent graphically how your ideas hang together. And if your readers would find it helpful to have an overview of your material so they can see how your ideas hang together, then make a nice formal outline (a table of contents), with every letter and numeral in place.

APPLICATIONS

1. Write a brief reflection on how you regularly use lists and outlines (however informal) made from lists. Are they usually mental? Do you ever write

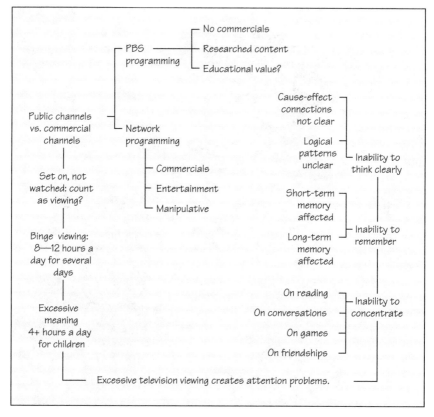

Figure 7.6 Tree Diagram Built from Bottom Up

them out? Do you ever regroup them for different purposes? Do you make working outlines when writing essay tests or papers? Why, why not?

2. Take any strong personal opinion you hold—perhaps on the same subject you clustered for Application 2 on page 150—and generate an informal writer's outline or tree diagram of it. In the outline or diagram, try to set forth your major reasons for your opinion. Line them up hierarchically, as major points and subpoints, in an order that makes sense so that you can explain them to a friend simply and briefly.

3. Based on your cluster for Application 3 on page 150, make a working outline of your life priorities. Arrange the different priorities under various headings such as *long-term, short-term,* and *daily,* or *past, present,* and *future.* Arrange your headings in an order you can quickly and simply account for. See if the grouping generates not only an order that wasn't there before, but also more ideas to order.

4. Find a magazine or newspaper article that you enjoyed reading and either outline it or make a tree diagram of it. (You might use the same article you clustered for Application 6 on page 151.) Show the article to classmates along with your outline or tree diagram, and see if they agree with your map of the article's organization.

5. Make an informal writer's outline or tree diagram of the television program, short story, movie, or novel you clustered in Application 7 on page 151. Remember to include characters, settings, action, conflict, and so on. Use your outline to write a brief essay that explains the various aspects of the work and how they fit together.

Flow Charts

Flow charts can help you understand complex situations that entail many decisions and possible consequences over a period of time. Such situations are not extraordinary, by any means. We're in the thick of them every day, starting when we get up in the morning, as Figure 7.7 shows.

Obviously, this chart includes only the basics: waking up, noting whether it's a work day and, if not, deciding whether to stay in bed or get up, deciding (once you get up) whether to put on play clothes or work clothes for the day. The process actually involves a lot more: deciding whether to shower before or after eating, what to eat, how much to eat, whether to wear sandals or shoes, a skirt or a dress, a bow or straight tie. Nothing is simple in life, not even getting going in the morning. But because we usually get going by habit, we're hardly aware that each act involves a choice.

As complex as the subject of morning choices can be, it's quite easy to follow with the flow chart in Figure 7.7. Indeed, using words alone to explain all those morning options would be much more cumbersome. Graphics can help simplify an enormously complex series of choices and possibilities by skipping all the niceties of written prose.

In general, flow charts are composed of five symbols.

An *oval* indicates the "start" or the "end" of a process:

A *diamond* is used for a decision point, a choice to be made, which is indicated inside the diamond with a word or phrase followed by a question mark:

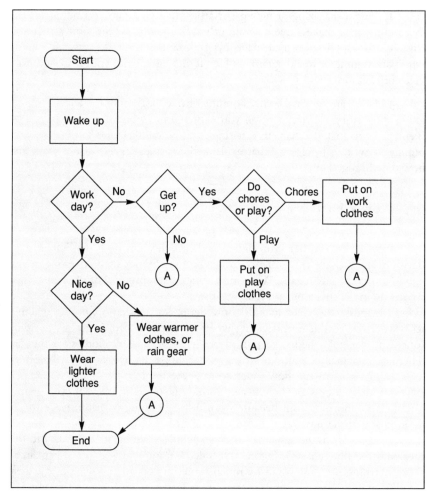

Figure 7.7 Sample Flow Chart

A *rectangle* is used for an action to be taken:

A *connecting line* is used to show the relationships among decisions and actions:

A *circle* is used as a connector from one section of a page to another, or from one page to the next:

With the symbols in mind and pencil and paper ready, we can go to work. Let's try a practical application.

Your old car just died. The mechanic says the distributor's shot, the main oil seal's broken, and the transmission is frozen in second gear. A junker to begin with, it's not worth fixing. You still need a car, though, and since you're not financially well-off, you have a decision to make. Here are your options:

1. Buy another junker, which costs little initially, but could eventually cost dearly in terms of time, trouble, and money;
2. Buy a better used car, paying more now but less later;
3. Buy a new car, paying so much initially you have to go into debt, but having the assurance that you'll eventually get some of your money back on resale;
4. Lease a new car, thus lowering your payments considerably but foregoing resale value;
5. Go without a car, relying instead on public transportation, a bicycle, and the generosity of friends.

The situation you're faced with involves many considerations and decisions, the effects of which you will have to live with for months, maybe years. How can you understand all these options and thus figure out a solution? Figure 7.8 provides a flow chart to help you see the choices you need to make in dealing with your car crisis.

Note that in a reasonably brief space this chart maps several complex decisions and their potential outcomes. The act of creating such a chart requires that we imagine *how* we would make each decision and thus implies some criteria. If we wanted to explore this further, we would break each "search" box into specific criteria which we could use to extend the original flow chart. Figure 7.9, for example, shows an extension for Figure 7.8's "Search for decent junker" box, using three criteria (there could be many more, of course). As you can see, sometimes making each criterion a separate decision point, rather than grouping them together as one, may clarify those complex areas.

Now, how can we connect all this with writing? Flow charting is useful for writing in two crucial ways. First, because it puts complex processes and procedures in quick visual form, it can serve as a strategy of discovery, helping you see new possibilities or old possibilities in a new light. For example, as a member of a committee trying to solve a complex problem—revising a grievance procedure or organizing a benefit concert—you could use flow charting to help you understand the problem more clearly and thus write about it more effectively.

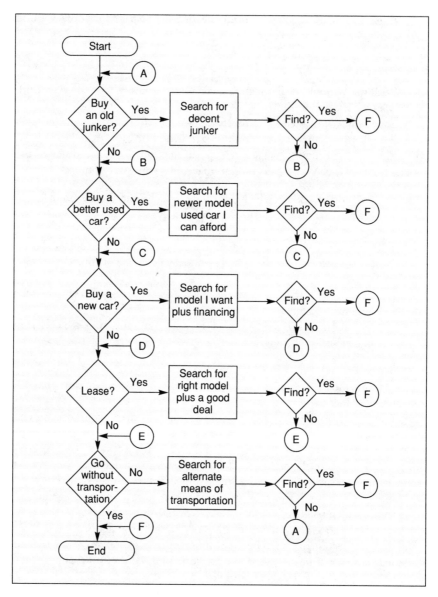

Figure 7.8 Flow Chart: Choosing a Car

Second, you can use a flow chart to help readers better understand your subject. For certain purposes words alone are often not as clear as words accompanied by visual aids. For a process or procedure with multiple possible outcomes, flow charts are one of the best visual supplements available.

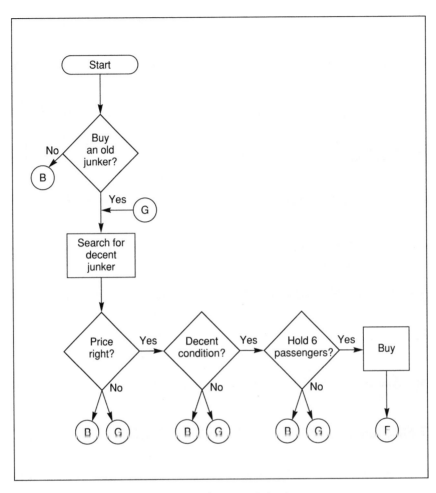

Figure 7.9 Flow Chart Extension Showing Criteria

APPLICATIONS

1. Flow chart any process with which you are familiar—such as starting a car or feeding a pet—showing the various decision points and actions as accurately and completely as you can. Ideally, choose a process which you've performed often so you don't have to do extensive research.

2. If you have a friend who has been complaining about difficulties with some procedure—such as getting organized or scheduling study hours or deciding what to do on weekends—ask him or her to describe the situation in detail.

Then create a flow chart for it. You may have to revise the chart several times before your friend gives you sufficient information to make it accurate: most people aren't used to examining processes in such detail.

3. Based on your cluster for Application 3 on page 150, choose one of your life priorities and construct a flow chart that shows the major decisions that have made it a priority. For example, if one of your priorities is "getting good grades," you probably have had to choose between partying and studying, between taking weekends off and spending weekends in the library, between having friends who support your study habits and friends who distract you, and so on. Discuss your decision points with your writing group.

4. Create a flow chart for the plot of a favorite novel, movie, or television drama you've seen lately. (You might choose the work you outlined for Application 5 on page 155.) Show the major decision points in the story and the various outcomes for each character. Examine *one* of those decision points and briefly explain how the story would have been different if the character had made a different decision. As a variation on this, you might try writing a brief story with alternative storylines giving the reader several plot options to choose from that lead to different outcomes. (Such stories are favorites with young readers.) Use a flow chart to help you construct the plot(s).

5. Consider any strong opinion you hold (perhaps the one you explored for Application 2 on pages 150 and 154). Then—and this is a challenge—use a flow chart to figure out *how* you arrived at your opinion. What were the major decision points that led to your opinion? What actions have you taken that grew out of your opinion? Where do you think your opinion might lead?

6. Find an article in a magazine or newspaper that includes some explanation of a process or procedure—an action of some sort. Make a flow chart for the procedure that could be used as a visual aid to accompany the article.

Ranking Tables

Sometimes we need to determine a simple hierarchy—of what's most important, what's best, what needs to be done first, and so on. A valuable strategy for creating such hierarchies is the *ranking table*. It's easy to use, it's fast, and it gives you plenty to think and write about as you develop it. Ranking tables are especially useful when you need to order a list of items so that no two items are equal, when each item must be rated either above or below another. Any time you're asked to write about items as priorities, you might use ranking tables to get started.

To illustrate, we'll list ten favorite movies, then make a ranking table to find our order of preference among them. We begin with the list in random order.

Gone with the Wind
It's a Wonderful Life
High Noon
Star Wars
Citizen Kane
Bonnie and Clyde
The Wizard of Oz
Close Encounters of the Third Kind
Psycho
Annie Hall

To make a ranking table, list all but the last item down the left side of the page. Use the last item to start a row across the top of the page. Finish the top row by listing the same items that are in the vertical column, starting with the bottom one and ending with the second. Then, if you wish, draw in a grid with each column one square shorter than the one to its left. Figure 7.10 shows how our table of favorite movies looks (using abbreviations to save space: AH = *Annie Hall*, P = *Psycho*, and so forth).

To complete the process, compare each item in the left-hand column with each of the items listed across the top. Then indicate your choice between the two in the proper box. In our example, we start by comparing *Gone with the Wind* to

	AH	P	CE	OZ	BC	CK	SW	HN	WL
GWTW									
WL									
HN									
SW									
CK									
BC									
OZ									
CE									
P									

Figure 7.10 Sample Ranking Grid

	AH	P	CE	OZ	BC	CK	SW	HN	WL
GWTW	GW	GW	GW	GW	GW	CK	GW	GW	GW
WL	WL	WL	WL	OZ	WL	CK	WL	WL	
HN	AH	P	CE	OZ	HN	CK	SW		
SW	AH	P	CE	OZ	SW	CK			
CK	CK	CK	CK	CK	CK				
BC	AH	P	CE	OZ					
OZ	OZ	OZ	OZ						
CE	AH	CE							
P	AH								

Figure 7.11   Sample Completed Ranking Table

Annie Hall, then *Psycho,* and so forth. When we prefer *Gone with the Wind* to the other movie, we put "GW" in the box; when we prefer the other movie, we put the abbreviation for that movie in the box. We do the same all the way down and across the chart. Figure 7.11 shows our completed ranking table.

All that remains is to count the number of times each title occurs in the table in Figure 7.11 and then construct the hierarchy. First we list the movies and the number of times each appears:

Gone with the Wind	*8*
It's a Wonderful Life	*6*
High Noon	*1*
Star Wars	*2*
Citizen Kane	*9*
Bonnie and Clyde	*0*
The Wizard of Oz	*7*
Close Encounters	*4*
Psycho	*3*
Annie Hall	*5*

Then we can order the movies according to the results of our ranking table, from number one to number ten:

> *Citizen Kane*
> *Gone with the Wind*
> *The Wizard of Oz*

It's a Wonderful Life
Annie Hall
Close Encounters
Psycho
Star Wars
High Noon
Bonnie and Clyde

Try using ranking tables the next time you need a simple ranking of any-thing—cars you're considering buying, influences on your life, presidential can-didates. It's simple, fast, and surprisingly thought-provoking, since you have to consider each item in relation to every other item. Ranking tables are also helpful when you're writing a set of instructions, for example, in figuring out which ac-tions have to occur before other actions.

SUMMARY
When you need more ideas or you sense that your ideas don't quite con-nect, try mapping them with one or more of these strategies:

- *Clustering* to brainstorm ideas visually
- *Outlining* or *treeing* to connect ideas according to some organizing plan
- *Flow charts* to examine sequences of actions and decision points
- *Ranking tables* to arrange items in a hierarchy

APPLICATIONS

1. With a good friend, make a ranking table on a common interest: fa-vorite television programs, restaurants, whatever. See how much you have in common (or how little, as the case may be).

2. Based on your cluster for Application 3 on page 150, use ranking tables to consider your life priorities in depth. Follow the procedure outlined here and see what you discover about your values in life, now and in the future. When you're finished, write a brief reflection on your current priorities for your writing group. If possible, consider how they have changed in the last couple of years and how they might change in the next five or ten.

3. Construct a ranking table for the required actions of any process: quitting smoking, changing the oil in a car, putting a meal together, getting acquainted with someone. After listing the actions in any order, compare each with all the others using the question "Should _____ occur before _____ ?" Establish a hierarchy, then write out the results as a set of instructions.

INVITATIONS FOR EXTENDED WRITING

As you write drafts for any of these invitations, be sure to use those concentrating or intuiting strategies from Chapter 2 that you found useful. Also listen to your yes voice for support. Remember that you only need your no voice when you revise and edit.

1. A Model for Succeeding in College You've just received a letter from your younger brother. As usual, he's struggling with school. But this time, instead of making jokes about it, he asks for your help. "Here I am a high-school senior already," he says, "and I've been accepted as a provisional student at State. You know my grades are low, and my ACT scores are likewise. But now that I've decided to go to a university, I want to do well. Besides, I've really gotten interested in biology—been getting A's all year from Mr. Burton—and I'd like to make it as a biology major. So what can I do to become a really good student? If I don't do well at State, I'll probably end up bagging groceries, which is no way to study flora and fauna. Can you help? I need all I can get."

You decide to give your brother the best advice you can. Start by listing several effective study strategies, such as:

- taking detailed, accurate lecture notes
- rereading the assignments
- talking about subjects with classmates
- debriefing after every class
- studying every day
- studying hardest assignments first
- studying at best times every day
- taking breaks
- concentrating
- cutting down on socializing

After a few minutes you can probably generate a good dozen ideas for someone who wants to know how to negotiate college successfully.

Now make a ranking table and decide which strategies are most crucial—generate a hierarchy, in other words. Once you have a hierarchy of what's critical to success in college, write your brother a letter about it. Or write an article describing how to succeed in college, and submit it to your former high-school newspaper.

2. A Flow Chart You Can Use Take any common procedure at your school—registration, signing up for and taking CLEP tests, applying for financial aid—and construct a flow chart for it. If your flow chart reveals that the procedure is well organized, write a complimentary letter to those in charge, and include your flow chart for their gratification. (They will be flattered—people in such positions are not used to receiving such letters.) If, however, your chart reveals that the procedure is not well organized, write a letter or an article for your school newspaper explaining what your chart has turned up and recommending the reorganization it suggests. Use the chart to illustrate and support your case.

3. An Opinion Essay for a Newspaper Most newspapers—especially large metropolitan papers—regularly publish opinion essays. Read several such essays in your local or regional newspaper, noting length, degree of formality, the use of illustrations (if any).

Then write an opinion essay of your own using clustering, outlining, flow charting, or ranking tables (whichever seems most appropriate) to help get started. You may want to include illustrations for readers if you think such models help clarify your points.

4. An Autobiographical Essay About Priorities One thing you can count on: people find their fellow humans fascinating. We look at each other, talk about each other, read stories and books, watch movies and plays that detail characters and their problems—the fascination is endless. So while writing an autobiographical essay may seem to you an exercise in vanity, members of your writing group will be interested in what you have to say.

Start with any of the material you generated for Application 3 on page 150, 154, and 159 and Application 2 on page 163. Then, write an autobiographical essay based on an extended examination of your personal priorities. The idea, in fact, is to explain your life in terms of your priorities. It should include:

- What each priority is. Offer a detailed explanation of what you mean by "making money," "travel," and so on.
- Why you rank each priority where you do. Explain why making money is more important than travel, for example.
- An introduction that presents a personal anecdote illustrating some of your priorities, and a conclusion that predicts how you expect them to change in the future.

5. Review of an Article Just as we are interested in each others' lives, so we are interested in each others' opinions. Hence, the popularity of reviews, of brief articles explaining personal responses and judgments of various subjects: books, plays, movies, concerts. When we are familiar with the thing reviewed, we read to see what others think, to see if we can learn more about it and whether we agree or disagree. When we are not familiar with the thing reviewed, we read to see if we want to take the time and trouble to experience it ourselves.

For this assignment, use any of the mapping strategies in this chapter to get started on a review of an article. Your review should be addressed to your classmates to help them decide whether they would like to read the article themselves. (You might review the article you explored in Application 6 on page 151 and Application 4 on page 154.) Include these four areas of emphasis (which you may find useful in organizing your review):

1. Summary. Describe the article's major points and their arrangement.
2. Strong Points. Describe what the article does well, including the style of writing, the ideas, the kinds of evidence presented, the sources and quotations.
3. Limitations. Describe any respects in which the article falls short, using the same items you evaluated for strengths.
4. Judgment. Explain whether you found the article worth reading. If not, consider whether it would be worthwhile for anyone to read. If so, say who.

6. Critical Essay on a Favorite Work Write a critical essay on a favorite novel, short story, poem, television program, or movie for your campus or local newspaper, or your classmates. (You might choose the work you explored in Application 7 on page 151, Application 5 on page 155, or Application 4 on page 160.) Your essay should be a balanced examination of the work, an attempt to understand its appeal, possibly in spite of its shortcomings. Cluster, outline, create flow charts, or use ranking tables for help in generating and developing your ideas.

For Further Reading and Research

Coleman, Eve. "Flowcharting as a Prewriting Activity." *CRLA*, Winter 1983: 36–38.
Rico, Gabriele. *Writing the Natural Way*. Los Angeles: Tarcher, 1983.

CHAPTER EIGHT

Connecting

But the greatest thing by far is to be a master of metaphor.
—ARISTOTLE

A metaphor is an implied comparison of two things, ideas, or states of mind that may not literally have much in common. A closely related figure of speech, the simile, is an explicit comparison of two such things. Although distinct, metaphors and similes have enough in common that we will discuss them together as *metaphor*.

"O, my Luve is like a red, red rose, / That's newly sprung in June" is a famous simile. "All the world's a stage, / And all the men and women merely players" is an equally famous metaphor. Neither sentence makes sense if taken literally. The poet's love doesn't actually have petals, leaves, and thorns, nor does she bloom in June. If the world's a stage, where's the audience, the director, the script, the payroll? Good metaphors create *unusual* comparisons, unlikely connections, in order to make the strange familiar or (just as often) the familiar strange.

Why would anyone want to make the familiar strange? Consider an alternative: "My love is a beautiful person." This sentence makes instant and literal sense, yet it actually doesn't communicate much at all. Of course one's love is a beautiful person; if he or she weren't beautiful to the lover in some way, there could be no love. *Love* and *beautiful* in this pairing are virtual synonyms.

To learn something new about anything that's familiar, we need to see it differently, and nothing opens the eyes like a metaphor. A good metaphor is a comparison that hadn't occurred to us before. (Although you may have heard the love/rose and world/stage figures many times—they *are* popular—we'd wager that they hadn't occurred to you before you first heard them.) To see the familiar in even stranger terms, here's Robert Frost speaking of love in his poem "The Silken Tent":

She is as in a field a silken tent
At midday when a sunny summer breeze
Has dried the dew and all its ropes relent,
So that in guys it gently sways at ease,
And its supporting central cedar pile,
That is its pinnacle to heavenward
And signifies the sureness of the soul,
Seems to owe naught to any single cord,
But strictly held by none, is loosely bound
By countless silken ties of love and thought
To everything on earth the compass round
And only by one's going slightly taut
In the capriciousness of summer air
Is of the slightest bondage made aware.

In this extended comparison of a loved one and a silk tent, Frost is able to explore the flexibility and the strength of love in a memorable way, as the play between independence and bondage.

Whether we're aware of it or not, metaphor is indispensable to all thinking. For example, we cannot think of something as literal as the body or the world without using a metaphor. The very origins of the words are metaphorical. *World* derives from the Anglo-Saxon *wer*, which means a man; *body* comes from the old German *boddike*, which means a tub for brewing. And they make a marvelous kind of sense, these metaphors: my body as a kind of fermenting process, a chemical plant, and the world, as I see it, made in my image. Put them together and we can see the world itself as a brewing vat, a fermenting drink that nourishes, that raises us up, then sinks us down, wipes us out.

Children often play with metaphors, hardly knowing how fresh their language seems: "My hands have a headache," said the young skier, when his hands grew uncomfortably cold. Scientists find metaphor indispensible, as well. Physicians and physiologists think of the body as a mechanism. Some ecologists conceive the earth as *Gaia,* a living organism. Even the most precise and abstract of sciences, physics, is rooted in metaphor. We talk of gravity in terms of attraction, of space in terms of extension, of light in terms of particles and waves, and so on. As writer Norman Mailer says, "If the universe is a lock, then metaphor . . . is the key." That, of course, is also a metaphor.

In his book *Metaphor as Meaning,* Weller Embler suggests how crucial metaphor can be:

> When we wish to speak of our *being* in the world, when we wish to utter what we have felt in moments of deepest insight, when we bring to the surface those thoughts which really occupy us most, thoughts of our existence and of our relationship to heaven and earth, we use [metaphor], the language of the arts.

Many people assume that metaphor is colorful but imprecise, vague, like a fuzzy lens for soft landscape shots. But as the very figure "fuzzy lens for soft landscape shots" demonstrates, a good metaphor can be extremely precise.

Consider Sir Thomas Browne's metaphor expressing mortality: "For the world, I count it not an inn, but a hospital; and a place not to live, but to die in." John F. Kennedy's "Life is not fair" may be memorably honest and succinct, but it is not nearly so precise as Hamlet's "slings and arrows of outrageous fortune." Describing a serious construction accident involving a 2,000-foot television tower, one reporter noted that the tower "telescoped" into a heap, and the word fit perfectly: the higher, smaller sections of the tower slipped into the lower, larger ones right on down to the bottom, like the barrels of a telescope all sliding into one. Saying that the tower "collapsed," "fell apart," "fell down," or "crashed" would not have expressed as precisely what actually happened.

Thousands of metaphors form the stuff of everyday talk: "Chill out." "He thinks he's hot stuff." "She made a mountain out of a molehill." "That expression is dead as a doornail." Most of these are little more than corpses of deceased metaphors, otherwise known as clichés. We use old metaphors because they are so handy, but, of course, they have no force and little explanatory value. (What, after all, is a doornail?) George Orwell recommended *never* using a metaphor that we are used to seeing in print (to which should be added, "that we are used to hearing on the air"). To be effective, a metaphor must be fresher than a rose in June when lovers spoon singing a tune by the light of the moon.

Nearly everyone enjoys a fresh metaphor, but they also believe that making one is beyond their ability: metaphor is the province of genius, of Shakespeares and Robert Frosts. Wrong. Everyone makes metaphors now and then. We'll first discuss a way to generate potentially effective metaphors. Then we'll show you how to generate and develop analogies, thought patterns that are similar to metaphors, but different enough to warrant separate treatment. After analogy, we will demonstrate another technique for prompting the kinds of connections that constitute both metaphor and analogy.

Metaphors

When you are writing and find yourself about to use a cliché—"in a rut," "bottleneck," "open-minded"—stop for a moment and see if you can vary the metaphor so that it will be fresh. Suppose, for example, you want to describe an office on campus that takes an inordinate amount of time to get its work done, financial aid perhaps. Instead of calling it a bottleneck, try some elaboration of that metaphor that makes its meaning clear: "That office corks up paperwork for days." One figure can lead to another: from water stoppered in a bottle to water contained in another way ("That office dams up the work-flow."), from one kind of flow to another ("That office is a traffic jam without a cop."), from slow-flow to no-flow ("That office is gridlocked."). Usually you need to try several metaphors because, chances are, not all of them will be very good. But if you keep going, trying one variation after another, chances also are you'll come up with a good one, one that will tell readers precisely what you have in mind.

As for new metaphors rather than variations on old ones, here's a method that can help you generate them. First, make three lists, one of *abstractions* followed by the word "is," another of specific *things,* and a third of *adjective phrases:*

LIST I
1. Love is
2. Death is
3. Education is
4. Knowledge is
5. Religion is
6. Faith is
7. Power is
8. Sleep is
9. Work is
10. Play is

LIST II
1. a wet hound dog
2. a popular song
3. a landfill
4. a black hole
5. a new Corvette
6. a frozen TV dinner
7. a circling vulture
8. an ancient temple
9. a melting popsicle
10. a festering wound

LIST III
1. waiting for its time.
2. old to the wise, new to the foolish.
3. silly to those who think, serious to those who feel.
4. needed only by the poor in spirit.
5. unused by all but the rich.
6. unused by all but the poor.
7. quietly known, unquietly felt.
8. strange in twilight, common in daylight.
9. barbarous to the truly civilized.
10. productive only of couch-potatoes.

Next, choose any three-digit number. Start with the phrase from List I that corresponds to the first digit, and connect it to the phrase in List II that corresponds to the second digit and the phrase in List III that corresponds to the third. Then, read the resulting sentence. For example, the number 847 yields "Sleep is a black hole, quietly known, unquietly felt." The number 193 gives us "Love is a melting popsicle, silly to those who think, serious to those who feel." And from 919 we get "Work is a wet hound dog, barbarous to the truly civilized."

As you can see, this technique can help you generate metaphors by the dozen. Some may turn out to be enlightening, while others may be just plain silly. Take care, though, not to dismiss a metaphor too quickly—it might have some merit in the right context. For example, love may not seem much like a melting popsicle at first, but the comparison does point out a common characteristic of being in love: it can be short and sweet. And the metaphor implies even more: the very heat of love often ends it. This could lead to an entire essay on romantic love.

The following applications will help you generate and use fresh metaphors to strengthen your thinking, your writing, and your personal voice.

APPLICATIONS

1. Make three lists like those described earlier. The first should consist of ten abstractions or general terms (*friends, war, education,* and so on) followed by *is* or *are*. The second should consist of ten words naming things, preceded by *a* or *the* and a descriptive word or two (*a broken VCR, a smiling football coach, a dented fender, a canceled television show, an unwed mother*—whatever your yes voice comes up with spontaneously, without hard labor). The third list should consist of ten phrases describing attributes, each of which could be applied to at least one of the items in your second list (*grinding away with no picture, trying to be a good loser, in desperate need of repair*). From these three lists generate at least twenty metaphorical sentences, using a three-digit number as described on page 170. Print the better ones in block letters and give them to family and friends.

2. Take the most important thing in your life, and try to imagine it as (1) a famous person, (2) a plant, (3) an animal, (4) a machine, (5) a place. Suppose that you have an old Volkswagen Beetle that you love, and have driven for years. If it were a famous person, who would it be? Danny DeVito? Jesse James? Roseanne Arnold? What kind of plant would it be? A dandelion? A rose? An artichoke? What kind of animal? A bulldog? An armadillo? (Someone has already thought of it as an insect.) Suppose it were an appliance. Would it be a popcorn popper? And if it were a place, enlarged in your mind's eye to the size of a house, where would you visit first? Where would you prefer not to go?

Once you've come up with your images, write a paragraph on your favorite object, using your newly created metaphors to make it come to life for your classmates.

3. Consider a couple of close friends. Imagine each of them as (1) a car, (2) an animal, (3) a plant, (4) a place to visit, (5) a city. Next, consider yourself for each of these categories. What might you be? Finally, write a short piece that compares you to your friends. What do you have in common? Where are you different? Use metaphors throughout your explanation.

4. Close your eyes and "see" in your mind an image of any one of the following: (1) a tree, (2) a blade of grass, (3) a pebble, (4) a starfish, (5) a rabbit. Hold the image of the object for several seconds, and imagine that it's at least several times its usual size—enlarge it to gigantic proportions. What would it be good for if it were so huge, if anything? (Would it have to be modified to be useful for anything? If so, how?) Would it be a threat in any way to humans, either psychologically or physically? What would you call this gigantic thing? Write a brief set of answers to these questions for your writing group.

5. Try Application 4 again, only this time imagine that the object is extremely tiny—not much larger than the head of a pin. Answer the same questions.

6. Get a daily newspaper and read several news stories, editorials, and columns. Make a list of all the metaphors (including similes) you find. Look for obvious ones ("The company was on the chopping block at a community meeting last week.") as well as hidden ones ("Striking a budget deal that could smooth the legislative session which begins Monday, the governor and legislative leaders agreed to spending cuts.").

Write a short essay on the metaphors you find, identifying those that seem most helpful for making the writer's point clear and the reasons for their effectiveness. Likewise, identify the ones you find useless and the reasons they seem ineffective.

Analogies

An analogy is a figurative comparison similar to a metaphor, but with two important differences: first, unlike many metaphors, an analogy compares two items that have some basic similarities (objects are usually compared to objects, ideas to ideas, and actions to actions); second, in an analogy the comparison is an extended, literal, point-by-point operation.

Metaphor occurs in every form of writing, although it is not used as often and as deliberately in technical and scientific writing as it is in fiction and poetry. Likewise, analogy occurs everywhere, but more often in certain kinds of writing than in others. It occurs frequently in argument—"high school is like day care," "the tax system is a jungle," "college a half-way house"—as the arguer uses a point-by-point comparison to develop a persuasive case. Analogy is probably used most often in explanatory writing, especially to describe complex concepts and processes: steering a plane is like steering a boat, the structure of the atom is like the structure of a solar system, grammar is to writing what fundamental ball-tossing and dribbling skills are to playing basketball.

Making analogies means making connections—the basis of all creative thinking. Many people find the word *creative* foreign, if not terrifying. If you're one of these, rest assured that making connections is a skill, not a mystery, involving techniques, not magic. Everyone can do it, and everyone in fact does. But like any skill, it can be improved. We want to help you improve yours by showing three basic types of analogies, using three basic approaches.

The first is *direct* analogy. Here, you simply put together two similar items, then jot down every point of resemblance you can find between the two. Don't get impatient and try to force the comparisons. Just turn your mind loose, let it play, and follow its lead on paper. An old example should give you the idea:

> The state is like a person:
> the leader is the head, directing
> the armed forces are the arms, defending
> the businesses are the midsection, transacting
> the farmers are the hands, planting and harvesting
> the truckers are the feet, transporting. . . .

The second kind of analogy is *empathic*. Here, instead of looking at an object, idea, or action from outside, you *identify with* it, a process called *empathy*. Like an actor, you put yourself in that thing's place, becoming as much as possible the thing itself, to see how matters stand from that perspective. Such a radical difference in point of view can often reveal possibilities that would otherwise have remained unknown.

In *Synectics,* a book on analogy, W. J. J. Gordon cites the case of a group of engineers who were trying to invent a mechanism to "run a shaft at speeds varying from four hundred to four thousand rpm so that the power take-off end of this shaft always turns at four hundred." They tried various approaches involving conventional solutions—gears, wheels, cones, clutches—none of which worked. Then they used empathic analogy. One of the engineers imagined himself to be inside a box where the two shafts met, then began to imagine himself as the mechanism they were trying to invent. Here is how he began:

> Okay, I'm in the damn box, I grab the in-shaft with one hand and grab the out-shaft with the other. I let the in-shaft slip when I think it's going too fast so that the out-shaft will stay constant.

The other engineers questioned him about what he felt, then they began imagining themselves in the same place, exploring the function of this undefined, unknown mechanism. Eventually they invented one that worked, based on the principle of a liquid made up of billions of rubber bands that would automatically tighten when the shaft reached a certain speed and loosen when the shaft slowed down to a certain speed, thus keeping the speed constant.

Engineering has a reputation for being an unimaginative business. Don't believe it. Creativity is not the exclusive prerogative of the arts. Imagination has a role to play in every endeavor, and analogy is one of the ways it likes to play best.

The third kind of analogy extends this point: *fantastic,* we call it. It involves fantasizing about a subject, deliberately suspending in our minds all the known laws of the physical universe and seeing how the subject behaves in such a place.

One of the most famous examples of a fantastic analogy—and one that proved wondrously educational—occurred to August Kekule, a Belgian professor of chemistry in the mid-1900s, as a dream. After struggling with a problem concerning molecular structures, Kekule fell asleep in his chair. He later described the dream as follows:

> Again the atoms were gamboling before my eyes. This time the smaller groups kept modestly in the background. My mental eye, rendered more acute by repeated visions of this kind, could now distinguish larger structures, of manifold conformation; long rows, sometimes more closely fitted together; all twining and twisting in snakelike motion. But look! What was that? One of the snakes had seized hold of its own tail, and the form whirled mockingly before my eyes.

From this bizarre vision Kekule awoke with a start and deduced by analogy that certain molecules are closed rings, a deduction that is regarded as one of the most brilliant insights in the history of organic chemistry.

An important point to remember: when making analogies (whether direct, personal, or fantastic) let yourself go and have fun. To make connections, you must play around, turn your yes voice loose, let it roam, sniffing and rooting at will in the world of objects, ideas, and events to see what analogies it turns up. Romp a bit; follow where analogies lead, draw the line from dot to dot until a picture emerges. Then—and only then—turn your no voice loose to determine the true value of your analogies. Many will not prove worthwhile—just gravel and sand and such—but some, like Kekule's, will turn out to be nuggets of pure gold.

Although analogy can often be very useful in making your point, beware of *false analogy*—an analogy that upon examination turns out to be *mis*leading because it is not sufficiently true. (No analogy is entirely true, because the items are never exactly the same.) Earlier, for instance, we cited an analogy asserting that grammar is to writing what fundamental ball-playing skills are to playing basketball. An argument based on this analogy might be "Just as basketball players must master fundamentals to play the game well, so must writers master grammar to write well." Let's extend this a little, though: the fundamental skills of basketball include dribbling, passing, shooting lay-ups, shooting jumpshots, setting picks, rebounding, and so forth. Mastery of grammar involves knowing the parts of speech, the rules for noun-verb and pronoun-antecedent agreement, the use of adjectives and adverbs, correct sentence structure, and so forth. So, are the fundamentals of basketball analogous to the fundamentals of grammar? Not really. While people who have mastered the fundamentals of basketball almost always play well, people who have mastered the fundamentals of grammar don't necessarily write well. Good grammar and good writing are not one and the same. The analogy breaks down rather quickly, and if we try to use it to persuade people of the necessity of mastering grammar, they would have the right to cry, "False analogy!"

We would have to reconsider the analogy to see if it is true in some other way. If so, we can use it in modified form. If not, we need to chuck it and turn our yes voices loose to find a different analogy that works.

The moral: analogy can make a case, but it can also blow up in your face. Be sure your no voice has a chance to give your analogies a white-glove inspection.

APPLICATIONS

1. Study your pen or pencil, looking for some direct analogy. What is it obviously like? Note that it is shaped like a projectile, so it is directly analogous to many things, ranging from fingers to spears and arrows to bullets. See if some resemblances lead to point-by-point comparisons.

Next, imagine that you *are* the pen or pencil. What do you feel when you are being used? When you are running out of ink or need sharpening? How do various people hold you? Can you tell their mood by the ways they grip and move you? Do you ever get frustrated with the way they handle you? Would you prefer to be a typewriter? A computer?

Then, fantasize that the pen or pencil is a jet, a Concorde. It's taking you and your friend, the reader you have in mind, away. Where would you like it to go? What kind of fuel does it use? What kinds of space/time limits can it violate? What kinds of facilities does it offer? Have you ever thought of a pen as a means of locomotion, a vehicle to "fly" places, taking the reader with you?

Finally, write a one-page reflection on what you've come up with concerning your pencil.

2. Suppose you were to become—literally—a lower animal: a fox, an owl, a gorilla, a mole, a praying mantis, a hawk, a giant beetle, whatever. What animal would you prefer above all others to become? Why that one? What is it about that particular animal (as you imagine it) that makes you prefer it?

Consider two further questions: Which animal could you choose that probably would not surprise your friends? Which animal could you enjoy being that *would* surprise your friends?

Write a page or so answering these questions. Then write a couple of pages working out, point by point, analogies between each of the animals you've come up with and yourself. Take account of both physical and psychological attributes.

3. Search for analogies in three recent issues of any newspaper or magazine you regularly read. Are they clear? Do the explanatory analogies help you understand the subject better than if they had not been used? Are there persuasive analogies that help convince you of the point? Can you find any examples of empathic or fantastic analogies? What proportion are direct? Write a page or two summarizing what you find.

4. Examine any problem you've tried to solve recently: which class to take, which major to declare, which car to buy, which person to ask out, which apartment to rent. Concentrate on the problem by applying all three kinds of analogy: direct, empathic, and fantastic. Write a page or two reflecting on what you discover.

5. Examine any analogies that caught your interest as you read this section or that grew out of any previous Applications. Write one or two pages on what you've learned about analogy and the possibility (or impossibility, as the case may be) of using analogy regularly as a tool for concentration and discovery.

Prompted Connections

So far we have been concentrating on writing *prose*, a word that literally means forward, straight on. The progress of your prose may not seem very straightforward, but you have been aiming straight ahead, whether you've been aware of it or not: one item after another, one thought after another, one sentence after another, line by line.

There's another way to operate, however. Many writers like to play around, to turn their yes voice loose and doodle and dawdle with lists. As a matter of sober fact, to write well you must play around with ideas and words, in order to come up with connections and combinations that make your meaning clear and interest your readers.

Here, we acquaint you with a method of list-making that can help prompt connections and combinations necessary to give your ideas (and thus your writing) a lift. Based on an idea described by Don Koberg and Jim Bagnall in their book *The Universal Traveler,* the strategy is called "morphological forced connections."

Take any object your eye or mind lights on: a coffee cup, a stamp dispenser, a stapler, whatever. Then, make a numbered list of ten or so possible colors it could be. (Feel free to go on as long as you like.) Let's take a coffee cup:

1. white
2. red
3. green
4. blue
5. gold
6. black
7. brown
8. pink
9. puce
10. chartreuse

Next, note any materials that the object is or could be made of, coming up, if possible, with the same number as on your previous list. For the coffee cup we might list:

1. ceramic
2. tin
3. aluminum
4. plastic
5. styrofoam
6. glass
7. steel
8. wood
9. wax-coated paper
10. porcelain

Next, list potential shapes:

1. round
2. square
3. rectangular

4. triangular (isosceles)
5. triangular (right)
6. triangular (equilateral)
7. oval
8. hexagonal
9. octagonal
10. trapezoidal

Now, consider the object's possible uses:

1. drinking coffee
2. the cat's water dish
3. breaking a locked window, in an emergency
4. hurling to express anger
5. paperweight
6. memento of special occasion (a trip, an anniversary)
7. weapon (either offensive or defensive)
8. sugar bowl
9. vase
10. decoration/objet d'art

Finally, note how the object might be decorated:

1. lettering that shows its origins as a souvenir
2. a solid primary color
3. lettered in Gothic script with the owner's name
4. with a Far Side cartoon
5. with a quip (*Coffee Builds Strong Bladders*)
6. with a calendar
7. with an image of Uncle Sam
8. hand-painted by one of the children
9. stenciled in a Shaker design
10. crawling with delicate flowers, like bedroom wallpaper

Now, by simply choosing any five numbers at random, we can "prompt" connections that might create some interesting cup-like objects. The numbers 9/10/8/3/4 gives us a puce, porcelain, hexagonal window-smasher that's decorated with one of Gary Larson's Far Side cartoons. With 8/4/4/5/7 we get a pink, plastic, isosceles triangular-shaped paperweight with the image of Uncle Sam on one side—exactly the sort of knick-knack that can make millions.

Using numbered lists of properties like these can help you find connections that probably wouldn't otherwise occur, and these connections can lead to some interesting thinking and writing. Of course, some connections won't work: 10/5/7/7/6 amounts to a chartreuse, styrofoam, oval weapon bearing a calendar; 6/9/10/4/10 creates a black, paper, trapezoidal anger-expresser crawling with delicate flowers. On the other hand, some unlikely connections add up to interesting possibilities: 4/8/7/8/9 which gives us a blue, wood, oval sugar bowl stenciled in a Shaker design, which might prove very attractive in a nostalgic, Early American sort of way.

You should regard our five lists as a standard set, comprising color, material, shape and/or size, purpose, and style or decoration. The order of the lists doesn't matter, and you may add or substitute criteria as you wish, even come up with completely different criteria. The longer the lists and the more lists you have, the greater the number of connections you can make and the more creative the possible combinations.

This technique works just as well for ideas and events as it does for objects. Consider watching television, for example. Let's start with the act itself. It may mean:

1. passively watching electronic images of made-up events
2. passively watching electronic images of actual events as they happen
3. passively watching electronic images of recorded actual events
4. actively watching electronic images by getting and giving feedback via electronic hookups
5. actively watching electronic images by responding (yelling at the referees, screaming with a rock concert, crying at the news)
6. actively watching projected images re-created electronically (broadcasts of movies, for example)

Next, we can make a list of various physical positions people may be in when they watch television:

1. sitting down
2. lying down
3. standing up
4. squatting
5. jumping about (doing aerobics, for example)
6. standing on their heads

Then, we can list various reasons people have for watching television:

1. for entertainment
2. for information
3. for the company of background noise
4. out of habit
5. to see someone in particular (a star, an acquaintance)
6. to have something to do with company

Finally, let's consider some purposes of the television industry itself:

1. to entertain
2. to inform
3. to sell products
4. to make money
5. to convey a point of view
6. to reinforce cultural identity

As you can see, these lists are based upon certain principles or themes: the nature of the relationship between viewer and image, the viewer's physical position, the viewer's motive in watching, the industry's motive in broadcasting. If you can think of other themes, add a list or two of your own.

Now, by lining up items on the lists, what might we be able to learn? Consider 5/2/2/6: actively watching a live football game while lying flat on your back in order to gain information from a broadcast designed to reinforce cultural identity. Does this make sense? Before you dismiss it completely, think for a moment. "Watching actively" does not necessarily mean standing at attention. "Active" is a state of mind, and at times we can be wide awake while lying down. And it is possible to watch a football game for information. Further, it is reasonable to construe the broadcast of a football game as designed to reinforce cultural identity. Consider how the advertisers for football broadcasts associate their products with big American guys—often ex-football players—having fun in some red-blooded American way. Consider also how often the promoters and announcers of football broadcasts paint a picture of the game as specifically American, which indeed it is. And consider *that:* how popular the game is in the United States but almost nowhere else. The more you think about it, the more likely it may seem that reinforcing cultural identity is indeed a motive behind football broadcasts. Thus you could, lying flat on your back, watch a game actively—like a tourist or an anthropologist—looking for information on that motive, on what the game says about American culture.

Without the prompting of the lists, we might never have made some of those connections, and they represent just one combination. Again, not all connections will work. When we put together 3/5/6/5, for instance, we get an impossibility: one cannot passively watch a TV program designed to convey a point of view while jogging in order to have something to do with company. But it comes closer than it may at first appear. Eliminate "passively" and the connections make a possible sense: people jogging together, watching an aerobics show that stresses the importance of physical fitness and fellowship—an exercise party. If a combination doesn't seem to make sense at first, don't give up on it too quickly.

Note that in putting things together from these lists, you may need to shut down the no voice altogether. Just turn the yes voice loose, and watch it play. When you have come up with a set of connections, then turn the no voice loose. Let the two voices have at it with each other, and out of their discourse find out which of the connections work and which don't. Since both sorts of connections are important in understanding something, you may well discover that you suddenly have a subject for an essay on your hands.

APPLICATIONS

1. Take any object you regularly use, and improve on it in some way by using prompted connections. Take paper clips, for example. You might list various ways paper clips can be used, materials they can be made of, possible shapes, possible colors, even possible textures. Then, trying as many different prompts as you need, see if you can come up with an improved model. If you do, write to two sets of readers about your discovery:

- Describe your "discovery" to some friends, including a request that they try it and inform you of the results.
- Write a letter to potential backers, explaining why they should support your product.

2. Consider your favorite movie, television program, or novel. What are the three parts you most like about it? For the movie *Gone with the Wind,* for example, these might be (1) Clark Gable; (2) the love story between the two main characters; (3) the elaborate historical detail. Now imagine another work that contains these three attributes, but is different in every other way. Make lists of other elements—situations, plots, settings, supporting characters—and apply prompted connections. You might end up with a historical love story starring Clark Gable that involves him with a beautiful, willful woman, but that is set in the court of Marie Antoinette, with the complication of parents who wish to interfere with the relationship, and a lecherous tutor as a new supporting character.

Finally, write a summary of the plot of this new work, either as a proposal for a book publisher or a "treatment" for a television or movie producer.

3. Ponder for a few moments what it takes to be a really good teacher, coach, parent, doctor, or whatever. Then, consider the "activity" of teaching or coaching or parenting or doctoring, coming up with as many categories related to the "activity" as you can. For a parent, these might be "physical," "emotional," "psychological," "social," "financial." For each category list specific examples of characteristics or attributes. Then, try some prompted connections to see if you can generate connections that will help you explain just what makes an ideal. If you find that most of the connections in this case don't work—that they don't describe, for example, people who would be good parents—ask yourself why? After trying several of the connections, write a brief reflection on what does constitute an ideal for your subject.

INVITATIONS FOR EXTENDED WRITING

As you develop drafts, be sure to call on any concentrating, intuiting, and gathering strategies that you've found work for you. Also use your yes voice for support, especially if you find yourself procrastinating or blocked in any way.

1. An Essay on Metaphors Using everything you've observed and learned about metaphors, write an essay of three to five pages for your peers on the subject. Include everything that would help to explain metaphors, including any striking examples you've found or used. Submit the essay to your campus newspaper, if it would interest general readers.

2. Examining Metaphors in a Poem Now that you understand something about metaphors, consider the form that uses metaphors most intensely: poetry. Find a poem that contains some striking metaphors and examine them closely. What is being compared to what, and why?

To help you get started, consider the metaphors in this poem, appropriately titled "Metaphors":

> I'm a riddle in nine syllables,
> An elephant, a ponderous house,
> A melon strolling on two tendrils.
> O red fruit, ivory, fine timbers!
> This loaf's big with its yeasty rising.
> Money's new minted in this fat purse.
> I'm a means, a stage, a cow in calf.
> I've eaten a bag of green apples,
> Boarded the train there's no getting off.
> —*Sylvia Plath*

Note that there are nine lines, and that "nine" is mentioned in the first line. What is the poet getting at here? What is being compared to what? (Hint: the "I" in this poem has to be a female of child-bearing age.)

Write a brief explanation of the metaphors in this or any poem for your classmates.

3. A New Product Design a new product of any kind using analogies and/or prompted connections. Let your imagination rove about—what might be useful and needed? What would be appreciated, even if not especially needed? Who might use it? How often? Once you have a product in mind, try one or more of these:

- Write a product description for potential buyers that explains exactly what the product is and how it works.
- Write an advertisement for the product that might appear on television.
- Write a newspaper or magazine advertisement for the product.
- Write a letter to financial backers trying to get support for your product.
- Write a letter to a store trying to get the manager to stock your product for customers.

4. Metaphors in Editorials or Columns Choose any columnist or editorial writer for a newspaper, and read at least six of his or her pieces. Keep track of all the writer's metaphors and similes, and see if you notice any patterns, any consistency in how the metaphors are used. For example, a political columnist might use a series of battle metaphors to describe the conflicts between factions in a political party. Or an issues columnist might rely on metaphors that see nature as a tired mother to make points about dwindling resources.

If you notice anything interesting or unusual about the writer's use of metaphors, write him or her a letter and comment on them. If not, describe what you found to your classmates in a brief essay.

5. An Essay on Clichés For several days, listen to the speech of your classmates, friends, and relatives. Try to identify the phrases that you hear over and over again (there should be several). Which ones are metaphors? Make a list of those you hear, and write an essay on commonly used metaphors—who uses them, in what context, and why. If you hear any especially fresh metaphors, notice those too, and include them in your essay. Write for your classmates and teacher.

6. A New Game The world is always looking for new games to play. Consider designing a new game using prompted connections. Start with various categories used to define games: object of the game, equipment used, number of players, special rules, and so on. Then list under these categories appropriate attributes of the best games you know—Monopoly, Sorry, table tennis, golf. After you have several substantial lists, see if you can find a winning combination of attributes.

When you have a game that makes sense, try any of the following:

- Write a set of "official rules" for the game.
- Write your friends and explain the game, telling them how to play.
- Write a short piece for the local newspaper, explaining your new game and how people can play it.
- Write a letter to potential financial investors explaining the game and why it should be marketed.
- Write an advertisement for the game.

7. Take a paper you have been assigned to write on some aspect of a novel, poem, play, or historical event that you have been studying. See if you can't approach it using some fresh metaphors, analogies, and connections. For example, if your subject were *Huckleberry Finn,* how might the novel be related to you? As a friend? A parent? A loved one? A street person? Why? What kind of animal would the novel be? A mutt? A Chihuahua? A rabbit, a turtle, a scruffy old crow? Again, why? You might list some of the major characteristics of the work or event, then change one and ponder how different the whole might be. (What if *Huckleberry Finn* were set during the 1950s? Or if it shifted points of view from Huck to Jim and back? Or if Tom were the narrator instead of Huck?) Play with your subject using some of the ideas in this chapter, and incorporate what you learn in your paper.

For Further Reading and Research

Adams, James. *Conceptual Blockbusting.* Reading: Addison-Wesley, 1979.
———. *The Care and Feeding of Ideas.* Reading: Addison-Wesley, 1986.

Embler, Weller. *Metaphor and Meaning.* Deland: Everett/Edwards, 1968.

Gordon, W. J. J. *Synectics.* New York: Harper, 1961.

Koberg, Don and Jim Bagnall. *The Universal Traveler.* Los Altos: William Kaufmann, 1973.

Lakeoff, George, and Mark Johnson. *Metaphors We Live By.* Chicago: U of Chicago P, 1980.

CHAPTER NINE

Forming

[L]imits are as necessary as those provided by the banks of a river, without which the water would be dispersed on the earth and there would be no river—that is, the river is constituted by the tension between the flowing water and the banks.

—ROLLO MAY

Without Form in every sense, the facts of the past, like the jumbled visions of a sleeper in a dream, elude us.

—JACQUES BARZUN

Many instructors begin teaching poetry by asking students to write haiku, a poetic form of three lines, the first of which has five syllables, the second seven syllables, and the third five syllables:

The falling flower
I saw drift back to its branch
Was a butterfly.

The haiku form contains no rhymes, and haiku are often, though not always, about nature. But, by definition, every haiku has three lines of five, seven, and five syllables. If you want to write four lines or three lines of six syllables each, you won't be writing haiku.

You can probably see right away how forming material develops it—forming and developing are virtually synonymous—but you may wonder how forming can *generate* material. If you haven't generated something already, how can you form it? As poets know, however, beginning with a set form—the sonnet, the heroic couplet, the standard 32-bar song—often gets the mind working on material anew, thus generating ideas, examples, and images. According to the poet W. H. Auden, "In poetry you have a form looking for a subject and a subject looking for a form. When they come together successfully you have a poem."

What works for poets can work for prose writers, as well. In this chapter we will acquaint you with four basic forms that will help you both generate and develop material. Look upon these forms as suggestions rather than commandments: as you write you may come up with variations on your own. Strive for a form that suits your subject and occasion, a form that does your purpose, subject, and audience justice.

First, we'll look at what we call *ABA form,* also known as "beginning-middle-end" or "introduction-body-conclusion." As old as composition itself, this conventional form is still useful (because, like many things that become conventional, it works). Next, we'll take up the *rhetorical modes,* eight classical strategies that date back to Aristotle: description, chronology, exemplification, definition, classification, comparison and contrast, cause and effect, and argumentation. These modes are as fundamental to writing (some say even thinking) as a ball and field are to soccer. Then, we'll look at the *line and circle forms,* two basic forms that are particularly effective in exploratory writing—writing for sheer discovery, to see where the mind winds up or what the mind turns up rather than to explain something or to persuade someone. Finally, we'll consider some important *professional formats* common to business, engineering, education, and government. These formats are designed to handle such tasks as reviewing the literature on a subject, filling in background information, explaining a particular approach, describing the results of a study along with implications and recommendations, and putting together abstracts and summaries.

ABA Form

Used poorly, the conventional ABA form can sink subjects and readers like quicksand. But, used effectively, it can provide a clarity and coherence that readers appreciate. In essence, ABA form is simplicity itself: a one-paragraph introduction that includes the essay's major point, stated in a single sentence (the thesis statement); a middle (usually three or more paragraphs) that develops points and subpoints to support that major point; and a one-paragraph conclusion that restates the major point. It's the old "tell them what you're going to say, say it, then tell them what you've said" formula, boiled down to a minimum of five paragraphs.

Given certain audiences and purposes, ABA form makes perfect sense. If you're trying to show an American history instructor on an essay test that you understand the major causes of discontent among southerners after the Civil War, ABA form offers an easy format. If you're writing a letter to the editor and want readers to get your point quickly, ABA form will serve your purpose, although it may seem rigid and academic to many readers. And if you receive explicit instructions to state a thesis early in a paper, develop it, and restate it at the end, then ABA form is probably your best choice.

ABA form can also help you generate and develop ideas. How can you use such a rigid form to develop ideas? The first task in using ABA form is to find your major point. Suppose your instructor suggests that you write a short essay on an object that has made a difference in your life. It can be anything—a computer, a bicycle, a car, a piece of jewelry, whatever. Your job is to write an autobiographical essay for your classmates that explains what the object is and the difference it has made to you.

You could begin by freewriting for three minutes using the prompt "I couldn't get along without my _____." You could then look back over your freewrite and select the one object that seems to stand out. This would serve as your tentative thesis (which you could, of course, change later if you found you needed to do so).

Next, you would ask yourself in what ways the object you have chosen has changed your life and list as many as you can think of. These are the subpoints that support your thesis. You would also jot down anecdotes that illustrate these subpoints—anything that comes to mind that would show readers your involvement with the object.

At this point, if you have the freedom (given your assignment and its requirements) to write in some form other than ABA, you might develop your ideas as a dialogue, as a story, maybe as a stream-of-consciousness monologue or an exploratory essay. The ideas you generate using ABA form don't necessarily have to result in an ABA form essay. However, if you know your instructor and classmates are expecting something like an ABA pattern, and if you're comfortable with it yourself, you can easily develop an introduction, a body, and a conclusion.

Let's consider these three parts of ABA form in greater detail.

Introduction

How do you introduce your subject and thesis using ABA form? Here are two examples:

(1) Years ago the flamboyant baseball player and manager Leo Durocher said, "Nice guys finish last." To many people, particularly in a competitive culture like ours, Durocher's statement sounds like a self-evident truth. But if we consider entire lives, and not just careers, we find that nothing could be further from the truth.

(2) Years ago the flamboyant baseball player and manager Leo Durocher said, "Nice guys finish last." To many people, Durocher's statement amounts to a cynical attack on morality and the values of civilization. But like it or not, the guy had a point.

As these examples show, it is not enough to begin with a quote or an anecdote. You must also show how it defines your subject and thesis. If you don't explain, the reader can't know, because a quote can be used to define different subjects and theses. Here, both paragraphs use the quote from Durocher to define the same subject—nice guys—but different theses: (1) Durocher was wrong, (2) Durocher was right. However, we could have used the quote to define an entirely different subject as well as thesis:

> (3) Years ago the flamboyant baseball player and manager Leo Durocher said, "Nice guys finish last." People have been arguing the statement ever since, some saying it is true, that nice guys *do* finish last, and some saying it's not true, that nice guys finish *first*. Both sides, however, along with Durocher, miss the mark by assuming that coming out ahead is the direct result of the way one behaves, whether one is nice or nasty. The truth is, being first has nothing to do with character; it's just a matter of dumb luck.

The subject of (3): finishing first. The thesis: it's a function of luck. (All three paragraphs, by the way, progress from a specific point—the quote—to a generalization that defines a thesis.)

Here are five types of introductions that, used well, can get a reader's attention: anecdote, description, direct statement of thesis and subpoints, lively quote, and startling statement.

Anecdote An anecdote is a brief story, the sort we often tell each other in conversation for no other reason than the human interest involved. In writing, however, an anecdote generally implies a point that we intend to spell out.

A word about the notion of "point." Remember the times you've told a story to make a point and, somewhere in the middle, forgotten what that point was? And you realized that if you didn't know the point, then your listeners wouldn't be able to figure it out from the story? The lesson here is that when you use an anecdote in writing, you should state your point clearly. Otherwise readers may miss what you're saying.

Here is an example of an effective opening anecdote:

> Fifty years ago a woman spent a pleasant Saturday working in her garden. She worked later than she had planned so that when she was done she had very little time to clean up for the party she was to attend with her husband. Her nails were a wreck. She could trim them, but she couldn't scrape all the caked dirt out. Desperate, for a moment she despaired, then she had an idea: she would hide the dirt and at the same time flaunt her fingernails, by painting them bright red. Thus fingernail polish made its first appearance in the world, testimony to the old truth that necessity is the mother of invention.

One could derive other subjects and theses from this anecdote: that disguise is the original motive of all makeup, that the best disguise is the bold disguise, that it pays to be willing to do something novel, that you never know when or where or how original ideas will happen. The important thing is to connect the anecdote to some point.

Description Another effective way to begin an essay is with description:

> He looked like a caricature of a professional wrestler—thick-waisted, thick-shouldered, thick-necked, thick-headed, thick-lipped. His forehead was low, sloping into a brow that jutted over his eyes. His arms looked like legs, his fingers like bratwursts. It was hard to believe, even after you knew, that Dick Major made his living at a bar not as a bouncer, but as a piano player and tenor. What you see is not always what you get.

Other possible subjects and theses: Dick Major was surprising in other ways; stereotypes are often misleading; agility has nothing to do with bulk.

Direct Statement of Purpose In certain circumstances—essay exams, for example—you may find it most convenient to introduce your essay with a direct statement of your purpose. In that case you won't begin with specifics, as the previous examples do. You'll lead off with your thesis statement, making it as simple as possible (no longer than a short sentence), then use the rest of the introductory paragraph to enumerate the subpoints your essay will cover. You may make it even more succinct. Ernest van den Haag published an essay with a *title* that defines the thesis: "The Collapse of the Case Against Capital Punishment." His introduction, a very short one, simply indicates how he intends to go about proving his thesis:

> Three questions about the death penalty so overlap that they must each be answered. I shall ask seriatim [in order]: Is the death penalty constitutional? Is it useful? Is it morally justifiable?

Now that is to the point.

Lively Quote Donald Murray, writing teacher and Pulitzer-prize winning writer, offers these cautionary words about quotes used as leads:

> The danger . . . is that the writer will use a dramatic quotation that is not vital to the story; the quote sends the reader off on a false scent. The quote lead is such a powerful device that the writer must be sure it is honest and on target.

But, as Murray implies, a carefully chosen quote can draw and keep readers, and is worth searching for. Here's how Alice Walker begins her famous essay, "The Civil Rights Movement: What Good Was It?":

> Someone said recently to an old black lady from Mississippi, whose legs had been badly mangled by local police who arrested her for "disturbing the peace," that the Civil Rights Movement was dead, and asked, since it was dead, what she thought about it. The old lady replied, hobbling out of his presence on her cane, that the Civil Rights Movement was like herself, "if it's dead, it shore ain't ready to lay down!"

In the colorful and authoritative language of a civil rights veteran—language that makes the reader sit up and take notice—this quote defines the subject and the thesis Walker will develop in the essay.

Jaime M. O'Neill, a community college teacher in Washington, began his *Newsweek* essay "No Allusions in the Classroom" in a similar manner:

Josh Billings, a 19th-century humorist, wrote that it is better "not to know so much than to know so many things that ain't so." Recently, after 15 years of teaching in community colleges, I decided to take a sampling to find out what my students know that ain't so.

O'Neill's use of Billings' catchy statement defines his topic—just how much his students know and don't know—and establishes his light but serious tone.

O'Neill quotes a writer of some fame, but as Walker demonstrates, you don't have to confine yourself to literary figures. Just use a quote that is sharp, surprising, and to your point.

Startling Statement Here is George Orwell's lead for his autobiographical essay "Marrakech":

As the corpse went past the flies left the restaurant table in a cloud and rushed after it, but they came back a few minutes later.

Few readers can resist reading on after seeing that opening image. It is compellingly grotesque in its own right, and it raises questions that demand answers: What corpse? Why wasn't it in a coffin? Was this typical or unusual? Where did this take place?

After giving his essay a startling title—"The Courage of Turtles"—Edward Hoagland begins it with an even more startling lead:

Turtles are a kind of bird with the governor turned low.

It would be hard to find a reader who'd thought of turtles that way, or who could resist following the idea once Hoagland put it in his or her head.

These five kinds of leads are not mutually exclusive. Often you can mix and match. Walker couches her quote, for example, in a quick anecdote, and Hoagland's startling statement is also a description. While you are researching a topic—by reading, interviewing, thinking, whatever—keep an eye out for items that could serve as an introduction—anecdotes, quotes, scenes, or persons to describe. In deciding how to introduce your essay, consider what your audience would like, what the subject seems to warrant, and what you have available. Remember that in ABA form the primary goal of the introduction is to define your subject and thesis precisely. If you can do so in a way that piques your readers' desire to read on, so much the better.

Body

Once you have defined your subject and thesis, you are ready to develop them, one major point at a time. You might want to develop each point with a single paragraph, or some points may require several paragraphs, including one-sentence transition paragraphs. And don't feel limited to only three points, as defined by the old "five-paragraph theme" rules. Your idea might require two points, or six or seven or more, depending on your subject, your audience, and your purpose.

If you want to follow the traditional "theme" formula, begin most paragraphs with a topic sentence stating the general idea of the paragraph, followed with specifics supporting the idea—examples, facts, images. You'll find that professional writers don't often follow this pattern: many of their paragraphs will have topic sentences in the middle or at the end or altogether absent, but the topic will still be clear and the development coherent. In such paragraphs by student writers, however, the topic is often not clear. Here's an example of the latter:

> Nightmares usually occur toward morning. They are the most frightening of dreams. When you awake during a dream you will be able to remember it. Many people believe that nightmares are something we outgrow. They do become less frequent, but they do not disappear. Adults have more nightmares than people realize. One of the most common nightmares that appears throughout adulthood is about taking exams. Surveys taken at many schools, including Princeton and Harvard, indicate that a large percentage of students have nightmares about exams. The types of nightmares change as we grow older. Younger children usually have dreams and nightmares concerning something they are involved in, such as playing house and baseball. Old people worry about money to live on. Teenagers dream of gaining independence and establishing a career and settling down for marriage. When they get older they dream about raising the children and getting them off to college.

Not only is there no development of the idea, here, there is no single idea—unless we want to regard dreams about playing house and baseball as nightmares. This un-paragraph demonstrates why instructors sometimes *require* students to begin paragraphs with a topic sentence and follow it up with supporting sentences. We suggest you at least consider using a topic sentence-support structure, unless you can *explain* both to yourself and to your readers how another is better.

Your paragraphs need to be more than just coherent individually, of course. They also need to follow each other in some meaningful order. Let's say the subject is pianist/tenor Dick Major, who looks like a wrestler. Your discovery writing has led you to realize that he's a man of many surprises (your thesis). To develop that thesis you have three major points: that besides being a musician, he's an avid outdoorsman, a stock car driver, and an Old Testament scholar. You might order these from least surprising to most surprising. Another effective order might be to start with a good surprise to hook the reader, then move to least surprising, and end with the most surprising point—the 2-3-1 pattern discussed in Chapter 4. (Not that you should ever use points that are absolutely weak and dull, but there will always be some that are stronger and shinier and sharper than others.)

Having your points in order, develop them one by one, giving at least a paragraph to each. Cite specifics (three to five, as a very loose rule) that illustrate or prove the point you are making, just as that point helps illustrate or prove the thesis you are arguing:

> When he's not earning a living Dick Major often turns to the outdoors, and I don't mean his backyard or the park across the street. He likes to go fly fishing in Idaho (he ties his own flies), spelunking in Pennsylvania, kayaking on the Colorado, scuba diving in the Caribbean, mountain climbing in Peru, and sky diving in the wild blue yonder. In the future, he says, he would like to take up one-man sailing, hot air ballooning, and wilderness survival training—the *great* outdoors.

You could develop the other two points in a similar way. (Note, in this example how a paragraph itself can use the ABA structure: topic sentence as introduction, then specific instances as body, then a concluding phrase that returns to the idea of the topic sentence.)

Conclusion

You may have been taught that, like an introduction, a conclusion is a summary of the paper. That is how the ABA form got a bad reputation: when you begin with a summary, then develop the subject, then end with a summary—when in 1,000 words or less you say the same thing three times—you are bound either to bore your readers or to give the impression of talking down to them.

In some formats a conclusion *should* be a summary—that is its purpose. But in the more casual ABA form—the sort you find in most writing for general readers—you can (and should) return to the beginning without merely repeating yourself. Shape your conclusion as you shape an introduction, by starting with something specific. Find a quote, an anecdote, or a description that reinforces your thesis:

> Toward the end of our interview, Dick said he was about to finish a translation of the Book of Job. I asked him what he was going to undertake next in his spare time—become an astronaut? He didn't answer at first, but stared out the window as he softly played some Chopin, the underbite of his jaw and the overhang of his brow giving him a studious, Cro-Magnon look. Then he turned to me. "This may sound funny to you, but I'm a little burnt out playing and singing for my supper, and I've been thinking of doing something really different, something really vulgar and wild and fun. I'm going to become a professional wrestler for a while. I'll make a terrific villain." There seems to be no end to the surprising turns that Dick Major takes.

Thus, we land right back at the thesis of the essay, but not in a way that merely repeats it word for word. We have a sense of closure that reinforces the thesis without being obtrusive.

Many people picture the kinds of paragraphs we have been discussing as funnels or pyramids in terms of their specific and general elements. The *introductory paragraph* we've described looks like a pyramid:

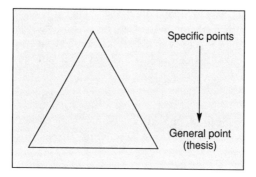

For the *body paragraphs* the pyramid is turned upside down and looks like a funnel:

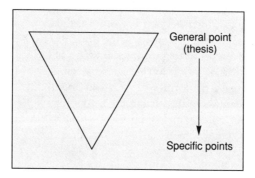

And the *concluding paragraph* looks like a pyramid again:

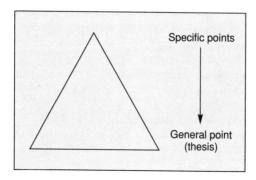

The solid structure of ABA form and general-specific/specific-general paragraphs provides a clarity that makes them particularly useful for on-the-spot writing tasks: essay tests, impromptu essays (and speeches), letters to the editor, and the like. Their simplicity makes them flexible enough to use for other types of writing as well, and in such a way that no one need notice the formula.

APPLICATIONS

1. Write an essay on the thesis, "Clothes reveal mood," using ABA form. Follow the form precisely, but feel free to get started by using any discovery strategies you find helpful. Draw your major points and your specifics from your own experience, from the experiences of others, from your observations, conversations, and reading.

After you've completed a draft, write a paragraph about your experience with ABA form: did you find it helpful, limiting, or what?

2. For your writing group, write an essay of two or three pages on an object that has made a difference in your life. Try to use ABA form both to generate ideas and to structure your essay. Write an introduction that both catches readers' attention and states your thesis explicitly, at least three body paragraphs that develop it, and a conclusion that restates it. Explain when and how the object came into your life and what a difference it has made using as many details as you think necessary.

3. Looking through anthologies, magazines, and the features section of the newspaper, see if you can find three pieces that use ABA form. If you can, use them as examples to prove the flexibility of ABA form. If not, try to adapt several of the articles you've read so that they fit ABA form. Write a brief essay about your findings.

4. Use ABA form to write a letter to a friend or relative that explains ABA form and its various uses. Before sending the letter, bring it to class and read it to your writing group for their constructive criticism. Rewrite it (if necessary) and mail it off.

5. Students are often intimidated by the idea of thesis, because they believe a thesis should be an important or profound idea. Not so. A thesis can be as small as a minor preference or whim, and still work. Here are some examples of theses, none of which is original or profound, but all of which can provide the basis for a perfectly respectable essay:

- CDs are a better buy than cassettes.
- Dogs are good pets for kids.
- Dogs are bad pets for kids.
- Paper routes teach responsibility.

- Paper routes teach irresponsibility.
- Television is a drug.

With these in mind, generate five theses of your own based on experience and personal preference. Then, generate at least three major points for each thesis. Put these points in their best working order, and make a quick ABA outline for each thesis. (This is good practice for writing essay test answers, by the way.)

Rhetorical Strategies

More than two thousand years ago, the Greek philosopher Aristotle described several different methods that *all* writers and speakers use to generate, develop, and support ideas. His descriptions were so apt that rhetoricians, with much modification, have used versions of Aristotle's "topoi" or "topics" ever since. (We prefer to call them "rhetorical strategies.") Like professional formats, they are not mutually exclusive. In fact, you will seldom see one strategy used in isolation. But they are distinguishable, and once you're acquainted with them, you will find them everywhere in both writing and speaking. You have probably used at least some of them yourself, whether you knew it or not.

While some disagreement exists about which strategies deserve an entire category, we are going to discuss eight in detail, based very loosely on Aristotle's original categories.

- *Description* explains how something looks, sounds, feels, smells.
- *Chronology* depicts sequences in time, from stories to technical processes.
- *Exemplification* illustrates a point with specific examples.
- *Definition* explains what something means.
- *Classification* divides things into groups.
- *Comparison and Contrast* puts two things side by side to find significant similarities and differences.
- *Cause and Effect* explains how one thing leads to another.
- *Argumentation* persuades the reader to adopt a point of view or a course of action.

Knowing these strategies can help you generate ideas and develop a subject from the beginning. Suppose you're assigned to write something about the mass media. One of your first concerns is to *define* the phrase: Exactly what are the mass media? Definition, you will find, often gets you involved in *classification*. The mass media fall into at least two groups—print and voice/image—each of which can be subdivided: print into newspapers, magazines, books; voice/image into radio, television, and film. But important questions remain: should the mass media be confined to print and broadcasting? Might you make a case that shopping malls be regarded as a form of mass media?

Let's say you decide to explore the idea of shopping malls as mass media. You would need to think of a mall in terms of, say, a newspaper, considering certain significant similarities and differences—that is, you would be involved in *comparison and contrast*. Thinking specifically of malls and newspapers, you would have to come up with particular instances of each, and of various aspects of each, thereby using *exemplification*. At the same time you would probably consider physical aspects of newspapers and malls—the way they look, sound, smell—and thus you'll have a go at *description*. You may know or learn something about how newspapers are produced, or you may remember a story about something that happened in a mall—and thus be concerned, however briefly, with *chronology*.

By entertaining the idea of a shopping mall as one of the mass media, you may wind up examining how malls affect the way we live, which is to say you'll use *cause and effect*. And you may wish to make a persuasive case that shopping malls should be considered mass media, thus relying on *argumentation*. The essay that grows out of these explorations would likely involve some, if not all, of these strategies, as well.

Thus, all the rhetorical strategies can help generate ideas from the outset by suggesting various ways to approach and develop a subject. Since they're so widely used, readers and writers alike turn to them almost naturally. Think of them as close friends, always helpful and available when called upon.

Description

Etymologically, the word *describe* means "to write down from, to copy." Generally, description is a copy in words of something in space—an object or mechanism, a person, a place—that is detailed enough to distinguish the subject from everything or everyone else. Descriptions of even the same subject can vary widely, depending on the audience and purpose. Here's a typical description from a "Wanted" poster:

> WANTED
>
> James Johnson: Age 43, 6' 1" Caucasian male, blond, blue-green eyes. Large "mother" tattoo on upper left arm and several large oblong moles on both forearms. Small scar on right cheek. Usually wears glasses. Athletic injury causes slight limp in right leg. Often wears sweatshirts, jeans, and sneakers.

With this description—even without a photograph—one could probably pick James Johnson out of a line-up or out of a crowd: the details here distinguish Johnson physically from other men. One could use other details that would distinguish him in other ways:

> James Johnson: Middle-aged, blond, blue-eyed male. A little taller than average. Enjoys Big Macs and chocolate shakes and brushes his teeth with Crest. Refuses to drive cars with automatic transmissions. Has been married five times. Prefers plaid boxer shorts. Reads much at night and goes south in the winter.

This description wouldn't help one pick James Johnson out of a line-up, but it gives a better picture of Johnson's personality than the first. If the purpose of the description were to recommend Mr. Johnson for a job or for a blind date, still other detail would be more appropriate.

The purpose of description is to enable a reader to see not in general but in particular, according to a certain purpose or function. No description can include everything. You must select. And to select effectively, you need some principle of selection. Defining audience and purpose gives you the principle of selection you need.

In selecting detail, also keep in mind the need for accuracy and surprise. Find the details that illustrate precisely the point about your subject you are making. And be on the lookout for detail that readers probably don't expect.

Let us show you what we mean. Here is a description of a place, the underground of a city, from Maxine Hong Kingston's *China Men:*

> The floor under the building was gray soil, a fine powder. Nothing had ever grown in it; it was sunless, rainless city soil. Beyond the light from one bulb the blackness began, the inside of the earth, the insides of the city. We had our flashlights ready. We chose a tunnel and walked side by side into the dark. There are breezes inside the earth. They blow cool and dry. Blackness absorbed our light. The people who lived and worked in the four stories above us didn't know how incomplete civilization is, the street only a crust. Down here under the sidewalks and the streets and the cars, the builders had left mounds of loose dirt, piles of dumped cement, rough patches of concrete tamping down and holding back some of the dirt. The posts were unpainted and not square on their pilings.

Note the many unanticipated twists and turns, some of them matters of fact (the cool and dry breezes inside the earth) and some of them similes and metaphors referring to the underside of the city. Here is a description of an object by the same author from her book *The Woman Warrior:*

> Once in a long while, four times so far for me, my mother brings out the metal tube that holds her medical diploma. On the tube are gold circles crossed with seven red lines each—"joy" ideographs in abstract. There are also little flowers that look like gears for a gold machine. According to the scraps of labels with Chinese and American addresses, stamps, and postmarks, the family airmailed the can from Hong Kong in 1950. It got crushed in the middle, and whoever tried to peel the labels off stopped because the red and gold paint came off too, leaving silver scratches that rust. Somebody tried to pry the end off before discovering that the tube pulls apart. When I open it, the smell of China flies out, a thousand-year-old bat flying heavy-headed out of the Chinese caverns where bats are as white as dust, a smell that comes from long ago, far back in the brain.

Again the passage is full of surprising twists and turns ("gears for a gold machine," "the smell of China," "a thousand-year old bat flying heavy-headed.")

In effective description, details are ordered according to some logical progression: from top to bottom or bottom to top, from left to right or right to left, from more conspicuous to less (as Kingston describes the diploma tube) or less conspicuous to more. When descriptions are haphazard, readers have trouble seeing what you want them to see.

One last point about description: writers not only describe what *is,* but also at times what *may be* or *might have been.* Fiction writers and poets do so most obviously, but we all describe what may be every time we plan something. The houses we live in, the cars we drive, the products we use, the clothes we wear—all were only imagined until description helped bring them to reality.

Chronology

There are basically two kinds of chronology: narration and process analysis. Narration deals with specific events, process analysis with procedures or natural phenomena that consistently take place in the same way. Both follow the logic of time: that is, actions and activities are related in the sequence they occur. Sometimes the relationship between actions is strictly one of sequence: I went downtown, I ran into an old friend, I looked at some jewelry, I bought a hat. Sometimes the relationship is one of cause and effect: I got a letter from the Internal Revenue Service, [therefore] I called my lawyer, and after reading the letter he [therefore] advised me to go to Argentina.

While we often think of narration as concerned with fictional events, as the stuff of novels and short stories, many essayists use narration, as well. Some essays consist primarily of narration: in his essay "Trapping Days," for example, Kurt Stadtfeld tells about the time he inadvertently trapped his cat, and in "Take the Plunge . . ." Gloria Emerson tells about making a parachute jump. Like all essayists, Stadtfeld and Emerson tell their tales to support and develop a point. At other times, essayists use one or more anecdotes—brief narrations of stories that illustrate specific points. In his essay "The Car," for example, Harry Crews begins with an anecdote to define his thesis, then relates several further anecdotes about cars he had owned to illustrate that thesis. Stories and anecdotes illustrate points effectively because they involve people, and we are all interested in people. Indeed, it is a principle of many writers to get people into their essays whatever their subject may be—a motorcycle shop, a fish market, a park, a line of shoes—simply because we find each other interesting.

Like narration, process analysis can be used to illustrate a point, but just as often—as in a recipe, for example—the point is the explanation of the process itself. Many essays are concerned with detailing processes: how to cook crawfish etouffe, how chocolate candy is manufactured, how Hopis get married, how the Marines make soldiers, how a swing set is to be put together, how to apply for a loan, how to generate and develop ideas. Scientific writing is often concerned with explaining natural processes, as in the following where Harold J. Morowitz compares the way iron is produced commercially and in the human body:

Commercial iron is produced by mixing ore (containing the oxides) with coke in a blast furnace where it is subject to a stream of very hot air. At the high temperature the oxygen combines with the coke, yielding reduced iron and carbon dioxide. The method is large scale, high temperature, and brute force.

Living systems have a much more subtle, low temperature, atom-by-atom method of solving the problem. The bacterium synthesizes and excretes into its surroundings molecules which have an extremely high affinity for binding iron at a very specific site. . . . The next step in the process is carried out by a transport system in the cell membrane which pumps the complexed metal back into the cell. Within the cytoplasm the chelator retains the iron so that it is unavailable for biochemical reactions. Two different schemes are used to pry the iron loose from the molecular claw. In one of these, the enzymes digest the binding structure. . . . In the other method, the iron is chemically reduced to the ferrous form which is then released. In either case, the metal atom is free within the cell where it is quickly utilized in making various ferroproteins.

When you begin thinking about a subject, then, consider any chronological sequences that are part of the subject, any anecdotes or processes that can help readers understand the subject more fully. You might even find that the best way to present your subject is as a narration, a story that relates a specific single experience of your own. Because one of the most basic ways we approach both the world and ideas is through stories, almost any subject can be presented chronologically in some sense or another.

Exemplification

Here is a rule that many writers live by: every time you make a general statement a reader could disagree with, back it up with specific examples. Unless it is a self-evident truth, a generalization without examples amounts to an assertion suspended in midair, like a cartoon character who has just run off a cliff. And like that character, it will fall—unless you put some specifics under it, examples that prove your point precisely.

For example: in his essay on Napoleon, Ralph Waldo Emerson asserts that Napoleon was "thoroughly unscrupulous." Without specifics that generalization could mean practically anything. To some readers it would mean that Napoleon was ruthless in war, to others that he was willing to use people in his quest for power, to others that he was a tyrannical ruler. But Emerson meant something both larger and smaller than those possibilities:

He would steal, slander, assassinate, drown, and poison, as his interest dictated. He had no generosity; but mere vulgar hatred: he was intensely selfish: he was perfidious: he cheated at cards: he was a prodigious gossip; and opened letters; and delighted in his infamous police; and rubbed his hands with joy when he had intercepted some morsel of intelligence concerning the men and women about him, boasting that "he knew everything"; and interfered with cutting the dresses of the women; and listened after the hurrahs and the compliments of the street, incognito.

By "thoroughly unscrupulous," Emerson means that Napoleon used people for his own purposes, that he abused people for the mere pleasure of it, that he wallowed in praise from any source. We understand Emerson's meaning because of his examples, and we accept that his generalization is true because his examples (assuming *they* are true) prove it.

Beginning writing students often have difficulty finding enough to say in an essay, whatever the subject. Such difficulty sometimes indicates the need for exemplification; rather than writing abstractly and generally, they need to write concretely and specifically. Effective exemplification shouldn't result in mere padding, however, adding material just for the sake of length. Exemplification means using specifics, concrete detail for a purpose—so that readers can better understand what you are talking about. For example, when a friend insists that her hometown is a great place to visit but a lousy place to live, you might want more information. Some specifics, in fact. What makes it such a lousy place to live? The high rent rates? Crime problems? Lack of parking? Pollution? What will clarify that assertion and make it vivid? If your friend can't give many specifics, you may be sure that she hasn't given her assertion much thought.

The same goes for your own assertions. Here is where the generative power of exemplification comes into play. Whenever you make an assertion, consider whether you can clarify and support it with solid examples. If you can't, consider how you might need to change the assertion, or dig deeper for better examples. This activity—moving between examples and assertions—can make you discover stronger assertions and more effective examples.

As you probably have inferred, exemplification is basic to all writing. Using examples may involve description, chronology, comparison and contrast, definition, and so on; well-chosen, telling examples sit at the heart of virtually all understanding.

Definition

Let's say you are going to write an essay on some aspect of liberal education. The term has an honorable history and a place in the dictionary, so you might think that a definition wouldn't be necessary. But it is. You can't assume that all readers will understand the term: some might think you mean education designed for or by political liberals. To spare everyone confusion—and to make sure you yourself know exactly what you mean—you need to begin with a definition:

> By "liberal education" I don't mean education designed for or by liberals in the political sense. Rather, I mean an education that gives one at least a nodding acquaintance with humanity's greatest accomplishments in both the arts and the sciences.

Note that this definition has two sides. The first tells readers what the term does *not* mean, but what it might be mistaken for. The second tells readers what you do mean by the term, equating it with something they will understand: "liberal education" equals "nodding acquaintance with humanity's greatest accomplishments in the arts and sciences."

In addition to defining something in familiar terms or in terms of what it is not (negation), you might also use one of the following modes of definition:

1. *Synonym.* X means approximately the same as Y: "A liberal education is a general education."

2. *Analytical.* X is a member of a group, characterized by several traits: "A liberal education is an introduction to major fields of knowledge. It includes theory and (where possible) practice in the arts, the sciences, history, psychology, health, philosophy, and religion."

3. *Similarity.* X is much like Y: "A liberal education is similar to a tour, only instead of visiting faraway places, you experience humankind's accomplishments, thoughts, and deeds."

4. *Example.* Instances of X are A and B: "The University of Chicago's liberal arts program involves reading and discussing great books, whereas Harvard's program offers a variety of courses in multiple disciplines, leaving students some choice."

5. *Function.* X does Y: "A liberal education helps students understand that they are part of a long cultural tradition rather than isolated beings."

6. *Stipulation.* X should mean Y, or I am using X to mean Y: "An effective liberal education means an awakening, a "coming to" as if from an unconscious state."

If you find it necessary to define something in more than a sentence or two, then you will likely use a number of these modes, perhaps even all of them. In their book *Ethical Dimensions in the Health Professions,* for instance, Ruth B. Purtilo and Christine K. Cassel identify three types of patients that health professionals dislike working with. These types are referred to derogatorily as "gomers," "gorks," and "crocks," names that obviously require defining:

> A "gomer" is typically an older man who is both dirty and debilitated. He is often a chronic alcoholic. A derelict or down-and-outer, the gomer subsists on public funds of some kind. He has an extensive history of multiple admissions to the hospital. He has real organic disease, which is usually related to poor personal hygiene, to inadequate nutrition, and to self-destructive habits such as alcohol or drug abuse and smoking.
>
> A "gork" may start out as a "gomer" but is a much sicker person. A gork is a patient who is moribund or unresponsive, generally having suffered irreversible brain damage of one sort or another. He or she is often also referred to as a "vegetable."
>
> A "crock" is someone who has many complaints for which no organic basis can be found. Such persons are often suspected of being hypochondriacs

or malingerers. (A hypochondriac is a person who genuinely believes that he or she has organic disease, but whose symptoms can be traced to neurotic personality problems. A malingerer, on the other hand, is a person who intentionally deceives the health professional to obtain secondary gain, such as disability payments or time off from work.)

Together, these definitions use many of the modes described earlier. By defining the three terms together, the authors *imply* the negative: a gomer is not a gork or a crock; a gork was once a gomer but is not a crock; a crock is neither a gomer nor a gork; a hypochrondriac is not a malingerer. We see extensive use of the familiar to define the unfamiliar: a gomer is an older man who is both dirty and debilitated. We see analysis: a gomer is a member of the genus derelict, characterized by alcoholism or drug dependence, welfare subsistence, frequent visits to the hospital, real disease. We see synonym: a gork is a vegetable. We see similarity: a crock is like a hypochondriac or a malingerer (hence the health professionals' suspicion). And we see function: a gomer lives on public welfare, abuses alcohol or drugs, smokes, eats poorly, he gets sick, he goes to the hospital a lot. The only two modes we don't see are example (although the authors do use an example in their discussion prior to the passage we quote) and stipulation.

There's a reason, in fact, that Purtilo and Cassel don't use the stipulative mode here: stipulation is most often used, not for concrete terms, but for terms that refer to broad concepts and that may have many meanings. To avoid ambiguity, you may want to stipulate exactly what you mean when you use the term or what you think the term *should* mean:

> By *love* I don't mean a feeling or an emotion or a sexual attraction between two persons, but rather the commitment of one person to serve another.

Sometimes writers find a subject important enough that they devote an entire essay to defining it, explaining in great detail what it means to them. In "Friends, Good Friends—and Such Good Friends" Judith Viorst classifies various kinds of friends, but her classification amounts to a definition of all that the idea of *friend* means to her. Norman Mailer's "The White Negro" amounts to an extended definition of "hipster" as he understands the word and the phenomenon it names. And the very title of an essay by Irving Kristol indicates that it is an extended definition: "What Is a 'Neo-Conservative'?" Such extended definitions involve not simply a literal "translation," but a detailed consideration of the concept or phenomenon expressed by the word. They always try to answer the question "What is —————?" in the broadest sense and thus amount to efforts at making sense through words of the world as we know it.

Classification

When Purtilo and Cassel describe the way health professionals divide undesirable patients into three categories (see page 200), they are using the strategy of classification. At its most limited, classification can result in this activity as stereo-typing, lumping people into categories based on superficial analysis or downright misperception. And yet to make sense of the world we must often organize it into groups and subgroups and sub-subgroups. Without a biological classification system, we would have to regard each organism not only as unique but as random, without any relationships to any other organisms. A university is a classification system students negotiate every day: it divides knowledge into colleges (arts and sciences, business, education) and it divides colleges into departments (physics, chemistry, biology) and it divides each department into different areas (mammalogy, entomology, herpetology, ichthyology, ornithology).

To realize how commonplace classification is, consider the supermarket: section by section you go through produce, bakery, dairy, meat, canned goods, beverages, cleaning aids. If the store were not classified, shopping would take much longer, stocking the shelves would be a nightmare, and taking inventory would be out of the question. Virtually everywhere you look—the classified ads in newspapers, any corporation, the American government, the library, even textbooks discussing rhetorical modes—you'll find a classification system in effect.

A couple of observations are in order. First, as the example by Purtilo and Cassel demonstrates, classification requires the use of other strategies as well—definition and exemplification most particularly. Second, no classification scheme works perfectly. Knowledge does not fall naturally into the neat categories of the university (astronomy involves mathematics and physics and chemistry, for example) any more than every grocery item finds a perfect spot on the supermarket shelf (are refried beans among the canned vegetables or in a special section of Mexican food?). In every classification scheme, there are inconsistencies, ambiguities, overlaps. There are always individual cases that don't fit. But the fact that no system is perfect does not mean that all systems are created equal. Some work better than others because they offer fewer difficulties.

Ultimately, the classification system that works best is one which serves your purpose in classifying the subject. You could classify trees, for instance, by their size, by their ability to thrive in a city, by their geographical distribution, by their foliage, by the hardness and softness of their wood, by their practical uses. Each of these criteria would provide a meaningful way of looking at trees. Classifying smokers according to the sorts of shoes they wear, on the other hand, is not likely to be meaningful. But classifying smokers according to the amount they smoke or how long they have smoked, or what they smoke—all of these can help you see the problem of smoking more clearly than you otherwise would.

When you engage in classification, you need to practice three principles:

First, *use the same criterion throughout*. Let's say you're running a workshop to help smokers break their habit. At the first session, you ask a few questions to divide your clients into coherent categories:

1. How many of you have never wanted to quit and are here now only because your doctor insists? (forced quitters)

2. How many of you want desperately to quit but have never succeeded for more than a day or two? (unsuccessful quitters)

3. How many of you have quit smoking before for at least a month and want to quit again? (temporarily successful quitters)

4. How many of you have recently quit and are here for fear of starting again? (possibly successful quitters)

These questions establish a consistent classification because they center in the same criterion: the degree of motivation to quit. Were you, after question 2, suddenly to start classifying people based on how many cigarettes they smoked every day, you'd end up with a collection of mismatched answers, a kind of information collage.

Second, *include all the parts of the subject.* If some items don't fit into any category, you need to establish either a new category (or more) or a whole new scheme. At the opening session of your stop-smoking workshop, for instance, you might find a few clients who have successfully quit several times for more than a year, and it might be necessary to give them a category of their own because they need a special treatment. Or you may find a few who have never tried to quit before but want to now that their doctors say they ought to.

Implied here is an important tip: in setting up a classification system, *look closely at the subject you're classifying.* Don't just make up categories out of your own head and then impose them on the subject. Rather, develop your categories based on your subject and the criterion you have chosen.

Third, *don't place an item into more than one category.* As we've said, no classification system is free of problems, among them the problem of overlap. But in a good classification system—one in which you've defined each category clearly—you will be able to place every item into a single category. Say you're classifying cars, and among your categories are family cars and sports cars. You note that some cars seem to have features of both these categories, their manufacturers wanting to offer the best of both worlds. But if you define your categories more clearly—based not simply on looks but on suspension systems and kinds of nonoptional equipment—you'll find that those cars giving you problems all have more characteristics of one category than the other: an Audi 5000 and a Ford Taurus are family cars, sporty though they be; the Toyota Supra is a sports car, even though it has a back seat.

Classification is one of the more popular pastimes among scientists, scholars, and writers. Judith Viorst has classified different sorts of friends. Lewis Thomas has classified different orders of medical technology. Gail Sheehy has classified six crises of adulthood. John Holt has classified three kinds of discipline. Norman Runnion has classified what he calls the different *species* of students. Greg Johnson has classified different faith healing practices. Aristotle classified the various strategies of rhetoric. Linnaeus classified the entire biological world.

Chances are, you will use this strategy in your writing lifetime many times. It is basic to the way the human mind deals with the world.

Comparison and Contrast

When we look in a mirror at our parts that come in pairs, we are first struck by likenesses: an ear on each side of the head, an eye on each side of the face, an arm on each side of the body. When we look more closely, we are struck by differences: one ear higher than the other, one eye squintier than the other, one arm thicker than the other. When we're noting likenesses, we usually say we're comparing; when we're noting differences, we usually say we're contrasting. In fact, they amount to two sides of the same activity, because we can't do one without doing the other.

We compare and contrast all the time, even more often than we classify. When we look at two things together we see both more fully than when we look at each in isolation. We're likely to emphasize likenesses if the items we're comparing seem at a glance unlike: How is a shopping mall like an ant colony? How is a city like a jungle? How is a prison like a monastery? When the items are essentially alike, considering differences will generate more interesting, illuminating insights: How does Steve Martin's approach to comedy differ from Eddie Murphy's? What are the differences between the "Today" show and "Good Morning, America"? Or between *Time* and *Newsweek*. In fact, writers commonly emphasize differences in their comparisons to bring out aspects of their subjects that might go unnoticed:

> [John] Havlicek stands in dramatic contrast to Julius Erving of the Philadelphia 76ers. Erving has the capacity to make legends come true; leaping from the foul line and slam-dunking the ball on his way down; going up for a lay-up, pulling the ball to his body and throwing under and up the other side of the rim, defying gravity and probability with moves and jumps. Havlicek looked like the living embodiment of his small-town Ohio background. He would bring the ball downcourt, weaving left, then right, looking for the path. He would swing the ball to a teammate, cut behind a pick, take the pass and release the shot in a flicker of time. It looked plain, unvarnished.
>
> —*Jeff Greenfield, "The Black and White Truth about Basketball"*

> Thin people make me tired. They've got speedy little metabolisms that cause them to bustle briskly. They're forever rubbing their bony hands together and eying new problems to tackle. I like to surround myself with sluggish, inert, easygoing fat people, the kind who believe that if you clean it up today, it'll just get dirty again tomorrow.
>
> —*Suzanne Britt, "That Lean and Hungry Look"*

In practicing comparison and contrast, you should keep in mind four basic principles.

First, *as a rule, work with two items only.* Peter Jennings and Dan Rather, *Time* and *Newsweek*, American and Chinese senses of space, black basketball players and white basketball players, fat people and thin people—writers almost always confine themselves to comparing and contrasting two items only. When more than two are involved, comparison and contrast may turn into something else—classification, for example.

Still, writers do sometimes compare and contrast more than two items, such as the speaking styles of four different candidates for a particular office. We see such extended comparison and contrast as well in consumer magazines: comparative analyses of five different cars or three brands of high chairs or ten VCRs. Generally, though, such comparisons and contrasts have to be considerably more limited than when only two items are involved.

Second, *compare and contrast only items in the same category.* Comparing and contrasting *Motor Trend* and *House and Garden* might seem easy, since the differences are so obvious, but—unless you are able to find some surprising similarities—such an exercise won't yield much interesting information. More useful would be to compare, say *Motor Trend* and *Car and Driver* or *House and Garden* and *Architectural Digest.* Unless your goal is to point out unexpected similarities, be sure to put together only things of a kind—luxury car and luxury car, teapot and teapot, love story and love story. That way you will turn up all sorts of subtle differences you (and your reader) hadn't noticed before.

Third, *use the same basis of comparison and contrast.* If you're comparing and contrasting cars on the basis of their fuel efficiency, looks and comfort are beside the point. To say that the Ford Escort is easy on gas whereas the Honda Civic has great resale value is only to confuse the issue—to such a point, in fact, that the issue itself gets lost. You may, of course, compare and contrast on the basis of more than one criterion. The principle, though, remains the same: give each criterion equal time for each item.

Fourth, *organize according to criteria or item consistently.* Whether you are comparing and contrasting two items or more, there are only two organizational patterns available, and when you choose one, you should stick to it all the way through. Organizing by criteria looks like this:

1. Initial cost
   a. Ford Escort
   b. Dodge Omni
2. Resale value
   a. Ford Escort
   b. Dodge Omni
3. Fuel economy
   a. Ford Escort
   b. Dodge Omni
4. Maintenance
   a. Ford Escort
   b. Dodge Omni

Organizing by item looks like this:

1. Ford Escort
   a. initial cost

        b. resale value
        c. fuel economy
        d. maintenance
  2. Dodge Omni
        a. initial cost
        b. resale value
        c. fuel economy
        d. maintenance

Organizing by criteria allows readers to see immediate contrasts but forces them to jump back and forth. Organizing by item allows readers to see each item whole, but, particularly if there are many criteria, it can strain readers' memories. Choose the one that is most appropriate for your subject and purpose. With both organization patterns the particular items or criteria are discussed in the same order each time. In an outline such order may seem unduly rigid and monotonous, but in a text it gives readers the sense that their needs are being looked after.

Comparison and contrast is one of the most powerful strategies for generating and developing and shaping ideas available. For almost any subject, if you find yourself at a loss about what to say, look for something *like* the subject, put the two side by side, and start noting the similarities, even the most obvious. When you have exhausted these, note all the differences, large and small. Pretty soon you will find yourself seeing significant things about each item you had never noticed before. For writing purposes your problem will be to fit everything you've learned into the limits of an essay.

Cause and Effect

One of the most common questions people ask is "why?" Why does the car keep breaking down? Why did the jet crash? Why can't I land a job? Why couldn't the North and South avoid the Civil War? In questions such as these, the motive is to solve a problem. The problem gives rise to the question, and if it's possible to find the cause of the problem, we assume, it's also possible to fix it.

We ask *why* for another reason, though—simple curiosity. Why do male dogs mark their territories? Why do some maples turn yellow in the fall, and some red? Why do blueberries grow so well in areas recently burned by fire? Such questions aren't prompted by a problem so much as the basic human desire to know, to understand. Sometimes the answers turn out to have practical value in solving some problems; more often they have the equally practical value of satisfying our curiosity and whetting our appreciation of the world we live in.

Writing that explores and explains answers to the question "why?" is also basic, and we call it *cause and effect* writing because it focuses on some phenomenon in those terms. In her essay "In Bed," for instance, Joan Didion focuses on migraine headaches in terms of cause and effect, as the following demonstrates:

> Migraine is something more than the fancy of a neurotic imagination. It is an essentially hereditary complex of symptoms, the most frequently noted

but by no means the most unpleasant of which is a vascular headache of blinding severity, suffered by a surprising number of women, a fair number of men (Thomas Jefferson had migraine, and so did Ulysses S. Grant, the day he accepted Lee's surrender), and by some unfortunate children as young as two years old. (I had my first when I was eight. It came on during a fire drill at the Columbia School in Colorado Springs, Colorado. I was taken first home and then to the infirmary at Peterson Field, where my father was stationed. The Air Corps doctor prescribed an enema.) Almost anything can trigger a specific attack of migraine: stress, allergy, fatigue, an abrupt change in barometric pressure, a contretemps over a parking ticket. A flaming light. A fire drill. One inherits, of course, only the predisposition. In other words, I spent yesterday in bed with a headache not merely because of my bad attitude, unpleasant tempers and wrong-think, but because both my grandmothers had migraine, my father has migraine and my mother has migraine.

Cause and effect writing, may also move in the other direction: not from effect to cause (Why does X happen?) but from cause to effect (What are the consequences of X?). In his essay "My Wood" E. M. Forster explores the personal consequences of owning property and defines four specific effects. Here he discusses one of these:

> In the first place, it makes me feel heavy. Property does have this effect. Property produces men of weight, and it was a man of weight who failed to get into the Kingdom of Heaven. He was not wicked, that unfortunate millionaire in the parable, he was only stout; he stuck out in front, not to mention behind, and as he wedged himself this way and that in the crystalline entrance and bruised his well-fed flanks, he saw beneath him a comparatively slim camel passing through the eye of a needle and being woven into the robe of God. The Gospels all through couple stoutness and slowness. They point out what is perfectly obvious, yet seldom realized: that if you have a lot of things you cannot move about a lot, that furniture requires dusting, dusters require servants, servants require insurance stamps, and the whole tangle of them makes you think twice before you accept an invitation to dinner or go for a bathe in the Jordan. . . .

One means of understanding virtually any subject—whether practically (as we see in Didion) or philosophically (as we see in Forster)—is through cause and effect: What brought it about? What else does it bring about? Regrettably, this strategy is one of the more difficult ones to navigate. It has four major pitfalls.

First, don't assume that because one thing precedes another, the first must be the cause of the second. It is true that causes precede effects; it is not true that *anything* which precedes something else is by definition a cause. You must establish a direct link between causes and effects.

It may be, for instance, that marijuana use leads to addiction to crack or heroin—but not necessarily and not simply because crack and heroin addicts once smoked pot. They also drank milk and chewed gum. Further, many people who smoked pot have never graduated to harder drugs. To prove that people are hooked on hard drugs *because* they once smoked marijuana requires more than a sequence of before-and-after.

Second, don't confuse effects with causes. It may seem odd, but we all fall into such confusion more often than we would like to admit. Have you ever thought that if you were only on the good side of your teacher or boss, you would get the grade or promotion you want? But being on your teacher's or boss's good side results from your doing good work, and is thus an effect of your performance. Likewise, your performance is the cause that gets you a good grade or a promotion. To be sure, an effect can become a cause, leading to another effect, which in turn can become another cause (as a result of the grade or raise, you work even harder). This dynamic cycle is what makes the confusion of cause and effect so common.

Third, don't oversimplify causes. Almost nothing happens in this world for a single, simple reason. Only in laboratory experiments, where all the variables except one are controlled, can it ever be said that a single factor is the cause. But when considering cause and effect in the mess of everyday reality, be sure you don't fall for a simplistic account. Consider all the causes. Make a list. You will find as a rule that you have more than you can reasonably explain. Emphasize the important ones, the indispensable ones, but acknowledge enough contributing causes to sound reasonable.

Fourth, don't confuse necessary and sufficient causes. Remember how Joan Didion distinguishes between the events that trigger a migraine and the fundamental cause—the inherited predisposition—without which those other factors couldn't trigger a migraine? In more technical language, those triggering events are called *sufficient causes* and the inherited predisposition is called a *necessary cause*. The difference is important but subtle.

Necessary causes are the *sine qua non* (without which nothing) of an effect—without the inherited disposition, no number of triggering events will set off a migraine. As a rule, though, necessary causes require an occasion, one or several sufficient causes, to set them off—in the case of migraines these can be "stress, allergy, fatigue, an abrupt change in barometric pressure, a contretemps over a parking ticket," or any combination thereof. The pitfall here is to think that a necessary cause must result in a certain effect, without taking into account the requirement of sufficient causes. You can't have a BB gun because you'll shoot someone's eye out. You can't drive because you'll get in a wreck. The other pitfall is to think that sufficient causes will bring about a certain effect without first defining a necessary cause. That woman is a whiz on the debate team and has a 3.9 average, so she's bound to go to law school. This man is six feet four, weighs 225 pounds, and can run a 4.6 forty; therefore, he must be a football player. All these factors amount to so many sufficient triggers, but without the necessary hammers these causes won't necessarily make anything go off: the woman may just as easily be a cab driver, the man a singer. Before leaping to certain effects, we must examine the various causes. And in examining the causes, we must distinguish between sufficient and necessary.

A common form of the cause-effect (or effect-cause) strategy is the problem-solution form. Many television commercials use some form of problem-solution. First, they depict a problem—bad breath, plaque, a desperate thirst—then they present a solution: mouthwash, toothpaste, a soft drink. This structure parallels the cause-effect strategy, but it's more specific: the cause is always some imperfection or problem that needs to be solved, and the effect is always a solution to that problem.

Indeed, whenever someone writes about a problem, he or she usually follows the problem-solution form of the cause-effect strategy. In "Politics and the English Language" George Orwell cites the deplorable style of most political writing, explains the consequences of bad language, then proposes solutions to the problem: specific rules for writing well. In the Declaration of Independence Thomas Jefferson cites the problems that colonists have with England, then proposes a solution: independence. In "Letter from Birmingham Jail" Martin Luther King, Jr. defines the problem—continuing segregation—then proposes the solution: pursuing integration via civil disobedience.

When you are motivated by a problem you want to solve, or when you're aware of a solution that you're sure will solve a problem, use the problem-solution form of the cause-effect strategy. Like other discovery strategies, cause/effect will help you explore aspects of the subject that you might not otherwise have considered.

Argumentation

Persuading people to agree with your point is perhaps the most common motive for writing. As Joan Didion puts it, "In many ways writing is the act of saying *I*, of imposing oneself upon other people, of saying *listen to me, see it my way, change your mind.*" In terms of argumentation we would add to her list *and act accordingly.* Argumentation has these two distinct but closely related objectives: to convince people to think a certain way, and to convince them to act a certain way.

You have developed a classification for something? You need to do more than explain it—you need to persuade your readers that it works. You have your own definition of family or enlightened self-interest? You need to persuade your readers that it makes sense. You have a solution for a problem? You need to persuade your readers that they should adopt it. In fact, the point of having a thesis is to prove it, to get your readers to say at the end, "You're right, you're absolutely right!" or at least "Hmm, maybe I'd better think about that again."

There are many goals for argumentation, but we'll concentrate here on one of the most common: arguing for a proposal that will solve a specific problem. To argue a proposal successfully, you must take care of four tasks.

One, *establish a need.* You must define and demonstrate the existence of a problem. If the status quo is in good shape, nothing new is needed. But if something is amiss, then a new way of thinking or acting is in order. In his famous "Letter from Birmingham Jail," Martin Luther King, Jr., details the pervasiveness and destructiveness of segregation to convince those who had misgivings about his tactics for attaining civil rights that blacks had to do something radical. In the Declaration of Independence Jefferson catalogs English mistreatment of the colonies at length to prove that something drastic had to be done.

Two, *set forth a solution*. You must define what will work to solve the problem—namely, your proposal or thesis or idea. You must explain it both in the abstract, as an idea, and in the particular, with detail and example. To make it perfectly clear, you must define and demonstrate what it is not, distinguishing it from anything that it might be confused with. In his "Letter," for example, King proposes civil disobedience, defining it as peacefully disobeying laws that unjustly discriminate against certain citizens in order to get those laws changed. He also very carefully explains that the civil disobedience he advocates does not mean disobeying the law just because it happens to get in one's way. In the Declaration, Jefferson just as carefully defines the proposal—severance of relations with England, self-governance for the colonies—and just as carefully distinguishes it from irresponsible rebellion.

Three, *show benefits*. Here you must get specific: Just what will your proposal accomplish? How will it remedy the situation or get the job done? Considering the proposal as cause, what specific effects will it have? You should also point out that these benefits don't currently exist, unless your description of the status quo has already done that job. King, for example, points out that civil disobedience can lead to the end of segregation, allowing millions of people to enjoy the civil rights guaranteed them by the Constitution but denied them under current laws. In the Declaration Jefferson points out that independence will enable the citizens of the colonies to enjoy their civil rights—life, liberty, and the pursuit of happiness—which, under English rule, they are consistently denied.

Four, *refute options*. You must demonstrate the superiority of your proposal to all other options. Without such a demonstration, your readers will remain unconvinced. In his "Letter" King points out at length all the other courses that blacks had tried to no avail—requesting, petitioning, bringing suits to court. He also refutes various arguments against civil disobedience and suggests that the only alternative to his proposal at this point could be violence. In the Declaration Jefferson lists the colonists' various futile efforts to redress their grievances in order to show that nothing less than severing relations would work.

The way we've ordered the tasks here is common, but it's not the only order possible. The Declaration defines and defends the solution before detailing the problem. Why? The remedy is short and simple, the ailment long and complicated. The recitation of grievances, as it goes on and on, makes the remedy seem more and more warranted, more and more reasonable. The order in which you take care of these four tasks, then, depends on the particular case.

Let's look now at how you can think your way through a subject and argue it effectively. You can use this method for arguing any part of your case (the need, the solution, and so on), or you can use it as a way of structuring your entire argument. We draw on Stephen Toulmin's scheme, which begins with *data* and *claim:*

DATA ──────────────────────────────→ CLAIM

Data are the facts and observations upon which you base your claim, or conclusion. *Claim:* Getting a bachelor's degree does not automatically mean landing a high-paying job. *Data:* A high percentage of students graduating in recent years found no work at all, or work in fields outside or beneath their qualifications.

Fairly simple so far. Data-to-claim may seem familiar as basic inductive reasoning. But now we need to add a crucial third factor, the *warrant:*

The warrant is a statement that shows a connection between the data and the claim, signaled by the word "since." If you claim that a bachelor's degree is no guarantee of a decent job, and your data show a high percentage of graduates not getting jobs in their fields, you need to include a warrant that connects the two:

> Since (*warrant*) college graduates are conscientiously applying for jobs in their fields in record numbers, and (*data*) a high percentage don't find jobs, then (*claim*) getting a bachelor's degree does not automatically guarantee a job.

You now have the rudiments of a helpful means of thinking through arguments. But we need to add three more elements: a *qualifier,* a *rebuttal,* and a *backing.* The qualifier and rebuttal allow you to add exceptions without losing your whole case. For our argument about college graduates, you might want to add "in most fields" as a qualifier and also an "unless" statement to rebut those who know plenty of graduates in certain fields who found jobs quite easily (say in computer science, applied mathematics, and science teaching). Thus, the nearly complete argument now goes something like this:

> Since (*warrant*) college graduates are conscientiously applying for jobs in their fields in record numbers, and (*data*) a high percentage don't find jobs, then (*qualifier*) in most fields (*rebuttal*) with the exception of computer science, applied mathematics, and science teaching, (*claim*) getting a bachelor's degree does not automatically guarantee a job.

Now all that's left is to add whatever backing is needed to support the warrant. Here is the full argument, with all six parts:

(*Backing*) Interviews with recent college graduates in the job market reveal that (*warrant*) college graduates are conscientiously applying for jobs in their fields in record numbers, and since (*data*) a high percentage don't find jobs, then (*qualifier*) in most fields (*rebuttal*) with the exception of computer science, applied mathematics, and science teaching, (*claim*) getting a bachelor's degree does not automatically guarantee a job.

That's a stiff, unwieldy sentence to say the least, but it contains everything you'd need to develop a case for, say, opening more job markets for college graduates. Here is a diagram of all six parts:

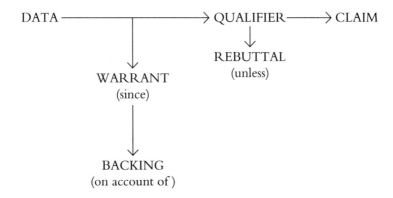

How does this scheme help you generate arguments? Being aware of these parts—not as a straitjacket into which all arguments must rightly fit, but as a free-flowing costume with many parts—you can consider where you need more material and more backing in order to dress your case for best effect.

Finally, remember that when you're thinking about making the best case possible, you need to appeal not only to the readers' reason, but also to their emotions. Emotions are indispensable and unavoidable. There is nothing wrong in appealing to emotion so long as the appeal is consistent with logic and fact. It is the argument that appeals to emotion at the expense of logic and fact that is false, cheap, sentimental, even propagandistic:

> We should keep the foreigners out of America. They are dirty and dishonest. Half of them are illiterate. They take good jobs from American citizens. They breed like flies. Most are communists, bound and determined to bury us. They rape our women and corrupt our children.

You can find "thought" of this order if you know where to look, and sometimes it temporarily succeeds (in the 1930s entire nations fell for it), but in the long run it dies of its own diseased logic.

An appeal to emotion consistent with healthy logic and fact is another story, as this excerpt from King's "Letter from Birmingham Jail" attests:

We should never forget that everything Adolf Hitler did in Germany was "legal" and everything the Hungarian freedom fighters did in Hungary was "illegal." It was "illegal" to aid and comfort a Jew in Hitler's Germany. Even so, I am sure that, had I lived in Germany at the time, I would have aided and comforted my Jewish brothers. If today I lived in a Communist country where certain principles dear to the Christian faith are suppressed, I would openly advocate disobeying that country's anti-religious laws.

King cites certain emotionally charged facts to show that we should not always obey the law, because the law (as these facts prove) is not the final moral authority by which we should guide and judge our behavior.

A last word: in appealing to emotion, don't stack your nouns with adjectives telling your readers how they are supposed to feel. Let your facts do the work. Put them down and explain what they mean, as simply and honestly as you can: don't just tell, show.

APPLICATIONS

1. With your writing group, discuss the "Clothes Reveal Mood" essay you wrote in ABA form for Application 1 on page 193. Did you use any rhetorical strategies, such as chronology, exemplification, description? Could parts of your essay be strengthened by using a more conscious application of those strategies? If so, revise the essay and discuss your revision with your writing group.

2. Answer these questions briefly, either for yourself in a journal or for your classmates and instructor:

    a. Which of the rhetorical strategies are you most comfortable with? Why?

    b. Have you consciously used any of them before? If so, which ones? If not, do you think you'll be consciously using them in the future? How so?

    c. Now that you've become familiar with several other formats, what do you think of the ABA shape?

3. Examine some books, magazines, and newspapers for examples of the rhetorical strategies. Bring an example of each to class. With your writing group, analyze these examples to evaluate their relative success or failure.

4. Write to a family member or a close friend, explaining the rhetorical strategies. Describe how you have used them in essays, and how they can help you generate and develop material for essays. Be specific—*show* the person you are writing what you mean.

5. Take any three subjects about which you're at least moderately curious and investigate them with the rhetorical strategies in mind—that is, use the strategies in exploring these subjects. See which strategies seem to turn up most for which subjects, and see which strategies simply seem to work better for you. See also the different sorts of things each strategy tends to turn up. Take notes. Then write an essay on each subject, using those strategies that suit it.

Exploratory Forms

Almost all writing involves both exploration and explanation. We explore a subject to find out what to say, and then explain what we have found so that readers will understand. Even when we know something inside out, writing about it helps us learn more about it. Still, in the forms we have considered so far, the emphasis is more on explanation than on exploration for its own sake. However, an essay can have as its goal not straightforward explanation but exploration, a setting forth into new territory to discover whatever it is you (and thus your readers) discover. We introduce you here to two forms that emphasize exploration.

Whenever you explore any new area, you have a choice of two basic strategies: either you go through it from one side to the other, making a line; or you establish a center from which you go out and to which you return several times, making circles that together make a larger circle. The same two basic strategies shape the exploratory essay: *line form*, otherwise known as incremental form, resembles beads on a string; *circle form,* otherwise known as theme-and-variations form, resembles a hub and spokes.

Line Form

"Line in nature is not found," said Emerson, but line is found in writing all the time. The very arrangement of the words on the page is linear, of course, but we mean something beyond that. In fact, a great deal of writing originates as lists. History begins as chronicle, a list of important events in chronological order. And such a list quickly becomes an exploration—as the writer tries to discover the relative importance of every event, very soon the writer starts exploring relations among events, leading to questions about the whys and wherefores of the past and, by implication, of the present.

Poets have enjoyed making catalogs from the beginning—and what is a catalog but a carefully shaped list? The poet explores a subject by following a train of thought, then shapes those thoughts to see where the subject has taken itself:

I hear America singing, the varied carols I hear,
Those of mechanics, each one singing his as it should be blithe and strong,
The carpenter singing his as he measures his plank or beam,
The mason singing his as he makes ready for work, or leaves off work,
The boatman singing what belongs to him in his boat, the deck-hand singing

on the steamboat deck,
The shoemaker singing as he sits on his bench, the hatter singing as he stands,
The wood-cutter's song, the plowboy's on his way in the morning, or at noon
  intermission or at sundown,
The delicious singing of the mother, or of the young wife at work, or of the
  girl sewing or washing,
Each singing what belongs to him or her and to none else,
The day what belongs to the day—at night the party of young fellows, robust,
  friendly,
Singing with open mouths their strong melodious songs.

— Walt Whitman, "I Hear America Singing"

Brainstorming—concentrating on a subject as an individual or a group to
see what turns up—always involves making a list, usually several: one thing leads
to another, which in turn leads to another, and so forth, from the familiar to the
not-so familiar to the unknown and strange. And a good many exploratory essays
are made in the image of that basic shape, or parts of them are. In her essay on
the Santa Ana, a sustained wind that periodically attacks Los Angeles from the
desert, Joan Didion uses the line shape to explore some of the effects of a particular Santa Ana:

> The longest single Santa Ana period in recent years was in 1957, and it
> lasted not the usual three or four days but fourteen days, from November 21
> until December 4. On the first day 25,000 acres of the San Gabriel Mountains
> were burning, with gusts reaching 100 miles an hour. In town, the wind
> reached Force 12, or hurricane force, on the Beaufort Scale; oil derricks were
> toppled and people were ordered off the downtown streets to avoid injury
> from flying objects. On November 22 the fire in the San Gabriel was out of
> control. On November 24 six people were killed in automobile accidents, and
> by the end of the week the *LA Times* was keeping a box score of traffic deaths.
> On November 26 a prominent Pasadena attorney, depressed about money,
> shot and killed his wife, their two sons, and himself. On November 27 a South
> Gate divorcee, 22, was murdered and thrown from a moving car. On
> November 30 the San Gabriel fire was still out of control, and the wind in
> town was blowing 80 miles an hour. On the first day of December four people
> died violently, and on the third the wind began to break.

Note that this line is a chronicle of sorts—it is a list of events in chronological
order—but the events have more in common than simple succession. They all
seem to arise from a common cause, and they all suggest mayhem on the increase.
This is why line form is also called incremental form: it builds and builds.

Clearly, using this line shape requires caution and discretion. You can string
beads endlessly, but no reader will be willing to follow after a certain point. What
is the readers' point of no return? Where do you stop? There are no formulas for
answering this question, as different readers have different attention spans and different interests. But two things can help. First, you can create suspense. You can

make a line that's clearly going somewhere without disclosing where it's going until you arrive. Look at how this essay begins:

> A bird that eats feathers, a mammal that never drinks, a fish that grows a fishing line and worm on its head to catch other fish. Creatures in a nightmare? No, they are very much with us as co-inhabitants of this earth.
>
> —*Jean George, "That Astounding Creator, Nature"*

Note that George does not push the suspense very far—three examples and a question: this essay appeared in *Reader's Digest* and, according to that magazine's style, had to be cut down to essential information. But by asking questions and withholding the answer for a moment, George provokes and holds our interest: What are these strange things anyway? Although the essay is not a whodunit, it still uses the principle of suspense.

In his essay "The Deltoid Factor" written for a more contemplative periodical, novelist Walker Percy also begins with a line, but at much greater length than does George:

> Why does man feel so sad in the twentieth century?
>
> Why does man feel so bad in the very age when, more than in any other age, he has succeeded in satisfying his needs and making over the world for his own use?
>
> Why has man entered on an orgy of war, murder, torture, and self-destruction unparalleled in history and in the very century when he had hoped to see the dawn of universal peace and brotherhood?
>
> Why do people often feel bad in good environments and good in bad environments?
>
> Why do people often feel so bad in good environments that they prefer bad environments?
>
> Why does a man often feel better in a bad environment?
>
> Why is a man apt to feel bad in a good environment, say suburban Short Hills, New Jersey, on an ordinary Wednesday afternoon? Why is the same man apt to feel good in a very bad environment, say an old hotel on Key Largo during a hurricane?

And the questions keep coming for over three more pages, creating an increasingly bleak picture of the human condition and thus increasing our desire to find the answer.

The second way to meet the challenge of keeping readers reading is to offer them surprise. Watch the surprises Shana Alexander springs on readers in discussing how America is essentially a "Kid's Country":

> Our civilization is child-centered, child-obsessed. A kid's body is our physical ideal. Weightwatchers grunt and pant. Sages jog from sea to shining sea. Plastic surgeons scissor and tuck up. New hair sprouts, transplanted, on wisdom's brow. One way or another we are determined to "keep in shape,"

and invariably this means keeping a kid's shape—which we then outfit in baby-doll ruffles, sneakers and blue jeans.

Alexander's line extends from dieting to working out to jogging to plastic surgery to clothes. It's coherent, but no reader can anticipate every item. Furthermore, within the beads, so to speak, Alexander springs more surprises: jogging "from sea to shining sea," for example, and growing transplanted hair "on wisdom's brow." Note how these surprises arise naturally out of the subject: if you travel from sea to sea, you'll find joggers; even better, she takes her phrase from a song about an ideal America very different from the America she's criticizing. Alexander springs surprises within surprises, yet not one of them comes out of nowhere. That's an important point. You can easily spring surprises on the readers, but unless they're something more than cute tricks—unless they grow naturally out of your subject and purpose—readers are likely to throw the work aside in disgust.

In making a line, then, you have an obligation to the reader. But you also have an obligation to the subject, to treat it well by exploring it in sufficient detail to find something significant. Don't make your line too short for fear of boring your readers. Consider the passage by Walker Percy. Had he stopped after the fourth question, out of deference for readers with a 30-second attention span, he would have seriously shortchanged the important ramifications of the subject. Wisely, Percy decided to do the subject justice.

Circle Form

Think of the opening four notes of Beethoven's Fifth Symphony. Think of them in full orchestra, with strings and winds and horns, the works: TAH—TAH—TAH—TAAAAAH! Also recall the next several measures after the opening, how the orchestra repeats the phrase and varies it and repeats it again. It is no accident that this opening phrase is unforgettable.

Beethoven was working with a *motif,* a recurring pattern that becomes a familiar theme and serves as a sort of home base, the place to which the melodic line keeps returning and from which it launches forth again into more variation. Thus the motif is sometimes thought of as the hub, the melodic lines and their return making spokes and arcs, all the lines and arcs together composing a wheel as in Figure 9.1.

Writers use motifs, too—images or lines that they repeat from time to time, bringing the work back around to that point. A well-known poetic form, the villanelle, repeats two lines a total of eight times (four times each) in only nineteen lines. Dylan Thomas wrote the most famous villanelle in English—note how different it is from the catalogue by Whitman:

> Do not go gentle into that good night,
> Old age should burn and rave at close of day;
> Rage, rage against the dying of the light.

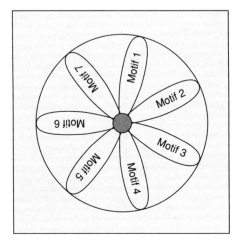

Figure 9.1   Motif Wheel

Though wise men at their end know dark is right,
Because their words had forked no lightning they
Do not go gentle into that good night.

Good men, the last wave by, crying how bright
Their frail deeds might have danced in a green bay,
Rage, rage against the dying of the light.

Wild men who caught and sang the sun in flight
And learn, too late, they grieved it on its way
Do not go gentle into that good night.

Grave men, near death, who see with blinding sight
Blind eyes could blaze like meteors and be gay,
Rage, rage against the dying of the light.

And you, my father, there on the sad height,
Curse, bless, me now with your fierce tears, I pray.
Do not go gentle into that good night.
Rage, rage against the dying of the light.

With the line you go on and on from A to Z; with the circle you return periodically, from wherever you've traveled back to A. The danger of the circle is that you repeat and repeat, beyond anyone's tolerance for repetition, but in fact you have to repeat yourself a lot before you get into trouble. More than most beginning writers realize, readers don't just tolerate various forms of repetition—they positively enjoy it. Public speakers know this well. The following is a famous example of repetition by Martin Luther King, Jr., one of the century's greatest speakers:

> I have a dream that one day on the red hills of Georgia the sons of for-
> mer slaves and the sons of former slaveowners will be able to sit down together
> at the table of brotherhood.
>
> I have a dream that one day even the state of Mississippi, a desert state
> sweltering with the heat of injustice and oppression, will be transformed into
> an oasis of freedom and justice.
>
> I have a dream that my four little children will one day live in a nation
> where they will not be judged by the color of their skin but by the content of
> their character.
>
> I have a dream today.
>
> I have a dream that one day the state of Alabama, whose governor's lips
> are presently dripping with the words of interposition and nullification, will be
> transformed into a situation where little black boys and black girls will be able
> to join hands with little white boys and white girls and walk together as sisters
> and brothers.
>
> I have a dream today.
>
> I have a dream that one day every valley shall be exalted, every hill and
> mountain shall be made low, the rough places will be made plain, and the
> crooked places will be made straight, and the glory of the Lord shall be re-
> vealed, and all flesh shall see it together.

The repetition builds excitement and intensity, creating an unforgettable speech.

Another way to use the circle form is to return at the end of an essay to its beginning, as ABA form does. E. B. White begins his short essay "Democracy" with this sentence:

> We received a letter from the Writers' War Board the other day asking
> for a statement on The Meaning of Democracy.

He ends it with this:

> Democracy is a request from a War Board, in the middle of a morning
> in the middle of a war, wanting to know what democracy is.

William G. Wing begins and ends his essay "Christmas Comes First on the Banks" in the same place:

> The Christmas sun rises first, in America, on trawlermen fishing the un-
> dersea meadows of Georges Bank. . . .
>
> Christmas came first to men on lonely meadows. It will come first again
> to the men on the lonely meadows offshore, fishing the Bank in boats
> wreathed by seabirds.

When an essay returns at the end to its beginning, making the circle complete, it actually takes us further, in a sense. Because of the journey in between, we see the beginning in a way we didn't at first. The essay explores the meaning of the be-ginning—a request from a War Board asking what democracy is, Christmas coming first to fishermen at sea—so that, when we wind up right back where we started, we now understand the theme or motif more deeply.

Whether you make a little circle within an essay or a big circle of the essay itself, keep in mind that the purpose is to explore the meaning of the theme you are repeating. Like White and Wing, Dylan Thomas repeats the two refrain lines in "Do Not Go Gentle Into That Good Night" in such a way as to discover their deeper meanings. King returns to the image of the dream to continue to discover all that it includes. If there is no exploration, the return amounts to simple repetition, just saying the same thing over and over again, like spinning wheels in the mud and sinking in deeper and deeper. Readers want to get somewhere, to an enlarged version of where they started.

In deciding which of the two exploratory forms to use, respect your intuition. You may find that the best one is the one you use spontaneously. But also be mindful that certain types of subjects lend themselves to the line while others lend themselves to the circle. Any type of event, for example, flows naturally as a line, because an event is a sequence of smaller events, one after the other. Ideas and issues, on the other hand, may be easier to circle, because they require investigation from different points of view.

Finally, how do you know whether a subject is appropriate for an exploratory essay? The answer: when it involves open-ended complexities rather than problems and solutions. The difference between the two is simple yet profound. Some questions are open-ended and don't lend themselves to simple answers or any answers at all: What is love? Why do good people die for no reason? What makes good people do evil things? Such questions are complex, mysterious; they won't be "solved" by any one answer or a particular course of action. Other questions, however, can be at least partially answered: What novels deserve attention at America's universities? What courses should a liberal arts education include? What's a reasonable way to teach writing? Should we continue to explore space?

We must all consider open-ended questions that don't lend themselves to easy answers because our speculations about such questions define us, our values, our sense of who we are and where we're going. Is space exploration more important than feeding the hungry? We cannot answer the question in the same way that we can figure out how to build a bridge. Yet we must consider the question, and come up with an answer of some sort, because we must decide whether to support such explorations. And while no answer may be definitive, some answers are better than others—they are better informed, better reasoned, better felt.

When your subject involves a mystery, then, it well may be the sort that deserves or even requires exploration. We make a try at it, then, an attempt to understand these issues that will always be a part of people's lives. And that is what the *essay* was originally all about—not a conclusion once and for all, but, as the word is translated from the French, a try, an attempt, an effort to make some sense of our lives.

APPLICATIONS

1. Explore any ideas you have about the relationship between clothes and moods. Let your mind roam freely over the subject to see if you tend to think in terms of a line or a circle—unfolding the idea step by step, or launching into it from some motif to which you keep returning. Make notes according to one shape or the other.

2. Bring to class examples of both exploratory forms that you turn up in your own reading, either for courses or for pleasure. A good start would be the editorial page of your newspaper. If one writer particularly strikes your fancy, read a number of his or her pieces, and see if you discern a preference for one form over another.

3. Make a list of all the motifs in your own thought and conversation— those themes you habitually return to over and over again. Note the ones that you might be able to use in a circular-shaped essay.

4. Make a list of anything you can think of about which you might be able to make a line-shaped essay. Write them out and save them.

Professional Formats

Even people who are not professional writers often have to write as part of their job: scientists, architects, managers, social workers, ministers, secretaries, and parents write reports, memos, speeches, proposals, announcements, sermons, letters, minutes, notes to the teacher. Invariably they need to explain something, to *expose* it, to make it apparent and thus understandable. For that reason, such writing is often called *expository*. Often they need to make a case for a thesis as well, and sometimes, therefore, they can use the ABA form. In many cases, however, they need to use some other format, one that is prescribed by their profession or the particular office they hold or their boss. Because these generic formats come with the job, we call them "professional." We're adapting them here to academic writing, but you will likely encounter some form of them in all kinds of on-the-job writing.

For our purposes, then, let's consider five professional formats: *literature reviews, statements of methodology, conclusions, abstracts and summaries,* and *prefaces.* These titles may seem somewhat obscure, but the formats themselves are essentially simple. (They are not mutually exclusive, by the way—one piece of writing can incorporate two or more, even all five.)

Literature Reviews

Occasionally you will find it necessary to review what others have written concerning a particular topic. This overview is designed to give a sense of what is known, as well as areas of agreement and disagreement. Writing such a review means first skimming lists of titles in the area under review, then, after reading the literature that seems to address the topic, deciding which articles and books are worth citing. For each of these, you write a quick explanation of its contribution and importance, ordering each according to some principle you've determined.

A review, then, amounts to an annotated list, one that often involves a hierarchy because the literature falls into various categories. As you can infer, you may do this kind of review with or without trying to prove a thesis.

In their articles and books scientists, scholars, and academicians often have to include reviews of other studies to make clear the need and value of their own. An example:

> In their introduction to *New Directions in Composition Research,* Richard Beach and Lillian Bridwell (1984) call for the development of a theory of writing that takes a global view of composing processes, incorporating, among other things, the important matter of context. "Studying the writer without taking the many dimensions of context into account," they remark, "is a little like studying animal life by visiting zoo cages (6)."
>
> This sentiment echoes that of Lee Odell and Dixie Goswami (1984), two researchers who have begun to look at writing within functional contexts of production. Citing a long tradition of studies of the relationship between social context and speech, they observe, "Writing does not exist in a vacuum; . . . a writer's purpose and knowledge of audience and subject matter shape the stylistic and substantive choices the writer makes" (22).
>
> Social context has not exactly been ignored in composition studies; it figures centrally in several seminal works, both theoretical and descriptive (e.g., Britton, Burgess, Martin, McLeod, & Rosen, 1975; Emig, 1971; Kinneavy, 1971). Other contextual perspectives have been offered by Crowhurst and Piche (1979); Myers (1980); Nystrand (1982); and Rosenthal (1983), who treats context in terms of the *meaning* sources available to a writer during composing. . . . But although widely acknowledged, context in composition remains largely unexplored.
>
> —*Deborah Brandt, "Toward an Understanding of Context in Composition"*

Note how Brandt runs through the literature to point out not only the acknowledged importance of her subject, but also its neglect, and thus the purpose and value of her study.

Sometimes it is necessary to survey the conceptual background of a subject—that is, to review the basic philosophical assumptions and attitudes that have existed or that now exist concerning the subject. Here is an example of such a review:

Pornography has been so thickly glossed over with the patina of chic these days in the name of verbal freedom and sophistication that important distinctions between freedom of political expression (a democratic necessity), honest sex education for children (a societal good) and ugly smut (the deliberate devaluation of the role of women through obscene, distorted depictions) have been hopelessly confused. Part of the problem is that those who traditionally have been the most vigorous opponents of porn are often those same people who shudder at the explicit mention of any sexual subject. Under their watchful, vigilante eyes, frank and free dissemination of educational materials relating to abortion, contraception, the act of birth, and female biology in general is also dangerous, subversive and dirty. (I am not unmindful that a frank and free discussion of rape, "the unspeakable crime," might well give these righteous vigilantes further cause to shudder.) Because the battle lines were falsely drawn a long time ago, before there was a vocal women's movement, the anti-pornography forces appear to be, for the most part, religious, Southern, conservative and right-wing, while the pro-porn forces are identified as Eastern, atheistic and liberal.

—*Susan Brownmiller, Against Our Will: Men, Women, and Rape*

A review of the literature that also surveys the conceptual background looks like this:

The current resurgence of interest in animal "rights" (Singer 1975; Regan and Singer 1976; Clark 1977; Frey 1980) has resulted in much greater attention being paid to the distinction between warranted and unwarranted exploitation of animals as opposed to the simpler and more emotive concepts of kindness and cruelty (Fox and Rowan 1980). While it is important to foster behavior favoring kindness and discouraging cruelty, these concepts are not particularly useful in helping to resolve conflicts between human and animal interests, such as the use of animals in biomedical research and education. For example, we are not being kind to a frog when we pith it for a classroom demonstration, but are we being cruel? For a small but vocal minority, the answer is an unequivocal "yes." For the majority, the answer is not so clear-cut, and this is where the concept of justified and unjustified exploitation is more useful in making social cost-benefit decisions. Education plays an important role in developing social consensus on such value-laden issues (Hoskins 1979; Kieffer 1979); but, to date, most educational efforts present very limited concepts of human/animal interactions.

—*Andrew N. Rowan, "Animals in Education"*

It is possible to write an essay that amounts in its entirety to a review of the literature or the conceptual background or both. You must write a literature review:

- When your field requires it as a convention for research (such as in the sciences and education)

• When your point builds upon or disputes points made in the literature or a review establishes the context for your point.

Statements of Methodology

When you intend to use a specific method in dealing with your subject, you need to explain that methodology in more or less detail. You may analyze the economic crash of 1929, for instance, from various perspectives: Marxist, laissez faire, Freudian, Calvinistic, to cite only a few. To best understand your point your reader needs to know your approach. An example:

> I feel like saying something about this abortion issue. My credentials as an expert on the subject: none. I am an M.D. and a novelist. I will speak only as a novelist. If I give an opinion as an M.D., it wouldn't interest anybody since, for one thing, any number of doctors have given opinions and who cares about another.
>
> The only obvious credential of a novelist has to do with his trade. He traffics in words and meanings. So the chronic misuse of words, especially the fobbing off of rhetoric for information, gets on his nerves. Another possible credential of a novelist peculiar to these times is that he is perhaps more sensitive to the atrocities of the age than most. People get desensitized. Who wants to go about his business being reminded of the six million dead in the holocaust, the 15 million in the Ukraine? Atrocities become banal. But a 20th century novelist should be a nag, an advertiser, a collector, a proclaimer of banal atrocities.
>
> —*Walker Percy, "A View of Abortion, With Something to Offend Everybody"*

In discussing his credentials Percy also defines his method: he will approach the abortion issue by considering the language that surrounds it.

Often the approach you need to explain isn't philosophical so much as practical: the steps you took and the order in which you took them. The following example written by a professional technical writer concerns tests performed on concrete:

> One cubic foot of concrete was mixed according to the preceding specifications [cited in a table in the preceding paragraph]. The concrete was poured into five wax cylinders and tamped three times during the pouring. When the concrete had hardened, the forms were removed and the concrete cylinders were placed in the curing room to be moist-cured at 70 degrees Fahrenheit. In the final stage of the procedure, a Tinius Olsen testing machine was used to test the cylinders under a compressive load. One cylinder was tested at 7 days, one at 14 days, one at 21 days, and the remaining two at 28 days.

Professional proposals—written requests to be granted a specific contract or special project—often include an explanation of the steps involved in the proposed project. Here's an example written by an academic applying for a leave of absence:

> I plan to refine three models of the creative process by interviewing those five artists involved in the early research. Then I will create a more polished single model of the creative process for presentation to those artists I plan to interview during Spring, 1991. This will take about a month.
>
> For the next two months, I will conduct as many interviews as possible with local, regional, and national artists. I hope to interview a minimum of 50 writers, musicians, painters. . . .

These two kinds of approaches, philosophical and practical, are not mutually exclusive. You well may find that your practical approach stems from your philosophical approach, or that your philosophical approach requires a certain practical grounding. In such cases, you need to explain both aspects of your approach in terms of the method you followed or will follow. In an article that explains research undertaken to investigate the creative process, the authors explain their method in the following manner:

> A group of five faculty recognized for their expertise in the arts (a painter, a poet, a sculptor, a novelist, and a photographer) met with the three authors for an initial three-hour session.
>
> Using the standard NGT process, which involves asking a question and having each participant generate as many answers as they can, the first session began with the question: "In as much detail as you like, list the things that you did, thought, or felt the last time you created an artistic product." Then they were asked to share each of their answers, round-robin fashion, one at a time.
>
> The five artists generated 83 answers, or "elements," during this one-hour initial session. During three subsequent sessions, the artists clarified their first choices, eliminated duplicates, and combined or divided overlapping elements. The group ultimately consented to 43 elements that they considered to be essential to the creative process.

Unlike literature reviews, which may either stand alone or serve as part of a larger whole, statements of methodology are never written to be read by themselves but always serve to provide a context for a larger piece of writing.

Conclusions

Professionals reading as part of their job are goal-oriented. They want to get to the point. The writer, therefore, must move them there as quickly as possible, and the conclusion of the trip must be absolutely clear. Conclusions generally have two aspects: results and recommendations. A conclusion may also include a consideration of implications.

Conclusions are answers to those questions raised in the study, research, or project being written about. How extensive is Lake Erie's pollution problem? To answer the question, the results should specify the details of the problem: which chemicals, in what proportions, and from what sources?

Implications, when they are noted, are various important side-issues involved in the results: "Lake Erie is more (or less) polluted than it was twenty years ago, and if the rate of increase (or decrease) continues, the lake will be at such and such a level by the end of another twenty years." "The fate of so many species of flora and fauna in the lake are at stake; these species include. . . ." "The laws passed ten years ago have (or have not) made a significant difference."

The recommendations follow from the results and implications, arguing that given the problem and situation as defined by the study, certain steps should be taken: "Existing legislation should be more strictly enforced (or rescinded)." "New legislation should be passed." "The enforcement agency should be beefed up (or cut back)." "The Sierra Club should mount a massive publicity campaign."

Conclusions can be divided into results, implications, and recommendations as distinctly as we have just done. These elements may also be combined in a continuous flow. The form you choose depends on the particular requirements of the person or office to whom you are writing or, in the absence of any requirement, on what seems most effective. If you choose a continuous structure for your conclusions, remember that it must be as clear as a conclusion that divides results from implications from recommendations. The following example concludes an extensive study of campus drug counseling at the University of Northern Iowa:

> The University of Northern Iowa (UNI) has recognized for some time that a number of its students have a drug problem, and has provided counseling services at the health center for students who want to overcome their dependency on alcohol or pot or hash or cocaine or whatever drug (or drugs) they use. The university has also encouraged students seeking help to contact the local chapter of Alcoholics Anonymous, which is open 24 hours a day, or the Northeast Council on Substance Abuse, which meets once a week. The question remains, however, whether the university should do more or less than it now does.

> Given the fact that American society as a whole is consuming drugs more and more, not less and less, one can assume that the percentage of students dependent on drugs will not decrease, and may increase. The university, therefore, should not cut back its services. On the other hand, at this point at least, students are not overwhelming the services available: the counseling service, AA, and the NCSA all report that they can handle the number of students seeking help. There is no reason, therefore, to increase any services at the present time.

> One must recognize, though, that many people who need help do not seek it, for a number of reasons—they don't see that they need help, or they are afraid of being ostracized by their peers if they seek help, or they are so dependent they are afraid even to try giving up their addiction. A basic truth of counseling is that no one "cures" anybody; all a counselor can do is facilitate recovery in behalf of those who want it. The university health center should, therefore, conduct an intensive and prolonged publicity campaign to persuade more drug-dependent students to want to take advantage of the services avail-

able. Then if demand should increase beyond the present capacity of the health center, the university should increase the staff of counselors to meet the demand.

This writer combines results and implications: there has been and is a substance abuse problem on campus (result), and given our society it won't simply go away (implication); present services are not overwhelmed (result), but many students who should be using them are not (implication). The recommendations are direct: do not decrease services available; do not increase services available; conduct a publicity campaign; if future demand should warrant, increase counseling staff. Though combined here, results, implications, and recommendations are spelled out clearly.

Abstracts and Summaries

When you write a formal proposal or a report, you will usually be required to include an abstract and a summary. An abstract is simply a summary in advance: it provides readers a preview in a nutshell of the paper they are about to read. A summary, on the other hand, is an abstract in retrospect: a nutshell review at the end of the paper.

A summary is always part of the paper it summarizes; an abstract usually precedes the paper as a sort of preface and because readers can refer to it readily, serves as a quick reminder of what the paper is about. You'll probably find it more efficient to write your paper, including your summary, before drafting an abstract.

Abstracts can be as short as a sentence and as long as a page. Often the length is specified. If not, base the length of the abstract on the length of the paper: an abstract should be no longer than a tenth of the total paper and is usually considerably shorter.

Like a summary, an abstract serves up the gist of the paper without any of the details. It's a stripped version, if you will, a skeleton, an X-ray. The following is an abstract of the report on campus alcohol abuse from which we quoted the conclusion:

> This report describes drug abuse at UNI and various services available to deal with it. It recommends that current services be maintained and that the health center publicize both the problem and the services.

When the length and complexity of the paper warrants it, an abstract or summary may also include a description of methodology and implications:

> The purpose of this report is to determine which adjustable-speed drive, ac (alternating-current) or dc (direct-current), should be purchased for production of the 19,500 steel crankshafts ordered by General Motors.
>
> The number 3-1505 lathe must be converted to an adjustable-speed drive because its constant speed of 1620 rpm (revolution per minute) is too fast for making steel crankshafts. The ac and dc drives are compared according to cost and capability.

Initial cost and installation of the dc drive is $122,000, versus $102,500 for the ac. The operation and maintenance of the dc is approximately $14,000 less per year, however. With all costs subtracted from the production of the 19,000 units, the dc drive would show a profit of $203,000 (12.3% increase) versus $197,000 (9.8% increase) for the ac.

The only difference in the capability of the drives is in their braking systems. The dc drive's system reduces the input power required by the lathe, but the ac's is slightly less efficient and costs about $3,000 per year more to operate.

The ac and dc drives are both capable of doing the job, and either would increase profits. The dc, however, has a 3% greater profit potential than the ac.

The dc adjustable drive should be installed on the number 3-1505 lathe. It should be purchased from the General Electric Company, which has given assurance that the drive will be installed within 2 weeks after purchase. With its implementation, a preventive maintenance program should be set up to check the drive's components continually.

In writing abstracts and summaries, remember that you are providing a quick overview so that the readers will have an accurate preview and review of your paper.

Prefaces

A preface is a courtesy, a letter to the reader explaining what the piece in hand is all about. It's like an orientation meeting where the writer introduces the essay or report with a brief description of its purpose and content. Thus the reader doesn't enter the paper blind, so to speak, but rather with some idea of what to expect. Prefaces come in two forms. The first you are familiar with—the familiar letter-type communication to readers at the beginning of a book, like this one. Such prefaces include, when appropriate, acknowledgments of support that the writer or writers received.

The other form is sometimes known as a *letter of transmittal*. When you submit a piece to someone in a professional capacity—an editor, a supervisor, your boss—you are usually expected to include with it a letter that accounts for it. Such a letter is not invariably necessary or even desirable: if you include one with an English or history assignment, your professor might find you formal to a fault. But should you hand in a paper under unusual circumstances, such a letter would be appropriate:

October 2, 1992

Professor George Richter
Biology Department
Baker Hall

Dear Professor Richter:

Enclosed you will find a copy of my final biology paper for last spring's "Elements of Microbiology" course. This paper completes the requirements for the course.

As you may recall from our conference last spring, you suggested that I write an annotated bibliography of recent articles in the *Microbiology Journal* that pertain to my current interest in cellular research. Therefore I have annotated all articles in the last five years that cover cellular research with lasers. There were a total of 16 articles.

Again, thank you for your patience in letting me extend the course work deadline. Because I was given more time, the bibliography is much stronger, and therefore more useful to me as a biology major.

Sincerely,
Samantha Jones

As you can see, a preface or letter of transmittal is an informal, somewhat personal abstract. Its purpose is to get your paper off to a good start, on the right foot with the reader. If you should need a preface or letter of transmittal, make sure not only that it accurately describes the paper, but that it establishes the proper tone, as well. You want your work to get the best hearing possible.

APPLICATIONS

1. Write a descriptive abstract of the "Clothes Reveal Mood" essay you wrote for Application 1 on page 193 or 213, or for another essay you've recently completed. Also write a letter of transmittal explaining the essay to your instructor.

2. Write brief answers to the following questions: Has working with these professional formats helped you see anything new about the ABA shape? What do any of these professional formats have in common with the ABA shape? Share answers with classmates.

3. Find and bring to class an example of any of the professional formats discussed in this chapter. We suggest you begin by looking at some journals in your major area of study. (Ask a librarian for titles or reference works.) Discuss these with your writing group.

4. Write a letter to a friend or family member in which you explain something you learned from your reading about professional formats. For example, you might explain the value of a letter of transmittal to your high-school age brother or sister.

5. Review a research or term paper you've written and see if you used any of the professional formats. Try to determine how you would write the paper now that you've read about professional formats, including formats you might now use that you didn't. Would you add material? Eliminate anything? Reorganize?

INVITATIONS FOR EXTENDED WRITING

If you're comfortable with any of the concentrating and intuiting strategies in Chapter 2, be sure to apply them as you write these essays. Also be sure to listen to your yes voice, bringing in your no voice only when you revise and edit.

1. An Essay on Clothes and Moods Consider all the material you've gathered on clothes and moods from Application 1 on pages 193, 213, and 229. Use as much of the material as you like to write an entirely new essay on the subject for a particular publication: a campus or local newsletter, a dorm or fraternity/sorority newsletter, whatever. If you want to make the case that clothes *don't* reveal mood, or any other aspect of the relation between clothes and moods, don't hesitate. Also, try to choose the most effective form for your audience and purpose; don't be tied to any form for its own sake.

2. An Essay on Forming Write an essay for either your instructor or a general audience on the concept of shaping. Consider the various strategies we have discussed. Make your essay either predominantly explanatory or predominantly exploratory, and use the various strategies and shapes that are appropriate.

3. A Letter to Classmates Look over any of the letters about shaping strategies you've written to family and friends in response to previous Applications in this chapter. Choose one form or strategy, and make a case for its superiority to all the others, at least for certain purposes or occasions. Be detailed and logical—specify the purposes or occasions, prove the superiority. Write your argument as a letter to your classmates.

4. An Exploratory Essay Using either of the exploratory shapes (line or circle), write an exploratory essay for a large and varied readership. Consider what you think is worth exploring in detail, and focus your attention on making it work, making it hold the interest of the readers. Use any of the earlier strategies you've learned—clustering, freewriting, flow charting, and so forth—to start and develop your essay. If you're happy about how it turns out, submit it for publication in a newspaper or magazine.

5. A Professional Format Report Find a piece of report-style writing that uses any of the professional format shapes in this chapter. If you've recently written such a piece, use that. For your classmates and instructor, explain which formats were used and point out the various shapes. If you found any problems with how the formats were used, explain those as well.

For Further Reading and Research

Brandt, Deborah. "Toward an Understanding of Context in Composition." *Written Communication* 3 (1986): 139–157.

Brownmiller, Susan. *Against Our Will: Men, Women, and Rape.* New York: Simon, 1975.

Didion, Joan. *Slouching Towards Bethlehem.* New York: Farrar, 1968.

————. *The White Album.* New York: Simon, 1979.

King, Martin Luther, Jr. *Why We Can't Wait.* New York: Harper, 1963.

Kingston, Maxine Hong. *China Men.* New York: Knopf, 1980.

Pauley, Steven E. *Technical Report Writing Today.* New York: Houghton, 1979.

Percy, Walker. "A View of Abortion, With Something to Offend Everybody." *New York Times* 8 June 1981.

Toulmin, Stephen. *The Uses of Argument.* Cambridge: Cambridge UP, 1958.

Eight All-Purpose Steps for Quick Writing

This book is concerned with discovery writing—writing that requires time for exploration and commitment. Yet much day-to-day writing—essay and short-answer tests, quick in-class responses, memos, letters of request and complaint, and so on—requires little exploration or commitment. You know what you want to say, and the trick is to get it down as coherently and quickly as possible.

Here is an eight-question checklist to help you with this kind of writing. Note that the first four questions focus on preparation: you need to answer these before you write. The final four you'll answer as you're writing.

1. **Do you know enough about the material, or will you need to consult sources?** If you know enough, go on to the next question. If you don't, what is the minimum number of sources you need to consult? Make a list and find the sources immediately, taking notes as necessary. If you don't have time, try to get an extension.

2. **Who are you writing for and why?** Are you writing a letter of complaint to a dorm counselor? A letter to the editor, complimenting or complaining? A short-answer test for a graduate assistant? Are you writing to persuade, inform, complain, request, refute? Define your purpose and audience as clearly as possible.

3. **Given the purpose, what kind of writing will fulfill it?** Do you need to show that you consulted sources? If so, you probably need to write more formally, at least mentioning sources. Will a less formal, personal approach fulfill your purpose? If so, plan to write your observations from your own point of view, in your own style or voice. Is format important, and if so, do you know the required format?

4. **Given the purpose, what is an appropriate tone?** Most often, for quick writing the appropriate tone is relatively formal and authoritative,

although for some kinds of business writing a friendlier, more personal tone may be suitable. In general, you're not writing to be liked on such occasions; you're writing to be respected and understood.

5. **What are the main points you need to make?** Jot these down quickly in a margin, on the back of the answer sheet, or on a piece of scratch paper.

6. **What is an appropriate order?** Number your points in the order you will develop them, and add more as necessary.

7. **How can you best develop each point?** As you write, support each point with as much factual detail as you can. Develop them in the order you have numbered them, and try to add appropriate connectives, such as "thus," "nevertheless," "because," "in addition," "also."

8. **Have you made any glaring mistakes?** Go through what you have written, looking for errors. For essay tests, make corrections as best you can—spelling, punctuation, sentence fragments, and so on—and, if necessary, add more points, using arrows and notes to show where they belong. For business writing you'll need to type a clean copy with your changes unless you're working on a word processor.

That's it. Remember, you're not writing for discovery in these circumstances, just to get down what you already know. If you don't panic under pressure, you can use many of the strategies we've discussed in this book even for essay test writing. Clustering, freewriting, even daydreaming can help if you get stuck. And keep ABA form in mind.

Conditions for Creating

When I am, as it were, completely myself, entirely alone, and of good cheer—say, traveling in a carriage, or walking after a good meal, or during the night when I cannot sleep—it is on such occasions that my ideas flow best and most abundantly. Whence and how they come, I know not; nor can I force them. Those ideas that please me I retain in my memory, and am accustomed, as I have been told, to hum them to myself. If I continue in this way, it soon occurs to me how I may turn this or that morsel to account so as to make a good dish of it. . . . What a delight this is I cannot tell!

—WOLFGANG AMADEUS MOZART

Although he was a genius of the first order, Mozart could not compose at will anytime, anywhere, under any circumstances. He did best under certain conditions: when he was alone and relaxed, traveling in a carriage, or walking after a good meal, or staying up late at night. Though few of us are as gifted as Mozart, we are all capable of creating. Like Mozart, we create best under certain conditions. Because the ideal conditions vary from person to person, we each need to discover which conditions best support our own creative work.

For convenience, we've divided conditions for creating into two categories: physical and mental. Incidentally, we make no distinction between creative writing and so-called expository writing (factual information, arguments, reports, memos, proposals): all writing requires some degree of creativity.

Physical Conditions

Obviously, the physical conditions that work for one writer won't necessarily work for another. Some creators prefer silence, others a certain kind of music; some prefer absolute privacy, others need movement around them; some even like smells, such as incense or candles. As varied as their favored conditions may be, however, writers implicitly agree on the following:

- Music that you enjoy dancing or listening closely to won't serve to enhance your creativity. It's more likely to distract you. If you like background music, find some that you tune into and out of easily without pausing to listen.
- Television seldom works for those who watch it only occasionally. For those who leave it on constantly without paying much attention, it does seem to offer background noise that doesn't distract.
- Anything that can interrupt you for several minutes should be avoided: phone calls, visits from relatives and housemates, a playful pet. Don't hesitate to turn down the ringer on your phone or disconnect it completely. Ask companions to respect your need to be alone, even if it's for only ten or twenty minutes. Put the dog outside. Remember Mozart again: "completely myself, entirely alone."
- Any moderately demanding physical activity should also be avoided. For actual writing, you probably have to sit somewhere. Even walking, which can work for incubating, won't allow you to follow your own thoughts for long, though some claim to have had success with portable tape recorders while walking. Obviously, strenuous physical activity will be distracting.
- Any physical discomfort—such as high heat and humidity, severe cold, even hunger—works against creating. It's best to be comfortably warm and well-fed (though not stuffed—this will put you to sleep).
- Any threatening environment—such as a room where fire or smoke alarms are constantly going off or where there are people who threaten one's safety—also must be avoided. Such distractions will constantly interfere with creating. Though notable writing has been created in jail, that's the sad exception rather than the rule.

Mental Conditions

Recent creativity research shows several mental states that support creating:

- *Receptivity.* "To get started," says poet William Stafford, "I will accept anything that occurs to me. Something always occurs, of course, to any of us. We can't keep from thinking. Maybe I have to settle for an immediate impression: it's cold, or hot, or dark, or bright, or in between! Or—well, the possibilities are endless." Stay open as you write; receive what comes with gratitude. Set aside your no voice for as long as possible.
- *Willingness to take risks and to fail.* Be ready to succeed, of course, but also be ready and willing to fail. Writer and teacher Paul Horgan observes: "I

have never ceased being amazed at the almost unanimous expectation of students (graduate and undergraduate alike) who look to the publication and the success of the very first works they commit to paper." Among other things, Horgan understands that students have not yet learned the willingness to fail. William Stafford suggests that writers, when creating, must be "careless of failure" lest they destroy their original idea-seedlings. Remember that one of the worst mistakes is failing to learn from mistakes.

- *Awareness of internal conflicts.* Writers constantly explore the conflicts among the ideas and feelings that recur over and over throughout their thinking lives. Often there is deep ambivalence about such ideas or feelings, and they write in order to understand what touches them deeply and why. Rather than avoiding what makes them uncomfortable, angry, or afraid, they embrace such conflicts.
- *Willingness to be immersed for a while.* Psychologist Mihaly Csikszentmihalyi insists that without the "flow" that results from immersion, there is no possibility of completing anything that's worthwhile. This flow is simply "the state in which people are so involved in an activity that nothing else seems to matter." This experience "is so enjoyable that people will do it even at great cost, for the sheer sake of doing it."
- *A clear head.* Don't buy into the popular myth that regular use of a psychoactive drug, such as alcohol or marijuana, will enhance your creativity. To be sure, a number of creators drink and take drugs, but they create in spite of the drug, not because of it, as they themselves are well aware:

> One of the disadvantages of wine is that it makes a man [or woman] mistake words for thoughts.
>
> —SAMUEL JOHNSON

> No one, ever, wrote anything as well even after one drink as he would have done without it.
>
> —RING LARDNER

The key piece of advice is also the oldest: know yourself. As you grow more aware of how you create, you will seek space and time that support and enhance your efforts.

Blockbusting

Every writer I know has trouble writing.

—JOSEPH HELLER

I went for years not finishing anything. Because, of course, when you finish something you can be judged. . . . I had poems which were rewritten so many times I suspect it was just a way of avoiding sending them out.

—ERICA JONG

Writers are notorious for using any reason to keep from working: over-researching, retyping, going to meetings, waxing the floors— anything.

—GLORIA STEINEM

"Writer's block" is an occupational illness from which no one seems immune, especially writers. Blocks seem to occur for any of four reasons.

First, blocks often occur when a writer has little commitment to purpose or audience. If a student writes only for the instructor and only for a grade, the essay is likely to be approached as nothing more than a classroom exercise. And since a classroom exercise may seem remote from the writer's vital interests, a block can easily result. Unless a writer is engaged in the subject and feels his or her ideas will make a genuine difference to some reader, there is little genuine incentive to write.

Second, writing demands serious concentration and a high energy level. It's plain hard work, in other words. Novelist William Styron was asked whether he enjoyed writing. His reply summarizes how many writers feel:

> I certainly don't. I get a fine warm feeling when I'm doing well, but that pleasure is pretty much negated by the pain of getting started each day. Let's face it, writing is hell.

Indeed, sometimes a block offers an attractive excuse for avoiding writing!

Third, all writing is a form of confession. Even the most straightforward factual articles reveal something of the writer. It's inevitable. And as Freud understood, most people would rather do almost anything than confess their deepest longings to strangers. Author Lawrence Durrell explains his own horror of confession as being almost normal:

> I have discovered quite recently that characteristic Freudian resistances to confessions of any sort, which are very well represented in all the writing blocks one goes through—the dizzy fits, the nauseas, and so on and so forth, which almost every writer has recorded—are a standard pattern for all kinds of creative things. They are simply forms of egotism.

Durrell admits that he gets blocks from reading reviews of his own work, recognizing how much he has revealed of himself:

> [E]gotism can be inflamed very easily by a good review, or a bad review for that matter, and you can get a nice tidy block which will cost you two days of work.

Finally, most writers fear critical reaction—from without, in the form of negative reader responses, and from within, in the form of their own no voice. In either case, the result can be a serious block.

Here we offer six specific strategies for breaking down blocks, whether they arise from procrastination, despair, a lack of purpose, a distaste for writing, a fear of confession, or that all-pervasive no voice. If you are blocked, you should find at least one of these strategies helpful. We end with twelve more quick blockbusting ideas that often work for people who find themselves suddenly unable to start or finish.

Positive Thinking

Doctors have known for ages that patients' perceptions of their medicines can directly affect healing. It happens so often that doctors call it the "placebo effect," named after "dummy" medications that patients are led to believe are real. If patients believe in the medication, they often respond, even though they may be taking a placebo. If patients do not believe in the medication, even a state-of-the-art drug may prove of little value.

Similarly, your attitude can directly affect your writing. If you believe you can't write, you may well develop a block. You may think there's serious evidence to support your negative attitude—you always get C's (or worse) on your essays, your writing never says what you mean. It just may be, however, that you had a negative attitude from the outset, a mindset that prevented you from writing as well as you could. Further, people can change if they want to, and everyone can improve his or her writing.

So, we invite you to try an attitude shift as a possible solution to your block. Unfortunately, changing your attitude isn't just a matter of willing it. "OK, now I'm going to think positively about this" won't work. And you may *have* a generally positive attitude about your writing but feel hopelessly blocked on a particular piece you're working on, like a .300 hitter in a slump. For either problem, developing a new attitude can take time. You need to replace the negative "tape" playing in your head with a positive one.

And we suggest that you do so literally. Using a blank cassette that will play thirty minutes on a side, you can record a blockbusting tape that will help remedy a long-term negative attitude toward writing or a short-term block that keeps you from finishing an already-begun piece.

In a calm, relaxed voice, read the following into a tape recorder clearly and slowly:

Relax. Let your muscles go limp. Take a deep breath now—inhale so that you imagine your body as an upside-down eyedropper. Inhaling, you're filling the eyedropper's bulb. Exhaling, you're emptying it.

Each time you empty it, let yourself relax more and more. For the first deep breath, let the tensions of the day out. Let them simply float out into the air, where they can no longer affect you. Now, inhale and exhale. (PAUSE)

For the second deep breath, let the tensions of the past week out; let them too float out of you into the air, where they can no longer affect you. Now, inhale and exhale. (PAUSE)

For the third deep breath, let all remaining tensions out; let them float away with your breath into the air, where they can no longer affect you. Now, inhale and exhale deeply once more. (PAUSE)

Now, you're in a totally relaxed state. It feels quite pleasant. Enjoy it for a few moments. (PAUSE)

You are now feeling quite pleasant, relaxed, and able to focus on the following. Know that the following is true: you have a strong desire to express yourself clearly and forcefully. You admire people who can express themselves so that people understand and respect them. You yourself have been able to do that occasionally, and you've been pleased and proud of yourself when that has happened.

Now, take a moment to think of some occasions when you were happy with how you expressed yourself. It may have been with close friends or relatives, in a classroom, possibly during a question-and-answer period after a lecture, maybe at work. Relive at least one of those occasions now. Try to remember how it made you feel—the sense of pride and accomplishment you felt. (PAUSE)

Know that you have the capability to express yourself just as clearly and forcefully again. You are entirely capable, willing, and able to express your ideas to anyone when you wish. There is nothing standing in your way that you can't overcome. In fact, you've overcome many barriers and obstacles to get where you are now.

Now, take a moment to consider just one obstacle that you had to overcome to get where you are today. It can be a financial barrier, a family problem, a health problem, an attitude block. Consider how you successfully overcame it, and allow yourself to feel pride that you were able to overcome that barrier. Relive that pride for a moment now. (PAUSE)

Know that you can overcome any obstacle. All you need is a willingness to try. And know that you will make great strides as a writer, sometimes all at once, sometimes a step at a time.

Relax now and enjoy the sense of your own capabilities. You no longer have to worry about being blocked; you can dissolve your blocks whenever you wish, and you have dissolved those that have been bothering you, completely.

Now slowly open your eyes as I count to five. At the count of five, open your eyes and sense your power. Write today out of that sense of power, and know that you have the capability to express whatever you wish.

One . . . two . . . three . . . four . . . five.

Play this tape back as often as you like—but especially just before you write. Be sure to listen to it where you won't be distracted, so you can concentrate on your own taped voice for the whole session. Don't try to listen to it while you're doing other things. And don't let your no voice persuade you it's only psychological trickery. Remember that your attitude can make all the difference in your performance, so that changing your attitude *can* improve your performance, significantly.

Rewards

Most of us recognize the need for rewards. The blocked writer, however, seldom thinks of rewards—only of punishment. Writing itself, or even the attempt to write, becomes punishment, creating a vicious cycle. You feel badly because the deadline is approaching and nothing is getting done. As each day passes you feel worse, making it even harder to finish. Perhaps you begin to find excuses to apply for an extension of the deadline; perhaps you start to visualize yourself as a failure, unable to complete any serious task. The result? Nothing gets done, and your misery over getting nothing done just intensifies.

One way to break this cycle is to reward yourself for completing a task. Start small. Identify something you enjoy that you can buy, do, or have around— a bon-bon, an ice cream bar, a song, a bike ride—and "insert" it in your writing time as a reward for an accomplishment, for writing a page or a paragraph, even if you don't judge what you've done very good. The important thing is to choose a reward that you'd really enjoy. Here are some suggestions, all readily available for little trouble and not much money:

- a hot bath or shower with some great bath salts or soap
- a short chapter by your favorite writer
- a movie on videotape that you've been wanting to see
- that new pen you've been wanting to buy
- a call to an old friend (three minutes long distance is still a good buy)
- a handful of nuts or a piece of exotic fruit

If you feel you can't do anything to deserve such rewards, you need to start from scratch. Sit at your writing desk for ten minutes and freewrite, nonstop. Write about your block, about the day, about your friends, even about the subject that you're supposed to be writing on. But write away, and don't stop until ten minutes is up. Then reward yourself, modestly, for writing *something.*

Next, plan a slightly larger reward, and jump to twenty minutes. Don't freewrite again; instead, doodle, brainstorm, write a short passage, maybe do a little background reading and notetaking. But only for twenty minutes. Then take another break and enjoy your reward.

Finally, write a section or passage that's actually for the piece you're having trouble with. Set no time limit—just work on it for a while. When you've written a passage you consider to be pretty good (and don't let your no voice tell you it has to be award-winning prose!), stop. Then—you guessed it—reward yourself again.

You can and should reward yourself often, to give yourself incentives to break the cycle and to prove to yourself that you're actually getting somewhere.

Time Management

In his fine book on time management for writers, Ken Atchity says "Work is infinite; time is finite. Therefore you must manage your time, not your work." Even so, many people let time master them—they're always behind, never really finishing anything to their satisfaction.

Yet unlike money, or health, or beauty, we all have the same amount of time to spend. People noted for their productivity have no more time than the rest of us. It's just that the rest of us are not focused or energetic enough to use the time we have. If you're having trouble getting your work done, especially your writing assignments, time management may be a real godsend.

Here's how it works. Start by making a list of everything you do that someone else can do. Don't use this as an excuse to permanently get out of your legitimate chores. But you can ask others to trade off duties with you for a while, to take over temporarily some of the errands or work that are normally your responsibilities. Do you usually take out the trash, do the laundry, straighten up your living space, get the mail, buy the groceries? That's probably five or six hours weekly that you could use to finish a project. Instead of writing, you're running errands that anyone else might do—if you ask—in exchange for some time later for themselves. Consider this to be time-negotiating. You promise to take over some of their chores for a while, after you've finished your project if they'll help you gain a few precious hours for a couple of days or even weeks.

Not only can you negotiate time, you can buy it. Make a further list of everything you do that you could pay someone else to do—items that don't require any special involvement from you, or any of your unique talents or expertise.

Too many people who are swamped with such work—daily housework, typing, yard and garden work, repairs, errands, and such—never consider occasionally paying someone else to take over these time-consuming tasks. We all know that time is money; we ought also to know that money buys time.

At this point you're down to those items that only you can do, for whatever reasons: call your parents, read assignments, do lab reports, write papers, attend lectures. These all deserve your serious attention. Separate this list into four groups:

PRIORITY ONE: *Must do* in the next two days.
PRIORITY TWO: *Must do* within the week.
PRIORITY THREE: *Can wait* for a week or more.
PRIORITY FOUR: *Needs regular attention,* but need not be completed for two or more weeks.

Let's look at all these lists. You've gotten rid of several responsibilities that would otherwise take your time (errands and chores that you can trade off or pay someone to do). You've decided what needs immediate attention (Priority One items). You've also decided what you can genuinely put off for a few days or a week or more (Priority Two and Priority Three items). Finally, you know exactly what you need to work on regularly as part of an ongoing project (Priority Four items).

Now, plan your work days, always, around your Priority One and Priority Four lists. Only these items need attention every day. Obviously, the others will eventually deserve attention, but not until you shift them to either Priority One or Priority Four. For now they can be set aside. And if you've found ways to get rid of errands and other duties for a while, you should have more time now to work on these crucial items.

Your Priority One list may actually be fairly small, probably two or three items at the most. From among these two or three items, choose the one that's most urgent, say a lab report due in a couple of days. Map out a schedule for finishing this task and work on it first.

Next, shift to a Priority Four item, say a speech you have to give in three weeks that you've done no preparation for yet. Today, spend just twenty minutes on it: read an article on the subject and take notes, for example.

Then, return to your Priority One list. Choose the item that's second most urgent and work on it. And if you have further Priority Four items, choose one to spend another twenty minutes on, perhaps simply writing down your goals for the project. There are few things more enlightening than seeing what you want to accomplish with a piece of writing in black and white. If goal setting doesn't work, freewrite on the subject for a while or doodle or dialogue. Sometimes one strategy will work when others fail. This will be enough for today, but remember that you'll need to do more with it soon—you should try to spend at least twenty minutes a day on Priority Four items.

Time management (sometimes called *prioritizing*) amounts to knowing those items you can negotiate or pay your way out of in order to get important work done. Then, it involves an honest assessment of what you need to do, and when. Then—and probably most crucial—it involves doing the tasks, one at a time.

Dialoguing

Nearly everyone who has thought about writers and writing has discussed the writer's different selves. First, there's the creator self who gets ideas out, who's enthusiastic about its discoveries, who experiments with new forms, who stretches the boundaries. The creator self makes itself known through what we've been calling a yes voice—the voice that supports, nurtures, encourages.

Then, there's the critical self. This is the voice that writers must listen to if they want to avoid embarrassing themselves. It says "no," this isn't right, this won't work here, this passage isn't quite right, this isn't the word you need. The no voice often represents the conventional, the tried and true, the stable, the predictable. And at times it can totally discourage even the most courageous writer. Actually talking, or dialoguing, with these voices will help you know exactly how they influence you, and may help you loosen up the block that comes from the no voice.

An experience with a student will help make this point clear. Dave was seriously blocked. Although he wanted to write, knew how to do research, and had plenty to say in class, he couldn't seem to get his essays into polished form. They remained collections of ideas, notes, fragments. His instructor suggested that he dialog with his yes and no voices. Dave was desperate enough to give it a try.

What he discovered was that whenever he tried to write, a strong sense that he was not up to the task came over him like a dark cloud. "Dave," the voice would start, "No matter what you write, it won't be much good. It will bore everyone. The teacher will pretend to like it, but secretly will wonder at your lack of perception. You really have no business writing anything, you know that?" Dave was surprised that he could articulate his no voice so quickly and accurately. In fact, he gave it a name—the "Commissar." His "Commissar" was merciless, and for months Dave had listened.

So, Dave initiated a dialogue with his "Commissar" voice, writing extended replies to its accusations. The results were astonishing. Dave wrote fast and furious, as though he'd never been blocked, and learned that his creative yes voice could put up a good fight:

COMMISSAR: *Now you think you're writing, but you're just scribbling away. Don't you even know that?*

YES: Just a minute. There's nothing wrong with this. It might be the start of something big.

C: *Oh, now you're lapsing into song titles. Can't you be more original?*

Y: I rather liked it. But the fact is that everything large begins with something small. And I already feel as though I learned something about you just by putting you down on paper.

C: *Now what might that be?*

Y: That you're overly critical, that you dislike everything I do, and that you're a pompous ass.

C: *You don't have to get personal. Let's face it, the fact is that you haven't written anything yet. And you have to recognize the facts. You're not really a writer, and you never will be.*

Y: I don't know that for sure, and neither do you. Some of the early pieces of great writers aren't really any better than mine.

C: *Come on, they all wrote better from the very beginning, and just got better and better.*

Y: Bull. They all struggled with words just like I do, and they all had to put up with a Commissar of some sort just like you. They even talk about it—many of them had to overcome enormous self-doubts in the form of a strong voice just like yours.

C: *Yes, but they had real talent. You just have hopes.*

Y: I'm going to reserve judgment on that for a while, and so should you.

And on it went. After an hour, Dave had written five pages of dialogue between his two voices and had made an exciting discovery: he also has a positive, supportive voice inside. Before this dialogue, he had no idea that he was simply listening to his "Commissar"—he thought that he genuinely had no talent, that he could never write. Dave's creative voice was so overwhelmed—until he literally gave it something to say—that he hardly knew it existed.

So, if and when you're blocked, dialogue. All you need is some time, some paper (or a typewriter or word processor), and a willingness to let those voices have a go at one another. Start by writing out the first sentence that occurs to you. Is it your critical no voice? Or is it more positive, supportive? Whichever it is, write a one-sentence reply to it from the other voice, then an answer to that reply, and so on until you've captured both of your voices.

Ask yourself: Is this dialogue accurate? Do you hear both of these voices when you write? Or do you tend to hear one voice more than another, like Dave's overwhelming "Commissar"? Also note whether the voices change with different kinds of writing: some writers sense a strong critical voice only when they try to write research papers, while others feel overwhelmed by their no voice when they try to write personal essays.

If your no voice tends to overwhelm your yes voice during any of your writing (and especially if you feel blocked), write an extended dialogue in which both voices actually talk it out. Let the less heard voice talk more, and strive for balance between them.

Goal Setting

One of the oddest facts of life is that many people live a long time without any goals at all. They accept what comes, hope for the best, and let tomorrow take care of itself. If you're in college, however, you can't live like that, even though a number of students seem to try. Those who do, not surprisingly, often wind up with a major writing block. Stewing, fretting, hemming, hawing, tearing their hair out over getting started or finishing, and getting nowhere in the process—all these struggles come from having set no clear goals for themselves.

Goals come in two basic dimensions: short-term and long-term. Short-term goals for an essay might include getting a good grade, impressing your instructor, or having an effect on members of your writing group: entertaining them or giving them useful information or making them examine an issue more closely. (These latter are analogous to the "real life" goals that all writers actually consider when they write for publication.)

Short-term goals are usually stepping stones for long-term goals. If you're writing for a good grade in the short term, your purpose in the long run might be to get a high course grade, to raise your overall average, to help you get a better job. These are mostly external goals, but you need to consider your long-term goals in personal terms, as well. One personal goal would be the satisfaction of being able to do something well, to express what's on your mind so that other people understand it or to gather and arrange information so that it's presented clearly and succinctly. Another long-term personal goal might be to make a positive difference in the world. You stand a much better chance of making such a difference if you can write well.

Keep in mind as you set goals for your papers that purpose is one of the key traits of any creative effort. According to David Perkins in *The Mind's Best Work,* "What makes creating special is not so much its component processes but their organization and direction, and that organization and direction derives from an end in view, however broad and vaguely grasped." Without a sense of moving toward some particular end, you may well not get anywhere.

So, if you're feeling blocked because you have no clear sense of why you're writing, consider your short- and long-run goals, both internal and external. The most important ones are internal; the more your goals arise from within, the more likely you are to finish tasks that take you toward those goals.

For any paper you're working on, list all the possible goals:

1. *Short-term external:* For whom are you writing besides yourself, and what difference will it make to them once your paper is done?
2. *Short-term internal:* What's in it for you, and how will you feel when you're finished?
3. *Long-term external:* What standards and expectations of others will doing this paper help you fulfill?
4. *Long-term internal:* What will finishing this paper mean to you in the long run?

The more detailed and complete you can make your answers to these questions, the clearer sense you will have of actually writing for some reason—and the more likely you can hurdle those blocks that come from having no clear purpose.

Directed Doodling

One of the sources of writing blocks is the pressure to make too much sense too early. Having to make words into sentences, then sentences into paragraphs, then paragraphs into essays that make sense to strangers is at best an intimidating business, and if you feel you have to rush it you can wind up with a major block.

To overcome a block of this kind, try directed doodling. With doodling, you needn't begin with words. It's a matter of playing with lines, circles, squiggles, dots, dashes—practically anything that helps you discover what's on your mind. Best of all, it doesn't have to be neat, or even make any sense to anyone but yourself. Great inventors have traditionally used doodling like this, and their sketches were anything but neatly presentable. Look, for example at Thomas Jefferson's sketch of a design for the U.S. Capitol building (Figure C.1) and at Thomas Edison's working drawing from which the original phonograph was built (Figure C.2).

The goal of directed doodling isn't just to relieve nervous tension, as most doodling can. Nor does it necessarily provide writers with specific structures and hierarchies, as do outlines, lists, and mapping. Rather, directed doodles offer a superb means of concentrating on a subject for an extended period of time without writing. You may generate insights worth exploring in writing, but there's no pressure to make sense (in words, anyway) until later.

Henning Nelms, author of the useful book *Thinking with a Pencil,* tells how he used doodling to interpret a play.

> A friend suggested that a drawing might be useful in interpreting a play. I chose *Romeo and Juliet* as an example because I had studied it for years and thought I knew all the answers. Five minutes' work on the chart revealed the striking symmetry in the organization of the characters. This symmetry is

Figure C.1   Thomas Jefferson, Suggested Design for U.S. Capitol. (*Coolidge Papers, Massachusetts Historical Society.*)

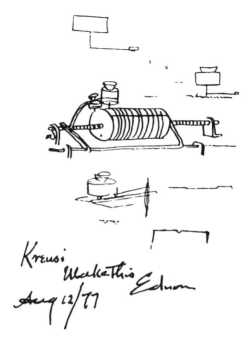

Figure C.2 Thomas A. Edison, Working Drawing From Which the Original Phonograph Was Built. (*Thomas Alva Edison Foundation Museum, West Orange, N.J.*)

certainly an important element in any interpretation of the play, and one that I had never suspected until the chart thrust it under my nose.

Figure C.3 reproduces the diagram that Nelms drew. Consider just how much you'd have on your mind about *Romeo and Juliet* after doodling up a chart like his.

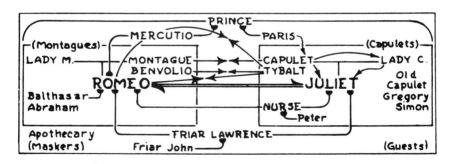

Figure C.3

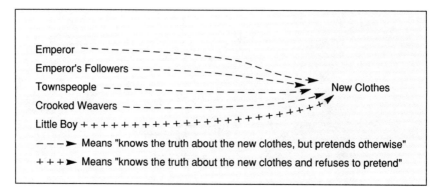

Figure C.4   Directed Doodle on "The Emperor's New Clothes."

Such charts will work for practically any literary work, complex or simple. Here's another example. "The Emperor's New Clothes," as you probably remember, is a tale about a foolish emperor who hires weavers to make him the perfect set of kingly clothes. The weavers convince the king that only the smartest people in the kingdom will actually be able to see the clothes; then they *pretend* to weave him an outfit literally fit for a king. Predictably enough, after the clothes are "stitched" and "tailored," everyone in the kingdom pretends to see them, including the poor emperor and his retinue. The emperor parades around his kingdom in his underwear, until an ingenuous little boy shouts, "The Emperor's not wearing any clothes!"

It's a liberating truth.

So, what insights about this simple tale might be derived from directed doodling? Figure C.4 suggests at least one: that all the characters except the little boy are on the same moral level as the crooked weavers. One could even infer that the crooked weavers are less reprehensible morally than the others; at least they're not cowardly or hypocritical.

This kind of directed doodling requires two components: a system of symbols and a subject that you know at least a little about. Here we'll develop a system of symbols to look at the intensity of personal relationships among a set of six people.

We'll let circles stand for females and squares for males, putting each of the six names inside either a circle or square:

Next, we'll use three kinds of arrows to indicate three levels of intensity. An unbroken arrow will stand for very intense feelings of one person towards another: Bill ──▶ Mary. A dashed arrow will indicate less intense feelings: Fred ◀-- Jean. And we'll use dotted arrows for the least intense feelings of one person towards another: Susan ·····▶ Ralph . The direction of the arrows

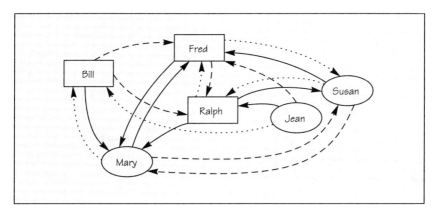

Figure C.5   Rough Sociogram of Relationships

indicates the direction of the feelings, and arrows can run in both directions (though they may indicate different levels of feelings).

Using these symbols, you can doodle out the relationships among your friends. (Sociologists call such doodles "sociograms.") Figure C.5 is an example of a "rough" sociogram of our model, while Figure C.6 shows a "clarified" version of Figure C.5. Here are a few things you can discover in a doodle such as ours:

- Which relationships are unequal (that is, where do different arrows run between two people).
- Who occupies the center of a group of friends (that is, who has the most solid arrows leading to him or her).
- Who exists at the periphery (that is, who has the least arrows leading to him or her).

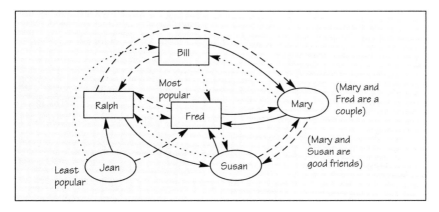

Figure C.6   Clarified Sociogram of Relationships

Directed doodling, whatever its form, often generates so many ideas that you have too much to write about rather than too little. The block disappears from the sheer momentum of the writer's involvement.

To experiment with directed doodling, take a problem you've been struggling with, whether it's related to writing or not. Try to doodle a picture of the problem first. Make a dark, confusing blob if that seems accurate. Or a series of interrelated circles if that seems more accurate. Or just two arrows pointing at one another (a standoff!) if that seems to picture it best.

Now, see if you can picture the problem another way. Try different shapes, different symbols. Can you picture it in three dimensions? Can you add what caused it to be a problem, or what effects it's likely to have if it continues? Can you doodle out some solution entering the picture and solving at least part of the problem?

Play with this awhile, using whatever images and symbols seem most appropriate.

Twelve Quick Unblockers

Here are twelve quick strategies for unblocking that don't require much time and energy. See if you can make any of them work for you:

1. *Quit and read awhile.* Find your favorite author and read for a few minutes. Sometimes this will get you back into your writing flow.
2. *Talk on tape.* Instead of struggling with language via written words, talk about your ideas into a tape recorder. Writers who struggle with every word at times find that just talking helps.
3. *Exercise.* Take a walk, a run, ride a bike, swim. Sometimes this breaks the physical tension that's been holding you back.
4. *Meditate.* If you meditate regularly, do it to unblock. If you don't, just sit quietly and count to ten using the rhythms of your inhaling and exhaling. Don't worry if you lose your concentration; gently bring yourself back to counting.
5. *Write nonstop.* Freewriting (see Chapter 1) allows you to create a flow, even when you may not be confident you're producing anything. Time yourself (5–10 minutes is fine), and don't stop. If you're writing at a computer keyboard, try turning off the screen so you aren't tempted to criticize what you've written as it comes out.
6. *Lower your expectations.* Remember you're creating a draft, and it doesn't have to be perfect the first time. Let it be messy, choppy, missing important information—just get it down.
7. *Write at a different time.* If you're writing at your "low" times, you may be fighting your own biorhythms. Try writing earlier, or later. Often what seems blocked at night flows in the morning.

8. *Talk to someone about your project.* Sometimes just a conversation can get ideas flowing again.

9. *Copy some prose you admire.* Find a few paragraphs and just copy them, getting the rhythms and sounds down. Sometimes this helps open the dam.

10. *Prime the pump.* Retype some paragraphs you have already written, paragraphs that you like. Doing so can get your rhythms and sounds flowing again so that you can begin writing where you left off.

11. *Switch to another project.* Let the project you're working on sit for a while. This is Isaac Asimov's strategy: "When I feel difficulty coming on, I switch to another book I'm writing. When I get back to the problem, my unconscious has solved it."

12. *Write a letter.* Direct your thoughts to one specific (and *real*) reader. Write to your teacher, explaining the problems you are having. Write to your friends about your paper and where you are with it. This offers a shift in perspective that often breaks a block.

For Further Reading and Research

Atchity, Ken. *A Writer's Time: A Guide to the Creative Process, from Vision through Revision.* New York: Norton, 1986.

Briggs, John. *Fire in the Crucible.* Los Angeles: Tarcher, 1990.

Csikszentmihalyi, Mihaly. *Flow: The Psychology of Optimal Experience.* New York: Harper, 1990.

John-Steiner, Vera. *Notebooks of the Mind.* New York: Harper, 1985.

Mack, Karin, and Eric Skjei. *Overcoming Writing Blocks.* Los Angeles: Tarcher, 1979.

Perkins, David. *The Mind's Best Work.* Cambridge: Harvard UP, 1981.

INDEX